Foreword

Welcome to the first edition of UCAS' new guide to getting into universities and colleges. You've already made the decision to apply for higher education, which is a very exciting step in itself. This publication is designed to guide you through the important decisions you need to make about what and where to study, and to help you make a realistic and successful application.

Undertaking a full-time undergraduate degree course is a big commitment and at UCAS we believe you need to have access to reliable and straightforward information that will help you make the right choice for your future. This guide will help you understand what sort of planning and research you need to do as well as what you can expect from different courses. In addition, we aim to guide you through the application process so you use your choices effectively, present yourself well on your application and get the offers you want.

We listened to applicants who have gone before you. They wanted a single source of answers for all the big questions and this guide provides you with everything you need to know. I hope you find it useful and I wish you every success in applying for higher education.

MARY CURNOCK COOK
CHIEF EXECUTIVE, UCAS

Introduction

Introduction

With applications to university and college becoming increasingly competitive, UCAS has produced this guide to help you in your research and planning so that you make informed decisions and the right choices about what, and where, to study.

Whether you're applying for full-time study, part-time study or distance learning, this comprehensive guide aims to direct you through the UCAS application process and tackle any questions that you may have about applying to higher education.

It will explain what UCAS' role is in your higher education journey and explain the application process in six easy steps. The steps will cover 'choosing courses', 'applying', 'offers', 'results', 'next steps' and finally 'starting university or college'.

Within these sections you will find comprehensive information on finance, open days, interviews, writing your personal statement, getting into Oxbridge, taking a gap year and much more.

Whatever your circumstances, whether you are applying through your school or applying independently; whether you are applying from the EU or a non-EU country; or whether you are a student with a disability, everything is covered in this guide.

Key to symbols

Key to symbols

You'll find these symbols throughout this book to make it easy to locate the information relevant to you.

Case studies. The experience of others.

Did you know? A great idea.

Frequently asked questions and the answers.

International students. Worldly advice.

Mature students. Older and wiser!

Myth buster. Blow those myths from your mind.

Students' tips. Advice from those who've gone before you.

Students with disabilities. Unlock your potential!

Top tip. Pinpointing key tips from UCAS.

Contents

Contents

www.ucas.com

Where to start?

So you're thinking about doing a higher education course. In this chapter we explore what higher education is, why you might want to do it (in case you're yet to be convinced!), what's available and what help there might be financially.

Higher education is an excellent way to pursue a subject that you have a passion for at the same time as meeting new people and developing independence. Student life can also provide opportunities to develop skills through involvement with societies and group work. The skills you learn will prove beneficial when applying for jobs in the future. So read on to fulfil your potential…

www.ucas.com

What is higher education?

Higher education offers a diverse range of courses and qualifications, such as degrees, Higher National Diplomas (HND) and foundation degrees. Many higher education courses take place in universities, but plenty are also taught at colleges, specialist art institutions and agricultural colleges.

Why choose higher education?

It's a must for some careers. A higher education qualification is essential for pursuing some vocational careers, like dentistry, chartered engineering and architecture. Some courses offer a vocational programme that is directly related to particular work areas, such as accountancy, sports science and teaching.

To improve your earning power. A higher education course, such as a degree or HND can improve your chances of getting a fulfilling job and your financial potential.

It can strengthen your understanding of different cultures and beliefs. Universities and colleges bring together students from a variety of backgrounds.

Higher education develops important transferable skills. Skills such as effective communication and timekeeping, management and delegation skills, research and creative thinking can give you an edge in the fast-changing world of employment.

To show other people what you can do. Your qualification will show employers what you can do and give them an idea of how well you might do in the future. It will also show people that you can learn.

For academic debate. If the course includes seminars, you can use this time to challenge each other's views in a neutral and stimulating environment.

To show yourself what you can do. Gaining a higher education qualification boosts your self-confidence and self-awareness, and you may be at a stage in life when you can study a subject for the sake of personal satisfaction.

Types of qualifications available

Higher education is not just about getting a degree. There are several other qualifications that can be gained at university or college and they cover both academic and work-related courses.

The main courses offered are:

Bachelor's degree

This is a three- or four-year course where graduates obtain a bachelor's degree. A degree helps you develop a thorough understanding of the subject and enables you to move into a job or profession or on to a postgraduate course. Sometimes known as a 'first' degree, it can lead to an 'ordinary' bachelor's degree or a bachelor's degree with honours. The latter generally requires a higher academic standard. Most first degrees are now assumed to be honours degrees, although ordinary degrees are offered by some institutions. Honours degrees in England, Wales and Northern Ireland tend to take three years to complete, or four years with an industrial placement or year abroad.

Honours degrees in Scotland normally take four years to complete, although you can enter into the second year if you have appropriate qualifications. An 'ordinary' degree in Scotland is usually a three-year full-time course, whereas an 'honours' degree is usually a four-year full-time course.

Case study

Name: Daniella Nzekwe
Studying: A levels

When I left school I knew that I wanted to do A levels but I wasn't so sure about university. I have always been ambitious but I seemed to think that my dream job would fall in my lap. Thankfully my college told me that careers in the media are really competitive and it helps to have a degree. This is when I started to think about all the things I was interested in. This changed many times, but some of the subjects were history, media, journalism, drama, until I finally decided that English was my true passion. After that, my tutorial classes helped me begin to research universities that offered the course I wanted. It was so stressful as many universities seem to be outside London and I wanted to stay at home. I found that the London universities asked for higher grades, which made me nervous as I am mainly a C student. After many weeks of thought I applied through UCAS with the help of my college.

I currently have an offer from Brunel University which is my dream university so I'm working really hard to get the grades.

The best of luck to everyone applying!

Part-time degree courses are taken over a longer period, usually five years or more. Institutions are increasingly able to offer flexible arrangements to suit your needs.

You're generally assessed by a mixture of exams and coursework as well as a written dissertation. Honours degrees are classified so that you are awarded a first-class (top mark), upper-second (2:1), lower-second (2:2), or third-class degree.

Higher National Certificate (HNC) and Higher National Diploma (HND)

The HNC is a one-year work-related course and the HND is a two-year work-related course, which, if completed with high grades, can lead to the second or third year of a bachelor's degree. Part-time courses take longer to complete. HNCs and HNDs are highly valued by employers as they are designed to give you the skills to put the knowledge you learn to effective use in a particular job. They're mainly assessed through assignments, projects and practical tasks.

Certificate of Higher Education (CertHE) and Diploma of Higher Education (DipHE)

These are the first year (the certificate) and second year (the diploma) of a degree course. They are academic, rather than vocational qualifications and can be used for entry to the second or third year of a related degree course.

Foundation degree

The foundation degree is a flexible vocational qualification combining academic study with workplace learning. A full-time course will usually take two years to complete; a part-time course may take longer. Often linked to a degree, there can be the opportunity to progress onto the third year of a bachelor's degree. You're likely to work on real projects which will enable you to pick up the technical and practical skills needed for your chosen line of work. As well as equipping you with the skills for a particular area of work, it also gives you general skills that are useful in any type of job. You'll be assessed in a variety of different ways, from project work to exams and presentations. There are courses you can study through distance learning, online, or at college.

Postgraduate

Higher education qualifications that require you to already have a bachelor's degree are known as postgraduate qualifications. They're often taken to build on the knowledge and skills gained during a bachelor's degree but you can also study a subject that's new to you. There are postgraduate diplomas and certificates, which can be academic or vocational, and there are master's degrees which are academic and can be research-based or a taught course, or a mixture of both. They can take around 12 months of full-time study to complete.

A doctorate qualification takes at least three years of full-time study to complete and you'd be expected to work independently, with guidance from a supervisor, on an original piece of research.

What level are these qualifications?

Each qualification has a different volume of learning. The government has indicated in a framework for higher education the level of each qualification - see the table over the page. The framework shows how different higher education qualifications compare in terms of the demands they place on learners. Each level tells you how hard the qualification is – the higher you go, the harder the qualification. The levels also indicate the differences in the range of intended learning outcomes. So, for example, the bachelor's degree is set at a higher level than the HNC.

Levels 1-3 (for England, Wales and Northern Ireland) and levels 1-6 (for Scotland) precede higher education and include A levels and Scottish Highers.

You don't have to do a qualification from each level in order to do a doctorate. Each qualification will have its own entry requirements but after completing A levels or Scottish Highers or similar, you can go straight into studying a bachelor's degree with honours.

Framework for higher education qualifications level in England, Wales and Northern Ireland	Scottish credit qualifications framework level	Examples of higher education qualifications within each level
4	7	- certificates of higher education (CertHE) - Higher National Certificates (HNC)
5	8	- diplomas of higher education (DipHE) - foundation degrees (eg FdA, FdSc) - Higher National Diplomas (HND)
6	9 10	- bachelor's degrees - bachelor's degrees with honours (eg BA, BSc, BEng, BEd, BMus)
7	11	- master's degrees (eg MA, MSc, MPhil, MRes) - postgraduate certificates - postgraduate diplomas
8	12	- doctoral degrees (eg PhD/DPhil)

Myth buster

Uni is not just for people who are good at academic courses

Universities offer many different types of courses. While some courses are mainly academic, others can be practical, physical or creative, where you leave the lecture hall behind to gain work experience, learn through scenario-based assessments or develop a practical skill.

Look at the different course structures to see which suits you – there are courses which offer time away from the university, like a year in industry and work placements in the UK or abroad.

The Entry Profiles in Course Search on **www.ucas.com** will tell you a lot about how academic a course is, and its method of teaching. So get to know what's available and choose those that you'll enjoy most.

The Choosing courses chapter has more information on Entry Profiles and Course Search

Single and combined courses

Single honours degrees are courses where one subject is studied. It allows you to focus on that one subject throughout the course, such as English.

Combined courses are designed for those who want flexibility and the variety and knowledge of skills offered by a combination of subjects, eg history and French. There are three types of combined courses:

- Joint honours degrees are where two subjects are studied equally, 50%-50%. They allow you to divide your time equally between two subjects.

- Major/minor courses allow you to study two subjects, one as a major part of your course, the other as the minor. The time spent is usually 75%-25%.

- Combined honours programmes are flexible courses that allow you to do two or three or four subjects, perhaps specialising in just two subject combinations as you move to the second or third year.

The use of 'and', 'with' and the ampersand ('&') in course titles
The course title should indicate whether a course is a single subject or joint subject course. Generally, the words 'and', 'with' and the ampersand ('&') have a specific meaning within a course title:

- Where there are two elements to a single subject, an ampersand ('&') is used to link the two elements, eg art & design.

- Where two subjects are studied (for a joint honours degree) in a balanced combination, the subjects will be joined with 'and', eg French and German.

- Where there are two elements to a main subject (within a joint honours course), the elements are joined with an ampersand ('&') and the main subject with 'and', eg physics & applied physics and French.

- For major and minor subjects, 'with' is used as the link word and the major subject is listed first, eg 'French with German' is French major with German minor.

Modular courses

The majority of higher education institutions have now adopted a modular structure for courses. This means that you can build a personalised course by choosing modules or units of study from different subject areas. Universities have a list of modules that can be taken for each course. Some might be compulsory and some you may be able to choose between. The university websites often list the modules that will be available to study, although you have to be aware of timetable clashes.

Sandwich courses

Some vocational courses include a year of working in the industry as part of the course. This will usually be for the third year of a degree course or the second year of an HND and, depending on the employer, may be full-time paid employment. The purpose of this is to introduce you to the world of work, while gaining valuable experience in a profession you might consider after completing your higher education course.

The universities often have links with some employers but you can also find your own placement, provided the university agrees it is suitable.

Foundation year - year 0 of a degree course

Some universities incorporate a foundation year into the degree. You can find this information using the Course Search facility on the UCAS website by searching on the subject 'foundation'. They're either designed to prepare students who have qualifications which are acceptable for entry in general but are not appropriate to a specific course of study or used as year 0 of a degree course to enable students with non-traditional qualifications to enter higher education by using year 0 as a preparatory year for a full degree programme. It is advisable to speak to the universities directly for more information about foundation years.

Foundation courses for international students

It is easy to get muddled with the different 'foundation' courses available. Foundation courses for international students are usually nine-months long and cover English skills and academic courses. They can help you prepare for university entry but are not accepted in every UK university. You can find information about them on the university websites.

Don't confuse them with the foundation year (year 0 of a degree course, detailed above), the foundation degree (a vocational qualification, see page 16) and the art and design foundation course, a one-year further education course designed to broaden and deepen the student's art skills before specialising and applying to an art-related degree.

Higher education – a different way of learning

Allow yourself time to acclimatise to the new teaching and learning environment.

Learning at a university or college is different from learning at school. At school you're dependent on teachers, the routine and timetable set by them and the protective structure of the school. You may be used to being directed to a resource and cutting and pasting or rewriting information. Achieving academic success at A level does not necessarily mean you can cope easily with the more independent and self-directed style of learning expected of universities. You may have to quickly learn these skills at the start of your course.

At university you're expected to take on a more independent way of learning. You will have to take responsibility for planning and organising your own work (as well as balancing work with pleasure). You will still get deadlines to hand in work but you might not have to hand it in for weeks and weeks. No one will tell you how many hours of study you should be doing – you'll have to work all this out for yourself. You might only get 15 hours of contact time per week (time in lectures, tutorials etc) so you'll be expected to study on your own the rest of time. This requires a lot of self-motivation and dedication.

You will need to discover your own learning style, when to work alone, when to work with others and when to seek advice. Independent learning is about asking complex questions, learning from resource materials, either in libraries or at home, analysing and evaluating the content, doing practicals and listening to feedback.

www.ucas.com

UCAS – our role in your journey

We're responsible for managing applications to higher education courses in the UK. We aim to help you make informed choices about higher education, guiding you, your parents and advisers through the application process. That's what this book is all about! But it is not your only source of help.

After looking at this book, you will need help with finding a course. We list all full-time higher education courses in the UCAS scheme (that's around 43,000 courses) on our website **www.ucas.com** along with the entry requirements for each course, and many list much more information in their Entry Profiles, such as course descriptions and student services.

When you decide to make your application to university, you will need to use Apply, our online application system. After sending us your application, we send it to your chosen universities and colleges where they can view it online but they will not see where else you have applied. The universities and colleges will consider your application and send their decisions to us.

Student tip:

'It all seems so horrifying at first but you have to remember that UCAS is there to make things easier for you.'

UCAStv

You will be able to see those decisions in Track. Track is the name of our online system that allows you to follow the progress of your application. In Track, you can see what's happening with your application, such as whether you've received any offers, and you can then make replies to any offers you have been made, accepting or declining them.

During the summer, we receive many exam results direct from the exam boards and pass them to the universities and colleges that are holding a place for you (see page 252). When you get your results, you can check Track to see if you've got a place on your chosen course. Depending on your circumstances, you may want to use Adjustment or Clearing (see pages 269 and 273) which allow you to search for further courses with vacancies.

Of course you can consult this book and our website at any stage to check what to do next. You can also watch video guides on UCAStv at **www.ucas.tv**, follow us on Twitter at **http://twitter.com/ucas_online**, ask us a question on Facebook at **www.facebook.com/ucasonline** or see your questions answered on YouTube at **www.youtube.com/ucasonline**. If you would like to speak to us, you can call our Customer Service Unit; details on **www.ucas.com/about_us/contact_us**.

UCAS' student network **www.yougofurther.co.uk**, an online community site, can then help you meet people before you go to uni or chat to people already on your chosen course. This helps to take away some of the fears of starting university on your own.

We have summarised our role in your journey in six easy steps…

Six steps to applying – the applicant journey

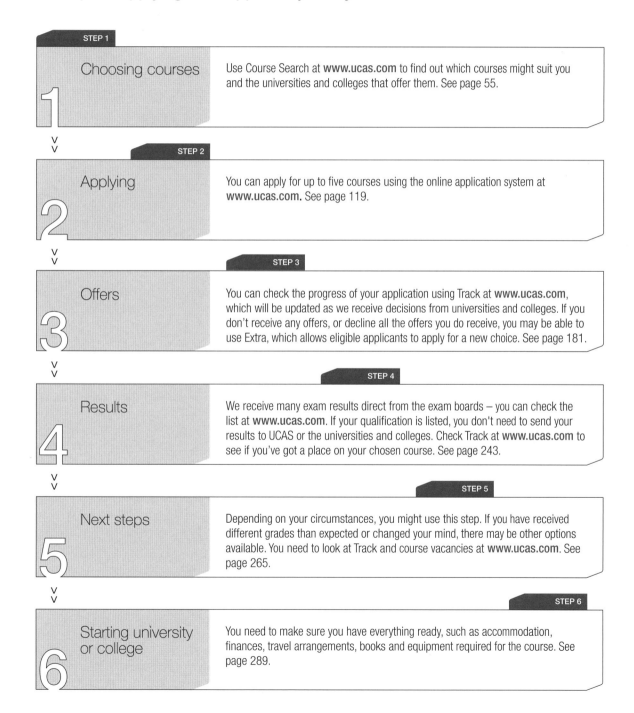

STEP 1

Choosing courses

Use Course Search at **www.ucas.com** to find out which courses might suit you and the universities and colleges that offer them. See page 55.

STEP 2

Applying

You can apply for up to five courses using the online application system at **www.ucas.com.** See page 119.

STEP 3

Offers

You can check the progress of your application using Track at **www.ucas.com**, which will be updated as we receive decisions from universities and colleges. If you don't receive any offers, or decline all the offers you do receive, you may be able to use Extra, which allows eligible applicants to apply for a new choice. See page 181.

STEP 4

Results

We receive many exam results direct from the exam boards – you can check the list at **www.ucas.com**. If your qualification is listed, you don't need to send your results to UCAS or the universities and colleges. Check Track at **www.ucas.com** to see if you've got a place on your chosen course. See page 243.

STEP 5

Next steps

Depending on your circumstances, you might use this step. If you have received different grades than expected or changed your mind, there may be other options available. You need to look at Track and course vacancies at **www.ucas.com**. See page 265.

STEP 6

Starting university or college

You need to make sure you have everything ready, such as accommodation, finances, travel arrangements, books and equipment required for the course. See page 289.

Mature students

People are increasingly taking up courses at every stage of their lives, so don't be put off higher education by thinking it's too late or that you might not fit in. Mature students are welcomed by universities and colleges for their experience, skills and enthusiasm.

Getting to know yourself and mixing with school leavers can be interesting and educational in itself! Mature students can play important roles as figures to whom younger students can relate. Your life and work experience will bring an extra dimension to seminar and tutorial groups, and will be valued.

When applying for university or college, you will need to provide evidence of your ability to study at the appropriate level, or evidence of relevant experience (or both). Course admission requirements are flexible for mature applicants and exact requirements will vary, depending on the course and university. If you have left school with few or no qualifications or not been in formal education for some years, you could take an Access course at a local college to brush up your study skills.

Lack of qualifications need not stop you from pursuing undergraduate study – universities and colleges will consider your experience and other qualities.

Access to higher education programmes

Access courses are known as Access to Higher Education courses in England, Wales and Northern Ireland and SWAP (Scottish Wider Access Programme) in Scotland. They're designed to provide a good grounding in the knowledge and study skills needed for entry to higher education.

Some programmes are linked to particular degree subjects and on completion may offer a guaranteed place at a particular university or college. Others are not tied to a subject area and concentrate on offering general progression to higher education by developing key transferable skills, English or communications, numeracy and information technology, all with tutorial support.

Most courses are modular in structure so you can build up credit at a pace that suits you and your circumstances. You can find out more information at **www.accesstohe.ac.uk** or **www.scottishwideraccess.org**.

Mature students' FAQs

Am I a mature student?

A mature student normally refers to anyone who is aged 21 and over or 20 if in Scotland.

Do I have to complete a different application?

No, it is the same application used for all applicants.

Whom should I ask to provide my reference?

If you are a mature student and cannot obtain an academic reference, you should ask a responsible person who knows you to provide your reference; they must not be a friend or relative. This could be an employer, training officer, careers adviser, a teacher on a recent relevant further education course or a senior colleague in employment or voluntary work.

Can I get funding?

Yes, you will still be eligible to apply for funding. The exact amount you can receive will depend on your personal circumstances. For further information visit **www.direct.gov.uk/studentfinance**.

Is there a maximum age for higher education?

No, there is not an age requirement for applying to higher education. Some courses may have specific requirements and therefore we advise you to contact the institution if you are unsure.

Will institutions consider experience if I don't quite meet the qualifications they have listed as requirements?

For a mature applicant many institutions will look at your life experience relevant to the subject you are applying to, therefore it may not always be necessary for you to specifically meet the entry requirements listed against your course. You should contact the individual institution for further advice on this.

Can the courses be more flexible to meet my needs?

The majority of higher education institutions offer either modular programmes, which enable students to build a personalised degree to allow flexibility, or part-time study options. There may also be the option of distance learning depending on the subject you wish to study.

I'm no longer at school so where can I get careers guidance?

There are many websites offering advice aimed at mature students, for example **www.careers.ed.ac.uk**.

Do institutions provide childcare?

Some institutions do offer this facility, however if you require childcare we advise you to contact the student services office of your chosen institution before applying to find out if there are childcare provisions. The charity, The Daycare Trust, promotes childcare in higher education and is a good contact point for advice on provisions and benefits.

Where can I live while I'm studying?

As a mature student you may have commitments meaning you would need to attend a local university and therefore stay living at home. However if you do decide to move away to study there are many accommodation options. Many institutions have halls of residence which may be an option for some mature students. However for students with spouses, children or both, some institutions are able to make specific housing provisions.

What are the basic study skills I will require?

Institutions will often look at a mature student's life experience rather than purely their formal qualifications. They will also consider whether you hold the basic study skills for higher education, which include being able to understand how to learn, organise time, read effectively, take notes, research, draw conclusions and write essays and reports.

The information for students with disabilities in this chapter and the rest of the guide has been contributed by Skill: National Bureau for Students with Disabilities

Skill is a UK independent charity that promotes equality in education, training and employment for disabled people.

Skill provides a free information and advice service for individual disabled people and the professionals who work with them, with a freephone helpline, email and the website **www.skill.org.uk**.

Students with disabilities

Definition of disability

A person has a disability if they have a physical or mental impairment which has a substantial and long-term effect on their ability to carry out normal day-to-day activities (Equality Act 2010).

Disability support

Under the Equality Act (2010), universities and colleges have a duty to make reasonable adjustments to their services, so disabled students are not placed at a substantial disadvantage. The Special Educational Needs and Disability Order (SENDO) 2005 is similar in Northern Ireland. However, it is still important to contact the disability support person at the institution to discuss how your individual needs will be met. They will usually be called the Disability Coordinator or something similar. You may find that some institutions have more experience in supporting people with a certain type of disability or impairment. The contact details of all the disability coordinators across the UK are listed in the Into Higher Education section of the Skill website.

All higher education institutions must have a Disability Equality Scheme, setting out how they intend to improve disability equality for staff and students across their institution. You may want to read an institution's Disability Equality Scheme to gain a better understanding of the institution's general support for disabled people.

Visit www.skill.org.uk for more information
Skill: National Bureau for Students with Disabilities promotes opportunities to empower young people and adults with any kind of disability to realise their potential in further, continuing and higher education, training and employment throughout the United Kingdom. Skill works by providing information and advice to individuals, promoting good practice and influencing policy in partnership with disabled people, service providers and policy makers.

Visit their website **www.skill.org.uk**, email them at info@skill.org.uk or contact them on 0800 328 5050 (telephone) or 18001 0800 328 5050 (textphone) or at Unit 3, Floor 3, Radisson Court, 219 Long Lane, London SE1 4PR.

Case study

Name: Shona Heath
Studying: BSc Human Biology with Psychology and Sociology
at: Glasgow Caledonian University

I had always planned to move away to university but this course was ideal so I chose Glasgow Caledonian University even though it's close to my home. I still wanted to have the experience of living away so I got a flat in the university's halls of residence in the first year and I lived there during term time for the rest of my time there. While I have been at university my condition, Friedreich's ataxia, has deteriorated and I now use my wheelchair all the time.

Disclosing my disability on my UCAS application was an issue for me as I hadn't accepted my disability at that time. I visited the uni over the summer and walked around, thinking that I could carry my bag and be able to walk from class to class on my own. In the end I accepted the help of a personal assistant and a wheelchair. Best decision ever when I look back on it as I was able to experience university life to the full.

My mum was the one who got things rolling for me; she got in touch with the social work department who assigned me to a social worker from Glasgow Caledonian University. My guidance teacher at secondary was also good support. I contacted the disability service during the summer beforehand and we set up an appointment to discuss my needs and see the uni. I also met the head of my department who showed me around the classrooms and laboratories I'd be in. We discussed in detail what support I needed and what was available...

...The second time I went to the university was to interview people to be my personal assistant. The disability officer made this process very easy for me, it wasn't a daunting experience. I picked people I got on with and they quickly became my friends. I also visited the student halls of residence with the disability officer to see if it was suitable and which room I preferred.

The personal assistants helped me get from class to class and helped with daily stuff like doing the washing and shopping. In my final year I opted not to have an assistant as I'll have to get used to getting around on my own when I finish uni and get a job. I can't believe how busy my life has become. I also get help such as extra time in exams, as I write more slowly. I now have a scribe to write my exam papers for me, which is excellent as it allows me thinking time. You can also get handouts before lectures, larger print, or coloured paper – you just have to ask.

Glasgow Caledonian's facilities and accessibility are great. In my time here, I have noticed changes being made to make it increasingly accessible, such as new, low desks and more wide doors. The university has its own disability team who are incredibly helpful. You'll get to know them really well and, again, you just have to ask.

I thoroughly recommend going to university. It's a great experience – you'll learn so much. A disability shouldn't stop you in any way. Just go for it. You'll find it easy once you're there – apart from the studying!

Case study

Name: Hameed Nazham Ahmed
Studying: HNC Construction Management
at: The University of Northampton

I have mobility problems and pain due to 11 disc protrusions into my spine. Three in my neck mean my hands and arms are permanently numb. My lower spine is also affected.

I chose The University of Northampton because it was my local university and it had an excellent programme. I'm married with three children and live at home. It can be very difficult trying to manage a family life, being disabled and studying; however, after settling into a good routine it doesn't seem so difficult.

How were you first put in touch with the university disability officer?
As soon as the university found out that I had some health issues they asked the local education officer from the county council to contact me. She did and later sent me a form for Disabled Students' Allowance (DSA) together with normal student loan forms.

When did you first contact the university disability officer?
Once my DSA form was being processed by the local authority, they wrote to me to let me know that I needed to have an 'Assessment of needs' and asked me to get in touch with the university's disabilities officer to arrange this. I did contact her and the assessment was arranged very promptly with an assessor at the Northampton Assessment Centre based at my university...

How were your needs assessed?
I had to go in to have a very lengthy appointment with the assessment centre; the appointment addressed all my health issues one by one. Every issue was tackled to find the most appropriate solution.

A lot of equipment like specialist chairs was tried out, as was software, reading accessories etc.

Did you need to visit the university disability officer?
Yes, after the appointment with the assessor I visited my disability officer. Having read a preliminary report, she started identifying things to make my life easy and arranged a note taker as well as comfortable chairs for my classes. She also arranged people to help me when I went to the library.

What information did the university provide for you?
They gave me a list of contacts at the university together with what additional support could be made available:

- extra time with assignments and exams

- arranging taxis when poorly

- how not to worry about renewing library books

- extra support for my surveying modules in the field such as collapsible chairs so I could have a rest when I got tired and how to arrange for a car and driver to take me to the various points outdoors on uni property.

They also told me about extra funding (access to learning funds) available when the DSA is exhausted.

What arrangements were made for you?
A lot of adjustments were made for me. I had a separate table and comfy chair to the rest of the class (at my request as working in an auditorium was not possible for me - too narrow a desk and uncomfortable chairs). I was allowed to give my presentation from my seat. My fellow students always encouraged me...

After my operation I needed a lot of emotional support which they provided in the form of psychologists and mental health nurses. I was regularly asked about any adjustments which would help me and I had a few, like keys to privileged lifts. They have arranged for me to have staff parking stickers and a barrier card to all car parks on campus. The note-takers were invaluable.

Did you discuss your disability with your academic tutor?
Yes I did. I had to negotiate deadlines separately and during exams they wanted to know if I needed anything else, like a separate room, which I did take them up on. The tutor was extremely sympathetic to my needs and privacy.

How have you found the help and equipment you've received?
The equipment has made a tremendous difference to my life as a student and a person. From comfortable specialist chairs to electric height-adjustable tables, speech recognition software (Dragon), mind mapping, digital tape recorders, portable back friend, electric staplers and punch machines, able table, allowances for printing, expert tuition at my home for IT and the note-taker were all invaluable.

Without all this help I would not have been able to take this course let alone pass it with a distinction. I am carrying on this year and taking my course to the next stage. Due to the fact I cannot hold books, I need to photocopy a lot more than normal to read chapters. The photocopying allowance came in very handy, together with printer, ink and internet which again the DSA covered.

Students with disabilities' FAQs

Am I eligible for extra financial help?
Disabled students' allowance (DSA) can help you with the cost of attending your course as a direct result of your disability. DSA is available for both full-time and part-time students.

Should I disclose my disability to the institutions I apply to?
We advise that all students with a disability should disclose any relevant information as it allows the institutions to ensure they can offer the correct support.

How much information do I need to provide about my disability?
We advise you to provide as much information as possible as this will ensure the correct support is provided to you when you attend your chosen institution. It will also ensure that the institutions are able to make clear decisions as to whether they can provide the support you require.

Will I be less likely to secure a place?
No, all applications gain equal consideration as long as they have met the required deadlines. If you have any concerns about this you can contact your chosen institutions for further information.

Is there an organisation that provides advice to me as a disabled student?
Skill: National Bureau for Students with Disabilities is a UK independent charity that promotes equality in education, training and employment for disabled people. It offers information, advice and support on DSA funding and applying for higher education.

How can I find out if my preferred institutions can meet my needs?
The best option would be to contact the institution directly as they will be able to discuss the facilities they have and they may also have a disability adviser who they can put you in touch with. An open day may be a good idea so you can gain firsthand experience as to whether the institution meets your needs.

Non-UK students

The UK has a long history of welcoming international students to study in its universities and colleges. The most recently available figures for 2008/09 for those studying full-time at publicly funded higher education institutions are:

European Union (EU) students	92,000
Non-EU students	214,000
Total	306,000

Source: HESA

In addition there are thought to be around 50,000 EU and non-EU students in publicly funded further education colleges (source: HESA). Through UCAS, there have been over 100,000 applicants from outside the UK in the past year from all corners of the globe.

When looking to study in the UK, there are many places and people that can help. There are people at each university and college who are ready to answer your questions, help you through the application process and support you while you are in the UK. Many universities and colleges organise a programme of events before you start your course to welcome you and to help you make new friends and get used to your new surroundings.

Social and cultural activities are often run for international students throughout the year. Universities and colleges also provide a variety of clubs and societies that you may wish to join.

UCAS is also here to help you in your journey into UK higher education. We understand what a life-changing decision this can be and we are here to help you every step of the way through to UK higher education. You may also meet some of our staff in your own country, as UCAS attends a number of international events to guide you, your parents and advisers through the application process. You can check where we will be visiting next by going to **www.ucas.com/students/ wheretostart/nonukstudents/internationalevents**. Many universities and colleges also visit a number of countries. You should check with their websites for further information. Finally, you might also want to check with your local British Council office to see if they can assist you in any way.

Immigration requirements for study in the UK

You need to give yourself plenty of time to deal with your visa application to come to study in the UK. The evidence you need to provide can take time, perhaps several months, to obtain and has to be in the required format, otherwise your application for entry clearance (visa) will be refused.

The UK Border Agency (UKBA) is responsible for considering applications to enter or stay in the UK, including student visas. For more information on the requirements to obtain a student visa, you should visit: **www.ukba.homeoffice.gov.uk/studyingintheuk**.

Similarly, UKCISA (the UK Council for International Student Affairs) produces information on immigration requirements at **www.ukcisa.org.uk/student/immigration.php** and **www.ukcisa.org.uk/student/info_sheets/applying_home_country.php**.

These pages also contain links to the UK government's relevant application forms and guidance.

There will also be staff at the universities and colleges where you plan to study who can answer questions you have about this process.

Non-UK students' FAQs

Can I apply from outside the UK?

Applications are made online so it is possible to apply from anywhere in the world with an internet connection.

Will I need to pass an English test first?

If English is not your native language, or if a university or college has a concern that your English language ability may be insufficient for the course you are applying for, they may ask you to take a recognised English language test, such as IELTS or TOEFL. The university or college may set a condition on an offer that you obtain particular grades in the test. Check with the universities or colleges directly to see which tests and what scores you would require.

How can I find out how much the fees are and whether I can get student funding or scholarships?

The profile of the course on the Course Search section on **www.ucas.com** will usually include the fees for both home and international students. Your chosen institutions will assess whether you will pay fees as a home or international student when they decide whether to offer a place. Funding information can be found at **www.ucas.com/students/studentfinance**. UKCISA also provides a detailed outline of fee status requirements: **www.ukcisa.org.uk/student/ fees student support.php**.

How can I tell if my qualifications will meet the entry requirements of my chosen institution if the qualification I've taken isn't in the UCAS Tariff or the Entry Profile for the course?

Contact the institution to discuss your qualifications. They will decide whether your qualifications will meet their entry requirements. Many universities and colleges will also have specific information listed by country on their own websites, which you should make sure to check.

Is there a different application for students from outside the UK?

Everyone applying through UCAS uses the same electronic Apply form available on **www.ucas.com**.

Will I need a visa to study in the UK?

If you are not normally resident in the UK you may need to apply for a student visa. Information on student visas can be found at **www.ukvisas.gov.uk/en**.

Will I be required to attend an interview and when will it be?

Each institution will decide whether they need to interview for their course and when interviews will take place. If you will have any problems attending an interview at the institution during the year you should contact the institution to discuss when an interview can be scheduled. Sometimes universities and colleges will come to your own country to conduct an interview.

Do I need to send academic transcripts and where should I send them to?

You must fill in details of ALL qualifications you have, or will receive, on your UCAS application. Although you cannot attach transcripts to your UCAS application, the institutions you have applied to might want to receive copies. They will tell you when they would like to receive a copy. Do not send any copies to UCAS.

Does my reference need to be in English?

Your reference must be written in English although it may be translated. Institutions may also wish to contact the referee directly for additional information so the referee should be contactable and able to respond in English if possible.

Can the institution help me find somewhere to live while I'm studying?

Contact your chosen institutions for information. Many have halls of residence which you can apply to stay in. They may also be able to help you find private accommodation.

Can I work while studying in the UK?

Currently, most students on a Tier 4 Adult student visa are able to work up to 20 hours a week during term time and full time outside of term time. However this may change. For more information on working in the UK, go to **www.ukcisa.org.uk**.

The information about student finance in this chapter and the rest of the guide has been contributed by NASMA.

The National Association of Student Money Advisers (NASMA) strives to relieve the poverty of students through the provision of advice, information and training. We aim to provide for the public benefit, the profession of student money advice.

Visit **www.nasma.org.uk**

Money: how to get hold of it!

Now that you have decided to study, you need to think about how you will survive financially. The 'money' sections in this book will advise you on the funding that may be available to you, and how to get your hands on it so that you can relax and enjoy your time at university.

Get sorted before you start!

If you have already been bored by budgeting sessions at school, and talk of student grants and loans leaves you cold, you might be thinking about skipping these sections and moving on to something more interesting. STOP!

These sections may save your life!

The cost of studying in the UK

As a student, you will usually have to pay for two things: tuition fees for your course, and living costs such as rent, food, books, transport and entertainment. Fees charged vary between courses, as well as between universities and colleges, so it's important to check these before you apply. Tuition fees are set by the university or college.

You can find out the tuition fee by looking at the university or college websites or on Course Search at **www.ucas.com/students/coursesearch** which has specific details on fees, bursaries and financial support for each course. The maximum tuition fee for 2011 entry for 'home' students is £3,375 (subject to final confirmation by the Government). If you are classed as 'overseas' for fee purposes, you are liable to pay the full cost fees which are set at a higher rate. See page 131 to see how your fee status is assessed.

For information on the proposed changes to tuition fees for 2012 entry for England, see page 47, and for Wales, see page 48.

If you're studying in Scotland, and already live there, you aren't normally required to pay tuition fees. Check the Student Awards Agency for Scotland (SAAS) website **www.saas.gov.uk** for further information.

Eligibility for student funding

Each country in the UK has its own rules and procedures, and you should check the website for the country where you're hoping to study as well as for the country where your family is living. See page 50 for a list of the websites to visit.

Eligibility is based on where you have lived before you start your course (your residency) and also if you have studied in higher education before. If you have studied before (even if only for a short time) it is strongly recommended that you seek advice before starting another course as there are restrictions on the number of years you can receive funding.

The rules are far too lengthy to go into here. You can find out all the information on the website **www.direct.gov.uk/studentfinance** or ask at your school, college or prospective university.

Cash support

For students entering higher education the financial support package available applies to the full term of your course and covers the following main areas. It is a good idea to get used to the different terminology so that you know what people are talking about and don't look daft!

Tuition fee loans – repayable

As long as you have not been to university before, and you meet the residency rules, you'll not have to pay your tuition fees upfront to cover the cost of being taught on your course. Instead you can take out a loan to cover the cost. If you take out this loan, the money will be paid directly to your university on your behalf.

If you want to pay your tuition fees yourself, and not take out a loan, you must make arrangements to do this with your university.

However, eligible Scottish domiciled students and EU students, studying at an institution in Scotland, are currently entitled to free tuition.

Changes to student finance apply to English universities and colleges for students entering higher education from 2012 onwards – see page 47 for details.

Maintenance Loans – repayable

You can have a Maintenance Loan to cover your living costs, such as rent, food and travel. Maintenance Loans are paid in three instalments, at the start of each term, into your bank account.

In Scotland, you can receive a student loan. The amount of loan you can get depends on the level of your family's income.

Maintenance Grants – non-repayable

Maintenance Grants are intended to help students from lower income households with their living costs. You do not have to take out a loan to be eligible for this grant.

Maintenance Grants are paid in three instalments, at the start of each term, into your bank account.

If you want to defer your entry to uni from 2011 to 2012, the 2012 student support package will apply to you.

Scottish students studying in Scotland can receive a Young Students' Bursary or Independent Students' Bursary. The amount available will depend on the level of your household income and is paid instead of part of your student loan, so it reduces the amount of loan you need to take out.

Special Support Grants – non-repayable

This grant is for students that are eligible for (but not necessarily in receipt of) means-tested benefits. As a general rule this would normally be students who are parents or disabled students.

Special Support Grants are paid in three instalments, at the start of each term, into your bank account.

Note: you can only apply for either the Special Support Grant or the Maintenance Grant in any academic year, not both.

University bursaries – non-repayable

Bursaries are usually linked to your household income. When you apply for your loans and grants you can agree to your university having access to your overall household income. It is really important that you do this as they will use this income figure to see if you are eligible for a university bursary.

You can spend this bursary as you wish – you can use it towards your rent, to pay off part of your tuition fees or to reduce the amount of student loan that you take out.

Bursaries are normally paid automatically to eligible students – you don't need to apply for them. They don't restrict the number of bursaries that they pay – if you are eligible you will get one.

However you should check on university websites for the rules, ask at open days and look on the student finance calculator on the **www.direct.gov.uk/ studentfinance** website.

Did you know?

Many bursaries go unaccepted each year.

There's more support on offer than you might think, so it's worth checking if you're eligible for any of the bursaries or grants available. Speak to your university for advice.

Scholarships – non-repayable

Scholarships are usually given to students because of achievement and excellence. This is one area of additional financial support where you may have to do some of your own research. (See more information on this in Step 2 Choosing courses.)

Cash support for uni entrants in England from 2012

At the time of writing (January 2011), the Government's Department for Business, Innovation and Skills (BIS) announced changes to student finance. The proposed changes only apply to English universities and colleges of higher education. Student finance for Northern Ireland and Scotland in 2012 has not been announced. The following proposed changes are subject to parliamentary approval and further information can be found at **www.bis.gov.uk/studentfinance**.

As is the case for students entering higher education in 2011, students going to uni from 2012 will not have to pay upfront for their tuition, and financial help will be available for tuition and living costs. However, any university or college will be able to charge a graduate contribution of up to £6,000 a year. And, in exceptional cases, universities will be able to charge higher contributions, up to a limit of £9,000, subject to meeting much tougher conditions on widening participation and fair access. It will be up to the university or college to decide what it charges.

Loans for tuition fees and living costs

The Government will lend any eligible student the money to pay the university or college for tuition costs. Also, Maintenance Loans will be available for all eligible students, irrespective of family income.

Be aware that there may be differences in loan rates for students living at home, those living away from home and studying in London, and loans for longer courses.

Maintenance Grants

Maintenance Grants will be available to help students from lower income households with their living costs. Students from families with incomes of up to £25,000 will be entitled to a student Maintenance Grant of £3,250 and those from families with incomes up to £42,000 will be entitled to a partial grant.

National Scholarships Programme

A new £150m National Scholarships Programme will be targeted at bright potential students from poor backgrounds. It will guarantee students benefits such as a free first year or foundation year.

Part-time students

- For the first time, subject to government approval, many part-time students will be entitled to a loan and will no longer pay upfront costs, so long as they study at least one-third of their time.

- The Government will lend any eligible student the money to pay the university or college for tuition costs.

- Part-time students will not be eligible for maintenance support.

Where to start?

Uni entrants in Wales from 2012

At the time of writing (January 2011), fees chargeable by Welsh institutions are likely to be set at similar levels to those in England but Welsh domiciled students are due to receive a fee grant, in addition to the fee loan, to pay for any increase above the current 2011 entry maximum tuition fee of £3,375 for 'home' students.

As for England, a non-repayable maintenance grant is available to help students from lower income households with their living costs. Welsh students will be entitled to a means-tested maintenance grant of up to £5,000.

Interest and repayments

Despite what you may have heard, Student Loans are not interest free, but the interest is linked to inflation (rather than a commercial rate). You are not likely to get a better deal on the high street. But be aware that you will be charged interest from the day you take your loan out.

The main difference between Student Loans and commercial loans are that the repayments on Student Loans are linked to how much you earn rather than how much you have borrowed.

The loan is only repayable when you finish your course and your income goes over £15,000 for 2011 entrants or £21,000 for 2012 or later entrants to English universities. It will be deducted from your salary (just like tax and national insurance) at 9% of your income over £15,000 or £21,000 respectively. All outstanding repayments will be written off after 30 years (25 years for 2011 entrants).

This table gives you some examples of monthly repayments:-

Salary £16,000	9% of £1,000	£90 per year	£7.50 per month
Salary £20,000	9% of £5,000	£450 per year	£37 per month
Salary £30,000	9% of £15,000	£1,350 per year	£112 per month

If you enter higher education in England in 2012 and on graduation earn a salary of £25,000, you would pay around £6.92 per week. If for whatever reason your income falls to £21,000 or below, you will have your repayments suspended.

For these students, the Government also proposes that a real rate of interest will be charged on loan repayments with a progressive taper:

- For graduates earning below £21,000, there will be no real rate of interest applied to their loan.

- For graduates earning between £21,000 and around £41,000, a real rate of interest will start to be charged, reaching a maximum of RPI* plus 3%.

- Above £41,000, graduates will repay at the full rate of RPI plus 3%.

* RPI (Retail Prices Index) is a measure of inflation based on the prices of goods and services.

Additional money or support you may be eligible for

Please note, at the time of writing, no decisions have been made by the Government about the following targeted support for students entering higher education in England from 2012. The information here is the current additional money and support available and it may change.

Care leaver's grant

If you have been in local authority care before going to university you will find that both your leaving care team and university have loads of additional support for you. Obviously you need to tell the university that you have been in care, but don't worry about other people knowing: it is all kept confidential. It is not like being at school where everyone knows all about you. At university you are treated like an adult – because you are an adult – so nobody will know anything about you if you don't want them to.

Child's play – extra help for students who are parents

Childcare – If you have children you will have different concerns and priorities when you are thinking about starting university. Universities employ specialist staff who will advise you about childcare, funding and benefits. The website **www.childcarelink.gov.uk** is a very comprehensive government website detailing national childcare places for children of all ages.

When you apply for your student funding you can also apply for help with your childcare costs. This is a means tested grant, which can cover up to 85% of your childcare costs.

You can also apply for a Parent's Learning Allowance.

These grants will be disregarded when Jobcentre Plus calculate your entitlement for benefits. They are both non-repayable.

Child Tax Credits – If you have children that are financially dependent on you and you receive Child Benefit for them, then you can claim Child Tax Credits from HM Revenue and Customs. You do not have to be working to receive Child Tax Credits. As a student you are not classed as employed (unless you are working 16 hours per week in addition to your studies) so cannot claim Working Tax Credits.

Disabled Students' Allowance

If you have a disability, ongoing health condition or specific learning difficulty you will be eligible for additional support from the disabled student's allowance. When you apply for your funding you will need to send some evidence such as an educational psychologist's report or letter from your specialist or doctor. Once this is accepted you will be sent for an assessment of your needs which will give a list of recommendations of support that you need to be able to do your course. This will then be paid for on your behalf.

Emergency and hardship funding

All universities have emergency money that they can use to assist students in hardship. This may be because your loan has not turned up or because something unexpected has happened. If your circumstances mean you will find it hard to work, perhaps due to the intensity of your course, your children or your disability, you may also qualify for additional financial support from your university.

Find out more about student finance from the relevant sites

England: Student Finance England – www.direct.gov.uk/studentfinance

Northern Ireland: Student Finance Northern Ireland – www.studentfinanceni.co.uk

Scotland: Student Awards Agency for Scotland (SAAS) – www.saas.gov.uk

Wales: Student Finance Wales – www.studentfinancewales.co.uk

Funding in summary

Check the websites opposite for what grants and loans you may be eligible to apply for.

Funding	How is it paid?	Where does it come from?	Additional information	Means tested or non-means tested	Repayable or non-repayable
Tuition fee loan	Direct to university	Student Loans Company		Non-means tested	Repayable – once completed and earning £15,000 for 2011 entrants or £21,000 for 2012 entrants (subject to government approval)
Maintenance Loan	Directly to students in three instalments	Student Loans Company	Used by students to live off, pay rent, buy food etc	72% non-means tested 28% means tested	Repayable – once completed and earning £15,000 for 2011 entrants or £21,000 for 2012 entrants (subject to government approval)
Maintenance Grant*	Direct to students in three instalments	Student Loans Company	Used by students to live off, pay rent, buy food etc	Means tested	Non-repayable
Special Support Grant*	Direct to students in three instalments	Student Loans Company	Used by students to live off, pay rent, buy food etc	Means tested	Non-repayable
Childcare Grant	Direct to students in three instalments	Student Loans Company	For students that have to pay for childcare	Means tested	Non-repayable
Adult Dependants Grant	Direct to students in three instalments	Student Loans Company	For students that have an adult that is dependent	Means tested	Non-repayable
Parents Learning Allowance	Direct to students in three instalments	Student Loans Company	For students that have dependent children	Means tested	Non-repayable
University scholarships	Will depend on university – check their website	University	Students that excel at certain things – may be sport, academic, arts etc	Not normally means tested	Non-repayable
University bursaries	Will depend on university - check their website	University	Dependent on income	Means tested	Non-repayable

* Students can only be eligible for one of these grants in any academic year

FAQs

FAQs

Is there an age limit for going to university or college?
No. People of all different ages apply for courses and those who are more mature are equally welcomed as they contribute not only their academic ability but also variety of life experience.

Where can I study? Is higher education limited to universities?
Traditionally, higher education has been associated with universities alone, however there are now a large number of colleges where you can study which means that with over 300 institutions there is currently more choice than ever. You can find out about each of the institutions by visiting **www.ucas.com**.

I have been educated overseas so which courses are right for me?
The UK welcomes many international students each year and so it's likely that you'll be able to find a course that is right for you. The institutions themselves can answer any questions you may have about their entry requirements and the support that is available. Don't be afraid to get in touch with them.

How does higher education in the UK differ from other countries?
Applications to higher education in the UK are usually made through UCAS which means that you have to submit only one application form. In other countries it is often the case that you must make an application to each institution separately, making the process time consuming and often expensive.

What qualifications do I need to reach higher education?
Institutions often set minimum entry requirements for their courses in terms of qualifications. You can find this information for the courses you are interested in by using Course Search at **www.ucas.com**, or by looking on the institutions' own websites.

Institutions will often accept a wide variety of qualifications, from both the UK and overseas. If you have any questions about their entry requirements then it's a good idea to contact them directly.

Is higher education just for school leavers?
Higher education is available to people from all stages of life, whether you have recently left school or you left some time ago. It is no longer the case that students

will all be embarking on courses at the same age as the choice to carry out further study can be triggered for different people at different times.

Do many employers look for graduates?

Many employers will seek to recruit individuals who have achieved a qualification at degree level as the relevant knowledge and experience this provides may be necessary for the job.

For jobs where there is fierce competition, knowledge at higher education level may help to provide an advantage over competitors. It is worthwhile visiting the websites of a few employers to find out what type of experience and qualifications they look for in their candidates.

What experience will I gain from higher education?

Higher education will expand your knowledge on a given subject and can sometimes include hands-on experience for more practical-based courses. You will learn to manage your time in order to meet deadlines and build on your analytical skills.

Aside from the educational aspects, there are many other ways that you can benefit from higher education. Living away from home at your chosen institution will help you to develop independence and mixing with students from around the world can broaden your cultural awareness.

How can I contact UCAS?

Our website **www.ucas.com/about_us/contact_us** has details of how to contact us.

You can email us at enquiries@ucas.ac.uk for an automated response with general information and guidance.

Do I have to apply through UCAS or can I apply to institutions directly?

For all courses listed on **www.ucas.com** you would have to submit an application through UCAS as we are the central admissions system. Your application allows you to apply for up to five choices.

Chapter summary

These are the things you should now know:

☐   Why you want to go higher education.

☐   The differences between the types of qualifications available:

-   bachelor's degree

-   Higher National Certificate (HNC) and Higher National Diploma (HND)

-   Certificate of Higher Education (CertHE) and Diploma of Higher Education (DipHE)

-   foundation degree

-   postgraduate.

☐   What are single subject and combined subject courses.

☐   What's meant by modular courses.

☐   What's meant by a sandwich course.

☐   How learning at university is different to learning at school.

☐   UCAS – our role in your journey.

☐   Six steps to applying – the applicant journey.

☐   Extra information for:

-   mature students

-   students with disabilities

-   non-UK students.

☐   Money: eligibility of student funding and cash support.

Step 1
Choosing courses

Once you know that you want to do a higher education course, you need to start thinking about what you want to study and where you want to go. There are lots of resources available to help you but at the end of the day it is you who will have to make up your own mind. You need to spend some quality time exploring what you want to do and what best fits your interests and abilities.

This chapter guides you through your research into a career, how to narrow your subject choices down using the Stamford Test, where to find course information and where to find information on universities and colleges.

Step 1 **Choosing courses**

Thinking of going to university or college?

No →

- Employment
- Apprenticeship
- Part-time course
- Gap year
- Re-sits
- Other ...

Yes ↓

Do your research!

Which subject?

Ask your school, family, etc

Visit **www.ucas.com** for Course Search, Stamford Test, links to uni websites

Library

unistats.direct.gov.uk

Summer school

Which career?

Careers service

Connexions

Work experience

Dreams, inspirations, heroes & heroines

Which course?

Which university or college? (see websites and prospectuses)

Check whether you need to sit an admissions test or are likely to be called to interview or audition (see **www.ucas.com**)

Joint degree – can restrict or open choices of career

Check out teaching and assessment methods

Attend an open day to look around and meet current students

Do your research

Choosing the right course can be crucial to your career path. So it's important early on to look into what you want to do so that when it comes to applying, you are sure of the reasons why you've chosen it.

Many potential applicants don't know what they want to study at uni or which subjects suit them best, so if you're not sure, you're not alone. It is essential that you spend quality time exploring and researching what to study. Every year a significant number of students discontinue their course because they failed to do the necessary research prior to application.

You can choose up to five courses to put down on your UCAS application, but you don't have to use all your choices - you can apply for just one if you know exactly where you want to go. You want to be realistic about which universities are likely to make you an offer.

Here's a list of the things you should be doing to research the right course for you. Each of these is explained in more detail under the appropriate heading.

Think ahead – going to university should be one of the most enriching and enjoyable experiences of your life. A big decision deserves a lot of thought. You can apply for five course choices and you want to arrive at the very best ones for you.

Think about your career path

Some careers require you to take a particular subject at a particular level while others will be happy with any subject. If you have an idea of what kind of a job you'd like after education, check what qualifications employers require. If you have an idea of what subject you'd like to study, see what career opportunities there are with it.

There are many places to check the career paths of courses.

- You can go to **www.direct.gov.uk/unistats** and see the employment prospects for a course. It shows the top 10 profession types of those students with a job six months after graduation.

- Visit **www.ucas.com/seps** to access the employability profiles which explain the broader skills you will have to offer a future employer.

- University and college prospectuses and websites often indicate what careers their graduates go into.

- *What Do Graduates Do?*, published every year and available from the UCAS bookstore for £14.95, provides destination statistics and articles to illustrate the variety of careers entered by graduates.

- Ask your school or college tutors and advisers, as well as your local Connexions, Careers Wales, Careers Scotland or Northern Ireland Careers Service offices.

- If you have a career in mind, talk to someone already doing the job and check to see if it has a professional representative body. Job advertisements can give a flavour of a career and how it might develop.

Students with disabilities

If you know what career you want to follow, discuss suitable degrees with a careers adviser. You could also talk to a professional organisation connected to the career in which you are interested. By talking to someone who is already doing the job, you can get practical advice about the best courses. You may want to do a foundation degree if you are already working and want to develop your skills, or if you have a specific career in mind.

In some cases you may need to think about how your impairment might affect your future career path. There are some courses and professions which have their own 'fitness to practise' regulations. These relate to the physical demands of the job and health and safety requirements. This might involve completing a health questionnaire and having an occupational health assessment.

No one should assume that a disabled person cannot enter a specific career. The Equality Act (2010) means that employers have to remove barriers in the workplace for disabled people and financial support is available to help them do this. Always start exploring your options based on what you want to do. Then you can think about any advice and support you might need.

No idea what to study? Start with the Stamford Test

If you know that a higher education course is for you but you find the choice of subjects too much, a good place to start is with the Stamford Test on the UCAS website **www.ucas.com**. It's a quick questionnaire that matches your personal interests, abilities and skills to potentially suitable higher education courses. It gives you a list of potential course headings to help you search for courses that are related to your strongest interests. Many students find it helpful when trying to make up their minds.

You can also ask yourself the following questions.

- Which subjects interest me?

- What are my talents?

- What job would I like to do after university or college?

- Which academic skills would I like to improve?

FAQs on the Stamford Test

What is the Stamford Test?

The Stamford Test is a short questionnaire designed to match your interests and abilities to possible higher education subjects.

What will it tell me?

If you are trying to make up your mind about what to study at university the Stamford Test could be useful in deciding which course and institution might suit you. It will give you a list of potential course headings to help you search for courses that are related to your strongest interests.

When should I take the test and where can I find it?

It is a good idea to take the test when you first start researching courses and institutions you might be interested in. The test will give you ideas as to what courses might be suitable for you and will help you narrow down your search. You can find the Stamford Test on the UCAS website.

Do I have to pay for the test or results?

No. However, once you have received your Stamford Test results there will be an option for a Centigrade Online program which will go into more detail and direct you to up to eight course areas. For a charge of £15 you will be sent a detailed bound report with well-matched selections.

FAQs on choosing a course

How do I choose a course?

You need to find a course that matches your interests, career aspirations and talents. It is important to choose a qualification that suits you. Universities and colleges offer a whole range of higher education courses including undergraduate degrees, foundation degrees, HNDs and HNCs, so you need to look into what these involve when deciding what to apply for.

You can take the Stamford Test. It is a short questionnaire which can help to match your interests and abilities to possible higher education subjects. Many students find this helpful when trying to make up their minds. Find it here: **www.ucas.com/students**.

Once you've decided which subject to study, you can decide which universities to apply for. You can visit **www.direct.gov.uk/unistats** to find information on what current students think about the course. You can also look at league tables, which compare universities by subject.

But the best way to decide if a university is right for you is to visit it. Arrange to go to an open day, or ask to arrange a tour.

How do I know if I'm eligible for a course?

Universities will list the entry requirements for their courses on their websites and on UCAS Course Search. Often they are listed in terms of UCAS Tariff points. If you are not sure if you have enough points, or your qualification is not included in the Tariff system, contact the university directly and ask them if you would meet their requirements.

Can I defer my place for a year?

You should check with the university or college you are interested in applying to in order to confirm they are happy to consider an application for deferred entry. You then need to state that you wish to defer on your application in the 'Choices' section by selecting the appropriate start date when adding the choice.

Choose a qualification that suits you

Most people think that higher education means studying for a degree, but there are many more qualifications that you can take at university or college. See the types of available qualifications on page 14.

Remember, you may get a better degree – which employers will like – if you study something you enjoy.

Consider combination courses if you would like to study more than one subject

If you are interested in more than one subject, you can choose to study a combination of subjects, eg English literature and psychology. Use Course Search at **www.ucas.com** to find out which combinations are available.

You can often decide for yourself how much time you would like to spend on each subject. See the section 'Single and combined courses' on page 18 for more information.

Did you know?

You can study waste management and dance…

It's amazing what combinations you can do. Over 1000 different subjects are available, in well over 43,000 different courses. So before jumping in with a favourite subject you're studying now, see what else is available. For example, if you're studying biology, have you thought about a course in zoology, marine biology or forensic science? If you prefer English, what about journalism, creative writing or primary school teaching?

International students

If you plan to work back in your home country, be sure to check with the professional body in your own country that the content of the course for professional qualifications is recognised.

Vocational or non-vocational course?

A vocational course is one which is job-specific while a non-vocational course is one which is not related to a specific job. A non-vocational course in something you have a passion about may make you more ready for a career than a job-specific course that you don't like much but chose for job-security reasons.

Consider taking a sandwich course, which includes a year of working in industry and gives you valuable experience in a profession. You can easily search for sandwich courses on Course Search at **www.ucas.com** by selecting 'sandwich' as your attendance type.

Think about how long it might take to achieve specific career goals and do this before you apply.

Studying abroad – Erasmus

Erasmus is the European exchange programme for higher education students. You get to study or do a work placement for a few months (anything from three to 12 months) in other European countries as part of your degree course. Students from all subjects can take part – it's not just for language students, although studying in another country will involve foreign languages in some way.

Student tip:

'Don't follow what your mates are doing or what uni they're going to – IT'S YOUR FUTURE!'

If you're interested, you need to choose a university or college that offers the Erasmus programme for the course you want to study. You can find out more information from the British Council website **www.britishcouncil.org/erasmus**.

It's a great opportunity to improve your academic experience and job opportunities and well as developing your personal confidence and maturity.

Look at Entry Profiles on Course Search at www.ucas.com

There is a wealth of information on the internet. Spend a few hours each week surfing and collecting information.

Course Search on the UCAS website lists around 43,000 full-time higher education courses, so narrowing your search down may seem daunting.

You will recognise the core subjects available to study, such as mathematics, English and chemistry. But you may not recognise the more creative and varied courses available which branch out from these core subjects. For example, if you enjoy chemistry, you could study chemical engineering, environmental chemistry or forensic science. If you prefer English, you could study English literature, journalism, creative writing or primary school teaching.

Course Search provides course information on:

- course title, duration, type of qualification and application deadline

- university contact details and website links

- links to the relevant employability profile

- link to the results from the National Student Survey on the Unistats website about the university or college

- link to the course Entry Profile which provides details about

    - the content of the course

    - entry requirements

Student tip:

'Course Search on the UCAS website is very helpful as it provides you with details about what the course is about, as well as the entry requirements.'

- skills, qualities and experiences admissions staff are looking for

- fees, bursaries and financial support

- details about the institution.

You can 'search by subject' on Course Search and it will bring up a list of all the courses with a significant element of your chosen subject in the content of the course. When you click on the course title you will find the Entry Profile link for the course. This link will take you to all the information which has been provided about that particular course. Entry Profiles are written by staff at the university or college which offers the course. They ensure you can find your way onto the right course. Check that you have the right qualifications, experiences and personal qualities to gain entry onto the course.

Many courses with the same title are actually very different in terms of content and study methods, so check the Entry Profiles to help you see which will suit you best.

Be sure of the entry requirements

When looking at the entry requirements, check the course-specific requirements in case there are any overall entry requirements which apply to you. There may be an admissions test you will have to take or an interview to attend. Then check if there are specific GCSE or Standard Grade subjects and grades which are required. Many will require you to have English and maths at grade C or above. The Tariff score or A level and Higher grades will be listed, as will any specific subjects and grades that you will be expected to gain before entering the course. Course Search lists the entry requirements for many qualifications so look for the one you're doing or have. If your qualification is not listed then contact the university to check whether the grade you have or are expecting to get would be acceptable for entry.

Tariff points are often used in entry requirements. The UCAS Tariff is the system for allocating points to qualifications used for entry to higher education. See page 341 for a list of the qualifications included in the Tariff or visit **www.ucas.com** to view the most up-to-date list.

Student tip:

'EARLY! EARLY! EARLY! I cannot emphasis this more!!! EARLY!!! Do not make the same mistake as I did, leaving it too late and getting all research, details and information just as the deadline is coming up.'

Often certain subjects will be required and you must be studying these in order to have your application fully considered.

Be realistic. A popular degree at a prestigious university will set challenging entry requirements.

Myth buster

If one course has lower entry requirements than another, it doesn't mean that it's not as good.

Try not to decide which courses to apply for based on just the grades or points they require – although you'll need to check that you can realistically meet these, you also need to think about the course itself. It's more important that you choose a course based on what it offers you, rather than whether it has high entry requirements or not.

Read through a course's Entry Profile to see if it's what you want, or check the university's website.

If you'd like to find out what other students thought of the university or subject that you're considering, take a look at Unistats at **www.direct.gov.uk/unistats**, where you can compare unis and subjects based on feedback from previous students.

But whatever anyone says about a course, make sure it's right for you.

FAQs on Course Search

How do I find out which universities or colleges run the course I want to apply for?

The Course Search facility on the UCAS website will allow you to do this research. You can simply search by subject or you can narrow down your search further by geographical region, a specific institution or course type. You can also look for courses leading to Qualified Teacher Status (QTS) or professional accreditation.

What qualifications do I need?

The majority of courses on the Course Search have an Entry Profile attached and this will allow you to look at the entry requirements for that course. Entry requirements differ between courses and universities so it is important to check these carefully before applying.

Can I search for a university or college that will accept my qualification(s)?

Unfortunately not, you need to find a course you are interested in and then check the specific entry requirements in the Entry Profile.

How do I search for part-time courses?

UCAS processes applications for full-time courses only. However, we have a part-time course search on our website from July until September where you can search for part-time courses at universities and colleges that recruit for their full-time courses through us. You can contact individual universities and colleges to find out if they have part-time options. This information should also be available on their website.

What information is included in the Entry Profile?

As well as the entry requirements for a course you will also find more details about the course, selection criteria, admissions policy, fees, bursaries and financial support, specific information about the institution, and details regarding any admissions tests required.

Can I search for courses in other countries?

No, UCAS only processes applications for courses in England, Wales, Scotland and Northern Ireland. You can find more information regarding studying in another country by contacting the Embassy for that country (see page 277).

Why are there two searches available, one for home and EU applicants and one for international applicants?

After their application has passed certain courses may be available only to international students so there are two searches to make it easier for you to find which courses have vacancies.

The reason for this is that publicly funded universities and colleges are required by the government to limit the number of students they accept who normally reside in the UK or the EU. However, there are no such restrictions placed on applicants living outside of the UK or EU.

International students

You should also contact your local British Council office (visit **www.britishcouncil.org**) as we work closely with them in providing up-to-date information to students. They may be able to help you search for a UK course.

Regardless of how old you are, it is important not to rush your choice.

Mature students

Deciding on the right course is crucial if you are to make the most of higher education. Looking at the Entry Profiles on Course Search at **www.ucas.com** will help to differentiate one course from another and will also provide links to university and colleges' own web pages with information specifically for mature students. If you find that the entry requirement information is only tailored for school leavers, contact the admissions tutor for the course and find out whether your experience and qualifications would be suitable.

Students with disabilities

Concentrate first on what you want to study. Most subjects can be made accessible with the appropriate support. Do not be put off by people assuming that you cannot do something because of your impairment.

- Visually impaired students take graphic design courses.

- People who are deaf or hard of hearing study music.

- People with dyslexia train to be teachers.

If you have very specific needs, you should visit all the institutions you are considering. It is better not to waste one of your UCAS choices by finding out that an institution is not suitable after you have applied. Many institutions welcome early, informal visits as they provide staff with an opportunity to discuss possible support arrangements with you.

Once you have an idea of what you want to study, start to do some more detailed investigation into each university that interests you.

Look at university and college websites and prospectuses

University and college websites and prospectuses should provide accurate information about the courses available covering course content, structure, study style and career destinations. You can find links to the university and college websites from Course Search or look for copies of prospectuses in your local careers office.

You can order prospectuses directly from universities or colleges. Ask them to send you a copy of their undergraduate prospectus along with any additional course-specific leaflets, or they may have an option on their website to enter your contact details to receive a prospectus or view a copy online. But remember, prospectuses also act as advertisements to encourage students to apply particularly to them.

Attend a higher education convention

Higher education conventions are an excellent opportunity to meet representatives from universities and colleges who will tell you about their institution. UCAS higher education conventions are held throughout the UK and run between March and July in England, Wales and Northern Ireland and between August and October in Scotland. Exhibitors also include further education colleges, Connexions, gap year organisations, student support services, professional bodies, student travel firms and student finance.

Outside of the UK, many events are held throughout the year, including many hosted by the British Council. You can check the following website to see what events are being held in your country: **www.educationuk.org/uk/events**. Examples of some of the locations are Hong Kong, Canada, South Korea and Cyprus. You should also check with the institutions you are interested in studying at to see if they will be visiting your country.

The events play a vital part in helping applicants decide what and where to study within higher education. Many of them have an extensive seminar programme. Recent topics include 'grants and loans', 'taking a year out', 'how to fill in your UCAS application' and 'entry into medicine, law and psychology'.

Education conventions are designed mainly for 16- and 17-year-old students, and schools and colleges make group bookings to attend. However you are also welcome to visit a convention as an individual on the day free of charge without any prior booking. A list of the higher education conventions can be found at **www.ucasevents.com/conventions**.

When you attend a convention or exhibition, it's a good idea to have a set of questions to ask the universities and colleges. Here are some examples.

Getting onto the course

- How many places are available for the course and how many applications are received each year?

- Are there any subjects or qualifications that are not acceptable for your course?

- What qualities do you look for when considering applicants?

- What key skills are looked for and what evidence of them is required?

- What special entry qualifications or other arrangements for mature students exist?

- For art and design courses, is an art foundation course necessary?

- Will I have to sit an additional test?

Interviews

- Is a formal interview part of the selection procedure?

- What proportion of applicants do you interview?

- What is the purpose of the interview, how important is it, and what form does it take?

The course itself

- How is the course assessed – by exam or continuous assessment?

- Is it possible to study abroad for part of the course?

- How flexible is the course? Is there scope to pursue special interests?

- How easy is it to change course or to study a subsidiary course?

Student tip:

'From going to a higher education event in my first year at college, I found out more about what universities have to offer, and also more about the information UCAS provides.'

- How is the course taught – through lectures, tutorials, seminars, laboratory work, other?

- How much contact time (in lectures, tutorials etc) is there per week?

- What is the staff to student ratio?

- Do departments give help or advice about obtaining sponsorship?

- Will I be expected to buy materials or equipment?

A year out

- Is taking a year out acceptable or encouraged? If so, is specific experience sought?

- Should I apply during my final A level or equivalent year for deferred entry, or apply during my year out?

- What are the financial implications of taking a year out?

The university or college

- Is it based on one site?

- Do students live in? Is there accommodation for all first year students?

- How far away is the accommodation from the institution?

- What is the typical cost of accommodation?

- Do I need to have personal transport? May I keep a car, motorbike or cycle? If so, can it be parked?

- Is public transport available from the halls of residence to lectures? If yes, what does it cost?

Student facilities

- Can you tell me about student services, the students' union, clubs, job shop, societies and sports and recreation facilities at your institution?

- What support services are provided, such as careers service, counselling, finance and medical?

- What support facilities exist for students with additional needs?

The future

- Where are graduates from this course likely to find employment?

- What exemptions does this course give with respect to professional qualifications?

Finding out more

- If I have any specific questions in the future, who should I contact at your institution?

- What are the arrangements for attending an open day or making a personal visit?

- Is there an alternative student prospectus? How do I get one?

Other recommended activities

- Attend university and college open days. These will help you decide if the university or college is right for you, and you can avoid the disappointment of starting a course and finding it is not what you expected.

- Arrange an interview with your tutor or personal careers adviser, if help is required.

- If you have not already done so, create an information progress file to record your research.

- Draft a personal statement for your UCAS application.

- Establish a personal timetable for ongoing research and your application.

FAQs on conventions and exhibitions

What is a convention or exhibition?

Conventions bring together universities and colleges to inform and guide prospective students. There is a lot of information available at conventions; as well as institutions there are often details about student finance and gap year organisations.

Exhibitions tend to focus on particular subject areas such as art and design or media.

Where and when are they held?

There are a number of conventions and exhibitions run throughout the UK. The events usually take place between March and October each year.

What use are they?

The conventions provide an opportunity to meet face-to-face with universities and colleges and obtain information regarding the course you are interested in and what the institution has to offer you with regard to facilities, support, clubs, etc. You will also be able to ask any questions you might have regarding the course or the institution.

How can I apply to go?

Tickets are not necessary for conventions, however invitations to book are usually sent out to schools and colleges prior to when booking commences. You are welcome to visit the convention on the day as an individual without prior booking.

You do need to book to attend an exhibition and you can do this online from the UCAS website.

Do I have to pay to come to an event?

No, all events are free of charge.

Choosing a university or college

There are lots of reasons why you might want to choose a particular university or college. The reasons will be personal to you and what is right for your friends might not be right for you. Here are some of the questions you might want to think about.

- **Near or far?** You might need to look for a local course so that you can stay with your family or you might be happy to move to wherever you need to go to do the right course.

- **Town or country?** Would you like to live in the centre of a big city to be close to all the facilities it has to offer or do you prefer a rural location?

- **Small or large?** Do you like the idea of studying on a really large university where there are large lecture theatres and something for everybody or would you prefer a small site where you can get to know everyone?

Student tip:

'Research the universities that are expert in your field and pick from there. All universities have the nightlife, the organisations and societies but not all universities specialise in your subject.'

Student tip:

'Choosing your uni. Well, it's not the easiest thing. All I can say is take what is important to you into consideration. I thought of:

- *Location – how far do I want to be away from home, friends and family?*
- *Cost – how far is it to travel? Is it an expensive area?*
- *Social 'n' nightlife – where do you think you can most enjoy and get the most out of?*
- *Relationships – is it going to be easy or tough? Well, just depends who you are.'*

- **Campus or non-campus?** Are you bothered whether you're on a campus where everything you need is located on one site or do you like the idea of moving around between sites?

- **What is the quality of study facilities, books and learning resources like?** Very important if you're going to be spending a lot of time there.

- **Hall of residence or rented accommodation?** Does it have guaranteed institution-managed accommodation for first year students? What's the cost of staying in hall? How easy is it to find a student house to live in?

- **Is there a range of activities, clubs and societies?** Many universities boast a vast array of clubs and societies from rowing and tennis to debating and religious clubs but some will be more active than others so check with the Students' Union and ask students when you visit on an open day.

- **Nightlife and social life?** Can you be assured of getting the social life you're after? Does it have an active Students' Union? What events does the Students' Union arrange? Are there clubs and pubs nearby that you want to go to?

- **Male to female ratio.** Are you interested in whether there are more females on campus than males, or vice versa?

- **What sports facilities are there?** Many universities have gyms, playing fields and swimming pools on site which are important if you like an active life.

- **What's the university's reputation?** The reputation of a university or college can be very subjective and it's important to choose a university that suits you rather than trying to fit into one that might not work for you. However, if you're thinking about your CV and the kudos a certain university will bring, then perhaps reputation is important for you. Maybe certain courses at specific universities are better regarded by an area of business or industry than others.

- **Does it have expert teaching staff?** What is the student to staff ratio? Are the academic staff experts in their field? How was the subject you were interested in rated in the latest Research Assessment Exercise (soon to be the Research Excellence Framework)? What teaching methods are used?

- **What's the general ambience of the university and the university town?**
  How does it feel when you visit? Do you feel safe and comfortable moving around the campus and town? Does it excite you? Does it have a view or a stunning piece of architecture that would inspire you? Does it have the space and support to be who you want to be?

You can find a map of the UK on page 367 or go to **www.ucas.com** to find a map plotting all the universities and colleges – click on 'where to study?'. The 'further details' link will help you answer some of the questions above. It tells you how many students there are (and what subject areas they study), what the male to female ratio is, more information about the campuses and whether they have institution-managed accommodation places for first year students.

International students
Check out the public transport to your chosen university so that you can fly in easily and get your luggage to the university without too much trouble!

Mature students
Look as widely as possible to find a university and course which best suits you. If you're limited to a single local university or college, you may want to look at the full range of courses it offers to see if there's something which appeals that you didn't originally consider. Alternatively higher education courses, or segments of them, are available in further education colleges.

Groups of universities

When reading about universities in the paper or doing your research, you may hear people referring to a specific group or category of university. The following is a brief explanation of each term.

1994 Group – a group of 19 internationally renowned, research-intensive universities established to promote excellence in research and teaching and enhance student and staff experience. It includes universities such as University of Bath, Lancaster University and University of St Andrews. A full list and details of the group is available at **www.1994group.ac.uk**.

Million+ Group – is a university think tank which uses rigorous research and evidence-based policy to solve complex problems in higher education. It aims to develop and shape public policy to enable people from every walk of life to benefit from access to universities that excel in teaching, research and knowledge transfer. It includes such universities as Kingston University London, Teesside University and University of the West of Scotland. Visit **www.millionplus.ac.uk** for more information.

Red brick universities – an informal term for six universities, originally civic colleges which achieved university status by the early 1900s. They are the universities of Birmingham, Bristol, Leeds, Liverpool, Manchester and Sheffield. More recently, due to their similar characteristics, universities such as Reading, Queen's University Belfast, Nottingham and Hull, among others, have also been classed as 'red brick'.

Russell Group – represents 20 leading universities which are committed to 'maintaining the very best research, an outstanding teaching and learning experience and unrivalled links with business and the public sector'. It includes universities such as Queen's University Belfast, Cardiff University, University of Edinburgh and University of Oxford. See **www.russellgroup.ac.uk** for a full list.

Post-1992 universities or new universities – an informal term referring to the universities who were formerly polytechnics or colleges of higher education and were given university status in (and after) 1992. Examples include the universities of Coventry, Worcester, Portsmouth, Glamorgan, and Glasgow Caledonian.

FAQs on choosing a university or college

Which institution is best for my chosen course?
Different places suit different people, so it depends what you're looking for. There are different guides and league tables that can help you, but check the source as it may be biased: some universities post league tables on their websites which show their courses at number one.

For information and impartial advice check the *Times Online* or *The Complete University Guide*, which is an interactive site where you can highlight your requirements and create your own unique table.

How can I find universities and colleges in my area that offer the course I want to do?

The Course Search facility on the UCAS website will allow you to search for the subject you are interested in and then narrow your search down by geographical region. This will just bring up the institutions in your area that offer the course you're interested in.

Also on the UCAS website there is a university and college map which will show you the locations of all the institutions across the UK.

Where can I find out more about the student experience?

There are several different places you can go to speak to current students and get tips on the application process and going to university. Attending an open day will mean you get to meet current students and prospective students to share your thoughts, questions and any worries you might have.

There is information from students on the Unistats and yougo websites, and you can use a social network site such as Twitter or Facebook — we have a UCAS adviser on both who can answer your questions and there is the opportunity to chat to other students as well.

Visit the Unistats website to compare universities

Visit website enables you to search, review and compare universities and colleges and the subjects they offer in order to help you to choose the best UK university and subject for you.

It includes results from the National Student Survey — where more than 220,000 students give their views about the quality of their higher education experience. You can also find links to Unistats in the course information screens on Course Search at **www.ucas.com**.

Visit **www.direct.gov.uk/unistats** to view and compare a range of university statistics and see how students rated their university experience. You can also find

links to Unistats on the course search course information screens at
www.ucas.com.

- See the best universities for your subject.

- See the national student satisfaction results.

- See job prospects.

Compare UCAS Tariff points… and lots more.

Open days and visits to universities and colleges

Visiting your chosen universities or colleges is a must if you want to be sure it's the right place for you. It will help with your expectations of university life as not only will you be shown lecture theatres, laboratories, libraries and IT suites but you're likely to get to see the student catering facilities, bar and halls of residence. Your visit will give you an idea of the distance between the facilities you'll be using, where they are in the city, town or country, how close you are to other public services and you will also find out how long it will take you to get there from home.

It is a good idea to aim to visit all of the universities and colleges you are interested in before you apply and certainly before you reply to your offers, to ensure you avoid the disappointment of applying for or starting the course and finding it is not what you expected.

Remember, if you're planning to visit a number of universities around the UK it may pay you to get the 16-25 Railcard or the Young Persons Coachcard. The 16-25 Railcard saves you a third off rail fares across Britain for a year. You can get one if you're between 16 and 25 years or in full-time education and over 26 years. See **www.16-25railcard.co.uk** for details. The Young Persons Coachcard saves you up to 30% off National Express coach fares for a year. Again you need to be between 16 and 26 or a full-time student. See **www.nationalexpress.com/coach/Offers/StudentCoachDeals.cfm** for details.

International students

If you can't visit, use video guides instead. **UCAS.tv**, **YouTube.com** and **unionview.com** all have really useful video clips to help you choose the right university for your needs, and to see its location.

FAQs on open days

What is an open day?

An open day is an opportunity to visit a university or college to see it first hand and confirm you are happy to go there before you apply.

When are the open days?

Each university and college will have its own date(s) for an open day. You should contact the institution directly for details and dates. You will find open day dates on our website at **www.ucas.com/students/choosingcourses/choosinguni/map** under 'further details' or go to the university and college websites for more details.

What do they involve?

Usually during an open day you will be shown around and have an opportunity to look at the accommodation and student union. You will also be able to meet current students and ask them any questions you have about the course and the university or college.

Are they worth going to?

Attending an open day will help you make an instinctive decision and confirm you feel right about attending that university and doing that course. You need to make sure it is what you want before agreeing to study there. Visiting a university will give you a feel of what the institution has to offer you and a taste of university life.

How do I register to attend?

This depends on the university or college and you should contact them directly to confirm whether you need to register – if it is necessary, you can usually do so on the institution's own website.

I can't make the official open day; can I still visit the university or college?

Probably – although it is unlikely the university or college will be able to offer you the same tour and so on, you will be encouraged to see the institution before accepting a place. You should contact the university or college directly to discuss an individual visit on a day that suits you both.

Case study

Name: Caryn Wright
Parent of A level student

My son is looking to go into higher education and as part of his research we have been attending a number of university open days.

I have been quite surprised at how differently the universities run their open days. Some just have a 'turn up on the day' policy, while others advised us that booking was either advisable or essential due to high numbers expected.

Once we had registered for the open days, we received some good communication ranging from a personalised prospectus to a welcome letter. We also received vouchers with discounts off on-site food while you were attending.

When we attended our first open day we really didn't know what to do, so we just marched up to the registration desk and asked. They helpfully gave us a bag full of information but also ran through all the different activities that were taking place and suggested that we attend a welcome session. We were also advised to check what time our subject talk was happening so as not to miss it and to make some time to visit some of the accommodation blocks. We managed to do all of this in a couple of hours and felt that we had a good understanding of what the university had to offer.

We then used this formula for the next five open days that we attended. On some occasions we found that the day finished too early and we did not get to see all that we wanted. I think the most important part of the day was attending the subject talks as you really got a feel for how you would get on with the lecturers and the course content.

They were usually followed by a tour of the department, which gave a good insight into the facilities available.

Remember, at the end of the day it is the course that is the most important thing. This was really highlighted when we attended a subject talk at one event and the audience were clearly not impressed. They either got up and left or fell asleep! We were certainly put off that subject at that particular institution. In contrast though, we attended a subject talk at a different university and the lecturers were so enthusiastic and passionate about the subject that it was clear they had the ability to completely capture the audience. My son was very impressed and felt a great sense of enthusiasm for that particular university.

The open days were attended by an equal amount of students on their own and students accompanied by their parents. As a parent I felt that I asked more questions than my son would have if he had attended on his own. Now that we have finished our round of open days both my son and myself have a better understanding about where he wants to go and what he wants to study. I think that they are an essential part of applying to higher education.

Visit www.ucas.tv and watch case studies

Our UCAS tv video site at **www.ucas.tv** is a great place to go if you're still not sure about what's important to you. It has loads of different case studies and video diaries that you can watch, ordinary students telling you their experience of choosing a university or college. As well as case studies and video diaries, we have put together some 'how-to' guides which explain each element of applying so you can get to know the process.

Go to the site and click on 'students' to find all the videos relating to you. Start with the 'how-to' guide for choosing courses and the 'how-to' guide on attending events.

International students

At **www.ucas.tv** you can watch videos about choosing courses, our 'how-to' guides and case studies for international applicants.

The information about league tables in this chapter has been contributed by Dr Bernard Kingston, author of *The Complete University Guide*.

Mayfield University Consultants has been compiling university league tables since 1995 and launched *The Complete University Guide* wholly online in 2007. The website is comprehensive and impartial and aims to help students to decide what to study where. It is free to access and a third of its users are based overseas. The interactive league table enables individuals to create their own unique university rankings. Visit **www.thecompleteuniversityguide.co.uk**.

Look at league tables

As part of your research for choosing what to study, you might well want to consult one or more of the league tables published on the web and elsewhere so here we outline their background, an insight into their composition and suggestions as to when and how to use them.

The tables

The compilers of these tables are trying to define the quality of the university experience you might expect and its outcome. They pull together a huge amount of disparate information about universities and courses and collate it to provide an at-a-glance summary. Some information can best be described only in words, not by figures and tables. However, league tables can be very useful at the outset in helping to draw up a long list of universities and colleges meeting your key criteria or for the subject or subjects that interest you. You might also want to go back to them at the end of your research to confirm that your short list is satisfactory. Remember there is no such thing as 'the best university', only the best university for you, not for your friends nor for your teachers and definitely not for your

Student tip:

'I consulted online newspapers for university league tables, which did influence my decision somewhat. Other influences included the distance from my home, and the course modules and specialities.'

First rule: approach the tables with caution, look at them with a critical eye and try to understand the assumptions behind the rankings.

Next, never rely solely on them, never use them in isolation.

parents. You are unique and this choice has to be a personal one. Be realistic, bordering on optimism not pessimism.

The higher education landscape is wide, diverse and complex, not easy to navigate. League tables can help by giving an overview and by simplifying the search. They do not, and cannot, tell the whole story but rather signpost you in the right direction. Their coverage is not comprehensive; typically the main table includes all the universities and university colleges but not the specialist institutions. The subject tables, on the other hand, do include the specialist colleges and institutes of agriculture and food science, art and design, and drama. These tables are based on the same raw data as the main table but some compilations use fewer measures. The data sets used are principally aimed at full-time, first degree applicants, not those of you interested in part-time or distance learning. Nearly all, therefore, are designed with students planning to do undergraduate courses in mind and yet most of their high profile supporters and detractors come from within the universities themselves. Most who comment on them have axes to grind, heralding good news emerging from them but vocal in their criticism or remaining silent when not so good.

How can you tell if they are fact or fiction? The first test has to be credibility – how impartial or independent are they? Most are tied to specific newspapers and possibly reflect their readerships but it is extremely doubtful that any editorial influence would ever be exerted on the compilers of the tables. On the other hand, conflicts of interest, actual or perceived, have to be guarded against if and when the compilers come from within any university or universities appearing in the tables. Then there is the issue of openness and transparency. All publish the methodology they use but some are easy to understand while others are complicated and remain decidedly opaque. See for yourself if you can follow how the raw data are manipulated to arrive at the final rankings. If you can't understand what it all means, don't be afraid to ask questions.

Much of the raw data come from the universities themselves, mostly from the Higher Education Statistics Agency (HESA) and, at this start point, many of the figures are common to all the compilers. This is because they are all looking for measures which are robust, consistent, comparable and, preferably, audited. However, there are inevitable time lags and this should be borne in mind when interpreting the outcomes. Likewise, some data are prone to erratic fluctuation from one year to the next and this is countered in some tables by averaging over two or three years. This, of course, results in an even greater time lag. Most datasets are available at the beginning of the calendar year and this determines the earliest time that the tables can be published. All come out in the spring or early summer apart from *The Sunday Times* supplement which appears in late summer or autumn. Fortuitously, this timing coincides with when most applicants are starting to think about universities.

The compilers

The producers of the four main university league tables of interest to would-be undergraduates are listed in Table 1 and the scope of their offerings in Table 2. Three are under the auspices of national newspapers and one is completely independent.

Table 1 The compilers of the tables (university league tables published in 2010)

League table	Website	Compiled by
The Complete University Guide	www.thecompleteuniversityguide.co.uk	Mayfield University Consultants
The Guardian	www.guardian.co.uk/education/universityguide	Intelligent Metrix
The Times	www.thetimes.co.uk/gug	Exeter Enterprises
The Sunday Times	www.thesundaytimes.co.uk/universityguide	Alastair McCall and Munro Global

Table 2 The scope of the tables (university league tables published in 2010)

	The Complete University Guide	The Guardian	The Times	The Sunday Times
No. of institutions	115	118	113	121
Measures used	9	8	8	8
No. of subjects	62	46	62	39
Measures used	4	8	4	6

Prior to 2007, *The Times* tables were compiled by Mayfield University Consultants, the instigators of *The Complete University Guide* and, when their association ceased, the task was assumed by Exeter Enterprises, a subsidiary of the University of Exeter. Similarities remain in both these sets of tables, although with each year that passes there is greater divergence within their methodologies. *The Sunday Times* and *The Times* both belong to the News International stable but they do not collaborate in the compilation of their league tables. You should regard them as unrelated and this is manifest in the very different rankings they produce.

Mayfield Consultants have been compiling league tables since 1995 and, early on, recognized the potential of a dedicated web-based university guide. *The Complete University Guide* was launched in 2007 in partnership with Constable & Robinson, independent publisher since 1795. It attempts to do what *The Guardian* and *The Times* do in their books and *The Sunday Times* in its supplement. To date, it has also given *The Independent* an exclusive right to publish its tables in the newspaper and on their website. The advantages of the web are obvious and all the compilers are now strongly developing their own sites. The tables can be interactive and are put into perspective by surrounding text thus allowing users to generate their own bespoke tables based on their individual preferences.

In most cases, there is a cost to gain access to the tables. The guide books published by *The Guardian* and *The Times* have always carried a price tag but recently these have been joined by pay walls on some newspaper sites. Thus, *The Sunday Times* and *The Times* web tables can now only be viewed in their entirety on payment of a fee. *The Guardian University Guide* can be purchased annually but its website remains free to access. A basic tenet of *The Complete University Guide* from its inception is that there should be no cost to the user. In summary, there are a variety of ways to access university league tables.

Methodology

The first thing to say about league table methodology is that it is not an exact science – but neither is it a black art! Compromises have to be made and proxies used but there is no doubt that publishing the figures has led to better data, not least because the university sector itself has improved the quality of the raw data returns to HESA. The universities always have an opportunity to check their HESA data and report mistakes before its release to the compilers. There is no brief for error and regular consultations take place online with institutions on key issues like missing data or subjects no longer taught. Most of the compilers have also established expert groups, mainly from the universities, who offer invaluable help and advice on key issues concerning methodology. One major criticism until recently has been the choice of measures used and the relative importance given to each one. This is completely down to the individual compilers who, in effect, impose their views of university quality on the user. The development of interactive tables has gone a long way to countering that criticism and you should take full advantage of customising your own table using only those measures which are of interest to you.

The raw source data are manipulated in a number of different ways en route to a university receiving a final score and, hence, its ultimate ranking. Compilers will deem some measures more important than others and give these greater significance in the total score awarded, perhaps by higher weightings. Secondly, there might well be an adjustment to allow for the differing subject mix from one university to another. For example, a university with a medical school will have higher entry standards and graduate prospects than one without simply because it has a medical school. Finally, a statistical technique is often used to ensure that each measure contributes the same amount to the overall score and so avoids the need for any scaling.

The main table ranking all the universities gets the headlines but most experts would agree that the subject tables are as important if not more so. You need to look at both sets because all universities, regardless of their overall ranking, have some academic departments with national, even international, reputations. Too much is also made in the press about this or that university climbing or falling a few places when this is usually insignificant. This is particularly the case in the lower half of the main table where there is close bunching of the university scores. As a consequence, there has been a consistent pattern over the years of considerable stability at the top of the table, much more movement lower down and interesting changes in the middle where many of the new universities are overtaking the old.

Measures

The measures used in the rankings published in 2010 are summarised in Table 3. Confusingly, these are usually referred to as the 2011 tables because they are aimed at applicants planning to go to university in 2011. Please go to the individual websites for a detailed description of the methodology and measures adopted by each compiler. Some such as Entry Standards are input measures whereas others like Completion Rates look at output. Most rely on hard objective data from HESA and the National Student Survey (NSS) and Research Assessment Exercise (RAE) commissioned by the Higher Education Funding Council for England (HEFCE). In a few cases where the data are not available, these are obtained directly from the individual universities. A consistent feature of *The Sunday Times* tables has been the subjective impressions of head teachers and academic peers but response rates have been low. There is also the potential for cartels forming with one group of academics singing the praises of a department at another university in return for a similar accolade for their own.

Table 3 The measures used in the tables (university league tables published in 2010)

	The Complete University Guide	The Guardian	The Times	The Sunday Times
Student satisfaction	✓	✓	✓	✓
Research assessment	✓		✓	✓
Entry standards	✓	✓	✓	✓
Student:staff ratio	✓	✓	✓	✓
Spend on academic services	✓	✓	✓	
Spend on student facilities	✓		✓	
Good honours degrees	✓		✓	✓
Completion rates	✓		✓	✓
Graduate prospects	✓	✓	✓	✓
Peer assessments				✓
Value added		✓		

We will now take a brief look at the individual measures using their most common titles.

Student satisfaction
Source: the annual National Student Survey (NSS) of final year undergraduates

This surveys student opinion on their experience of teaching and learning. It is a measure of satisfaction not quality, and satisfaction is affected by many factors, including prior expectation. The league tables use the survey results in different ways (see Table 4). *The Guardian* makes particularly heavy use of the NSS underpinning, as it does, no fewer than three of its seven measures which, in total, account for 25% of a university's overall score.

Table 4 The use of the National Student Survey's 22 questions (university league tables published in 2010)

	The Complete University Guide	The Guardian	The Times	The Sunday Times
The teaching on my course	✓	✓	✓	✓
Assessment and feedback	✓	✓	✓	✓
Academic support	✓		✓	✓
Organisation and management	✓		✓	✓
Learning resources			✓	✓
Personal development	✓		✓	✓
Overall satisfaction	✓	✓	✓	✓

Note

The Complete University Guide and *The Guardian* use 2009 NSS data, *The Times* uses 2008 + 2009 data, and *The Sunday Times* 2010 data. *The Guardian* uses its three NSS sections to create three separate measures. The other compilers use NSS sections as shown to produce a single measure of student satisfaction.

Research assessment
Source: the 2008 Research Assessment Exercise (RAE)

The RAE seeks to define the quality of a university's research and is an important source of university funding. Historically, The *Guardian* has always decided to omit any rating of research from its rankings.

Entry standards
Source: HESA Annual Survey

This is based on the full UCAS Tariff obtained by new students, usually those under 21 years of age. It gives their actual results, not the university offers made to them. Some universities have a specific policy of accepting students with a wide range of entry qualifications in order to widen their intake and this will tend to give them a lower score on this measure.

Student:staff ratio
Source: HESA Annual Survey

The number of students per member of academic staff, except those solely involved in research activities. A low ratio is good but it does not necessarily guarantee the quality of teaching nor how accessible the staff are.

Spend on academic services
Source: HESA Annual Survey

This is the spend per student on university services such as libraries and information technology. The spend figure is often averaged over more than one year to allow for uneven expenditure.

Spend on student facilities
Source: HESA Annual Survey

This covers spending on student (mainly) and staff amenities such as the careers service, the health and counselling services and athletic and sporting facilities. Again the figure is given as spend per student and averaged over more than a single year.

Good honours degrees
Source: HESA Annual Survey

The proportion of graduates achieving a first or upper second class honours degree. Degree class is controlled to a large extent by the individual universities themselves and is the subject of considerable current debate. It has been argued, therefore, that it is not a very good objective indicator of quality. However, it remains the primary badge of individual success and can often impact on graduate employment prospects.

Completion rate
Source: HESA Annual Survey
This shows the proportion of students projected to successfully complete their studies at the university or to transfer to another one elsewhere.

Graduate prospects
Source: HESA Annual Survey
Most compilers take this to be the proportion of graduates who obtain a graduate job – not any job – or continue with postgraduate studies within six months of graduation. If you want to read more about what constitutes a graduate occupation, see the classic study carried out by Peter Elias and Kate Purcell (Warwick Institute for Employment Research).

The Sunday Times uses graduate data on unemployment and those going into non-graduate jobs rather than the positive outcomes mentioned above.

Good employment statistics are often quoted by universities in their publications but be aware that some use all jobs, not just graduate jobs, in their figures.

Peer assessments
Source: Sunday Times Annual Survey
Academics were asked to rate departments in their own subjects for the quality of undergraduate provision. The level of response is not published but is reported to be 10-20%.

Value added
Source: HESA Annual Survey
The Guardian tracks new student qualifications on entry to the university and compares these with the degrees awarded at the end of their studies. Value added is based on entry standards and good honours data (but see comment above) and assumes students with low entry qualifications find it more difficult to obtain a first or upper second class honours degree.

This concludes our overview of those league tables of most interest to individuals interested in undergraduate courses and the universities which offer them. We hope you are now more aware of what these tables are and, more importantly, what they are not. Use them alongside all the other information sources available to you. You will find much more on the web, including more tables of particular interest to international students, on bursaries and scholarships, graduate salaries, safety and security, and sport and recreation, to name but a few.

League table checklist

- [ ] Never rely solely on league tables but only as part of wider research.
- [ ] Remember there is no such thing as "the best university".
- [ ] League table coverage is for full-time first degree study.
- [ ] Ask yourself how impartial or comprehensive any league table is.
- [ ] Remember there are inevitable time lags in the data used.
- [ ] Web-based tables have many advantages, including interactivity.
- [ ] The universities are given an opportunity to check their raw data.
- [ ] Tables are adjusted to allow for differing subject mix.
- [ ] The subject tables are at least as important as the main table.
- [ ] Movement by a few places in rank is usually statistically insignificant.

FAQS on league tables

What is a league table?

League tables are designed to help you compare universities and colleges by ranking them in order of specific categories. For example, the quality of teaching, the facilities available at the university, or student satisfaction in general.

How important should a university's ranking on a league table be in my decision on where to go?

There are a lot of universities and colleges to choose from so it is important to think about what is important to you and where you will be happy. If you know you would like to stay close to home it is probably not a good idea to choose a university 200 miles away just because it is higher in a league table – remember that different places suit different people and you should focus on which universities offer what you are looking for specifically.

How do I find out which university is best for the course I would like to do?
The Unistats website allows you to search for the subject you are interested in and then compare up to three universities offering related courses. The website will enable you to see what previous students have made of the course and to read their reviews of the teaching, support and so on.

www.ucas.com

Money: scholarships

Universities want to attract able students (and let's be honest, if you are going to university you are able). Some universities give huge amounts of money as scholarships and they will all have their own individual schemes and application processes. Some will ask you to complete an application form while others automatically assess from your UCAS information.

Some scholarships look at UCAS Tariff points only but many look at other things such as your ability to demonstrate a level of excellence and achievement above other students. This may be in the arts, sports or volunteering.

Look at websites and ask at open days. Generally, if universities have an application process, it will be necessary for you to apply well before you start the course because the basic idea of scholarships is to encourage you to go university 'A' rather than university 'B'.

What's the difference between a bursary and a scholarship?

Generally, scholarships are awarded on merit (ie you demonstrate excellence in one or more areas) while bursaries are awarded on the basis of financial need (ie you might be dependent upon your family income).

You can find out whether the courses you're interested in have a bursary or scholarship associated with them on Course Search at **www.ucas.com**. Find the link under the heading 'Bursary course selection' on the course information page on Course Search.

Did you know?

The bursary comparison facility on Course Search at **www.ucas.com** allows you to select bursaries and scholarships from up to six courses to view and compare them on a single page.

Summer schools and taster courses

Summer schools are taster courses held at universities and colleges which give you a taste of university life. They tend to be held during the summer after the students have gone home so that the halls of residence can be used for residential programmes and lectures, and other facilities are also available.

Some are subject specific while others are broad ranging with an emphasis on introducing you to university life and giving you an idea of what it might be like studying there. Subject-specific summer schools and taster courses are designed to help you decide if your chosen subject is a suitable education and career choice. They also help you decide which element of a subject you want to focus on, so if you know you like engineering, is it chemical, mechanical, civil or electronic engineering you should study?

There are week-long residential summer schools or one-day taster courses. Some cost, some are free to all and some are free but are only available to a specific group. For example, the Sutton Trust holds free summer schools for young people from non-privileged backgrounds. Many universities and colleges run short taster courses and, understandably, they're incredibly popular, so book early to reserve a place.

You don't have to want to study at the university hosting the summer school, you just need to think that you might want to do a higher education course in the future. Summer schools are aimed at learners from Year 9 (age 13) through to prospective mature students.

Your school should be able to tell you about possible summer schools or you can find them listed on university websites. Look at our publication Open Days which lists the open day dates along with summer schools and taster courses across Britain – find it on **www.ucasbooks.com**. In the meantime, here are a few websites which will get you started and help explain what's involved.

Aimhigher South West: **www.swsummerschools.ac.uk**

Aimhigher Greater Manchester: **www.aimhighergreatermanchester.co.uk**

Aimhigher in the West Midlands: **www.aimhigherwm.org**

Headstart courses: **www.headstartcourses.org.uk**

The London Taster Course Programme: **www.london.ac.uk/tasters**

The Sutton Trust: **www.suttontrust.com**

Case study

Name: Jordan Hodge
Studying: Mental Health Nursing
At: UWE, Bristol

I was concerned about not being clever enough for uni but I had a positive influence from family on my decision to apply to uni. My mum talked about Mental Health then the Leap into Health Summer School at the University of the West of England (UWE) was advertised in school.

The Mental Health workshop was really insightful on the types of treatment and I wanted more information on what you can do in the job. I want to go in to a profession that helps people. I also enjoyed Occupational Therapy and Radiography, which was presented really well. I could have seen myself doing that but once I had done the Mental Health workshop that swung it for me.

Summer School was the sole reason that I went to uni; if I hadn't gone I definitely wouldn't be doing Mental Health now. The Summer School gave me the taste of what uni is like. It also gave me a clear career plan; I made sure I redid my maths GCSE so I could get in and got the A level grades I needed.

Fear of the unknown puts a lot of people off like me. But having gone on the Summer School I felt educated enough and applying wasn't a problem.

Definitely go. It's a great opportunity. You'll learn a lot and have a great time, and it will help you decide your future.

Admissions tests

What is an admissions test?

It's a timed unseen written paper-based or online test, normally taken in the academic year before admission to a university or college, the results of which can be used by that university or college as one element in decision-making about an application.

The type of test used depends predominantly on the course and the attributes deemed appropriate for the professional, vocational or academic discipline. They can be aptitude tests, essay writing exercises, problem solving tests, critical thinking assessments, subject specific tests, cognitive and non-cognitive tests. Many tests are designed to enable a correlation to be made between test results and degree success; that is, they are designed to be predictive as well as testing aptitude. Whether evidence can be presented to support this will require long-term study and analysis.

The tests take place in the summer or autumn of the academic year before admission or at interview; in general, they normally take place from November onwards in the academic year prior to admission. A test can be a uni's own devised test or a test devised by a uni or group or consortium of institutions with one or more testing or awarding bodies. A test may be used by one uni for one or more subjects or may be used by many unis for the same subject.

What are tests used for?

A number of unis and test bodies argue that the use of a test can assist in assessing your potential regardless of your background. As all applicants sit the same test it is one element on which applicants can be judged equally. However, there may be issues around access to familiarisation or practice sessions that may weaken this argument.

Some unis use admissions tests to help differentiate between the most able applicants. A test score in this context has become more significant because of concerns about the large numbers of candidates who achieve high grades in entry level qualifications, eg the increasing number of A grades at A level.

Tests may also focus upon skills and aptitudes that are not assessed through academic attainment.

Universities' and colleges' own tests

In addition to the tests listed in the tables in this section, an increasing number of higher education institutions are using a variety of filtering techniques to decide whom to interview or to make an offer to. These are timed, in the sense that students are usually given a deadline by which they need to have submitted their response.

Examples include:

- submission of a sample essay from the student's A level coursework

- request to write 500 words on a set topic

- practical exercise based on use of statistics

- submission of a design brief.

While many of the universities concerned will have flagged up the possibility of candidates needing to provide extra evidence, as outlined above, in their course promotional literature and, in particular, within their Entry Profile (on UCAS' Course Search), others have not.

International students

If English is not your first language (and also if it is!), practise and practise the tests that are used; you can often find examples on the admissions tests' and university websites. However fluent you are, you need to improve your familiarity with the way the tests are set out and the fine detail of understanding the style for success in multiple-choice questions.

Examples of admissions tests

BioMedical Admissions Test (BMAT)	
Used for:	Entry to medicine, veterinary medicine and related courses
What it is:	The BioMedical Admissions Test (BMAT) is a subject-specific admissions test taken by applicants to certain medicine, veterinary medicine and related courses at the institutions listed below. The BMAT is owned and administered by Cambridge Assessment who is responsible for producing and marking the test, and also facilitates an extensive worldwide centre network at which candidates can sit the BMAT. BMAT was developed by Cambridge Assessment in response to a request by academics from some of the top medical and veterinary schools in the UK for an assessment that would: ■ enable them to differentiate between applicants who appear to be equally well qualified and suited to the course ■ provide a way of assessing the potential of students who have a range of qualifications. Cambridge Assessment has conducted research on data from previous years' BMAT sessions. The research shows that the BMAT: ■ is a good predictor of performance at year one undergraduate level ■ enables admissions tutors to screen out those candidates unlikely to take advantage of the best of higher education. The BMAT is a two-hour pen and paper test consisting of three separate sections. It does not require a great amount of extra study as it relies on skills and knowledge that candidates should already have.
Used by (for 2011 entry):	University of Cambridge, University of Oxford, Royal Veterinary College, University College London, Imperial College London
Entry method:	Through Cambridge Assessment – see the BMAT website www.bmat.org.uk
Duration of test:	2 hours
Other information:	BMAT website – www.bmat.org.uk

English Literature Admissions Test (ELAT)

Used for:	Entry to undergraduate courses in English
What it is:	The ELAT is a pre-interview admissions test for applicants to undergraduate courses in English at the University of Oxford. The test is designed to enable applicants to show their ability in the key skill of close reading, paying attention to such elements as the language, imagery, allusion, syntax, form and structure of the passages set for comment. ELAT is a 90-minute test and candidates write one essay comparing two or three passages. This is not a test of wide reading, nor is it based on the assumption that there are certain texts that all students should have read by this stage in their education. Marks will not be awarded for reference to other texts or authors, nor will candidates be expected to try to apply any theoretical frameworks to their essay. The test will be only one of the elements admissions tutors use to decide whether to invite a candidate for interview. Candidates will be given six poems or passages from prose and drama. The prose may include fiction and non-fiction. The six passages will be linked in some way, and this link will be made explicit in the introduction to the passages.
Used by (for 2011 entry):	University of Oxford
Entry method:	Via Cambridge Assessment – see the ELAT website www.elat.org.uk
Duration of test:	90 minutes
Other information:	ELAT website – www.elat.org.uk

Graduate Medical School Admissions Test (GAMSAT)

Used for:	Graduate entry to medicine and dentistry
What it is:	GAMSAT is a professionally designed and marked selection test developed by the Australian Council for Educational Research (ACER) for medical schools offering graduate-entry programmes open to graduates of any discipline. Applicants are selected for admission into the graduate entry programmes on the basis of three criteria. The schools may apply these criteria in different ways. The criteria are: ■ undergraduate honours degree ■ GAMSAT scores ■ interview. Non-school leaver applicants are selected into the Peninsula medical programme on the basis of performance in GAMSAT and in an interview. Performance in GAMSAT constitutes the only necessary information on an applicant's academic aptitude for the purpose of entry to Peninsula. Applicants who reach the threshold level in GAMSAT are invited to interview for assessment of non-academic attributes. Neither performance in a prior degree nor performance at secondary school will be considered. The programmes all build on the diverse interests and talents of the students admitted. Graduates of the programmes will have the skills and knowledge to practise effectively as pre-registration house officers under supervision, and to develop their careers through subsequent entry into further vocational training. Effective communication with patients and colleagues is seen as crucial. Teamwork and an awareness of community concerns will be stressed. In recognition of the fact that medical knowledge continues to expand and that doctors and dentists will continue to learn throughout their lives, self-directed learning is a major focus of the programmes. GAMSAT results are passed directly to the relevant institutions by UCAS, ensuring invisibility of choice is maintained.
Used by (for 2011 entry):	St. Georges Hospital Medical School, University of Nottingham, Peninsula College of Medicine and Dentistry University of Wales, Swansea and Keele University
Entry method:	Online via www.gamsatuk.org
Duration of test:	5½ hours
Other information:	On ACER website www.gamsatuk.org

History Aptitude Test (HAT)

Used for:	Entry to history or a joint honours degree involving history
What it is:	The colleges of the University of Oxford have introduced a History Aptitude Test (HAT) for use in the selection of candidates for all degree courses involving history. This test, which aims to examine the skills and potentialities required for the study of history at university, gives an objective basis for comparing candidates from different backgrounds, including mature applicants and those from different countries. It is designed to be challenging, in order to differentiate effectively between the most able applicants for university courses, including those who may have achieved or can be expected to achieve the highest possible grades in their examinations. The HAT is a two-hour test, which requires candidates to read two extracts and answer a total of four questions about them. One of the extracts will be from a work of history; candidates will be asked questions to test their comprehension of the arguments and ideas in it, their capacity to apply those ideas to historical situations they know about, and their ability to think and make judgements about the extract as a piece of historical writing. The other extract will be from a primary source, and candidates will be asked to offer thoughtful interpretations of its content without knowing anything about its context. The HAT is a test of skills, not of substantive historical knowledge. It is designed so that candidates should find it equally challenging, regardless of what period(s) they have studied or what school examinations they are taking.
Used by (for 2011 entry):	University of Oxford
Entry method:	Most UK candidates in full-time education will be able to take the test at their own schools or colleges. Mature candidates may take the test at the University of Oxford or at a regional test centre of their own choosing. International candidates will normally be able to take the test in their own schools or similar institutions, but may need to contact a local test centre.
Duration of test:	2 hours
Other information:	See University of Oxford's website – www.history.ox.ac.uk

Health Professions Admissions Test (HPAT)

Used for:	Entry to certain medical courses at the University of Ulster
What it is:	The Health Professions Admission Test (HPAT-Ulster) is a professionally designed and marked selection test developed to assess aptitude for study in the allied health professions. It has been designed in consultation with the University of Ulster to assess a range of attributes considered important to the study and later practice of the health professions. It is designed to complement academic achievement, by providing assessment of skills in the areas of reasoning, understanding and working with people, and written communication. These skills have been identified as important for a competent health professional. HPAT-Ulster is not based on any curriculum or body of knowledge and presumes no particular field or discipline of prior study. HPAT-Ulster has a strong focus on general skills and personal abilities. It does not test knowledge of the basic sciences. HPAT-Ulster is available to any candidate whose educational level at the time of sitting the test is final year of secondary schooling or higher, and who is capable of meeting the academic entry requirements (including prerequisite subjects at A level or equivalent) set by the University of Ulster.
Used by (for 2011 entry):	University of Ulster
Entry method:	Through HPAT – www.hpat.org.uk
Duration of test:	3 hours
Other information:	HPAT website – www.hpat.org.uk

The National Admissions Test for Law (LNAT)

Used for:	Entry to law and some combinations of law and other subjects
What it is:	The LNAT is a test run by a consortium of UK universities (LNAT Consortium Ltd) in partnership with Pearson VUE, the computer-based testing business of Pearson Education. The test helps universities to make fairer choices among the many highly qualified applicants who want to join their undergraduate law programmes.
	The test is professionally written and calibrated by Edexcel for Pearson VUE.
	The LNAT is a two-hour test in two parts: a multiple-choice element (80 minutes) and an essay element (40 minutes).
	The multiple-choice element consists of 10 argumentative passages, with three multiple-choice questions on each, making 30 questions in all. The questions are designed to test powers of comprehension, interpretation, analysis, synthesis, induction and deduction. These are the verbal reasoning skills at the heart of legal education. The questions do not test (and do not require) knowledge of any subject except the English language. This part of the test is machine-marked and the results are passed in numerical form to (only) those LNAT-participating universities to which the candidate has applied. Candidates will receive their marks after the admissions process is over.
	The essay element gives the candidate a choice of questions on a range of subjects. Although these typically require some rudimentary knowledge of everyday subjects, the point is not to test that knowledge. The point is to test the ability of the candidate to argue economically to a conclusion with a good command of written English. This part of the test is not centrally assessed. Instead the essays are passed unmarked to (only) those LNAT-participating law schools to which the candidate has applied. The essays will be used by each university in the way that best suits its own admissions system.
	The whole test is conducted on-screen.
Used by (for 2011 entry):	University of Birmingham, University of Bristol, University of Durham, University of Glasgow, King's College London, University of Leeds, University of Nottingham, University of Oxford, University College London
Entry method:	Through LNAT: see www.lnat.ac.uk
Test date:	Is booked during registration
Duration of test:	2 hours
Other information:	See the LNAT website www.lnat.ac.uk

Modern and Medieval Languages Test (MML)

Used for:	Entry to modern and medieval languages
What it is:	This written test will be taken by applicants, in the college by which they are being interviewed, while they are at the University of Cambridge for their interviews. (Applicants with disabilities or special learning needs are asked to inform the College so that they can take the test in an appropriate form.) There is no expectation that applicants will have practised this kind of exercise before. The test has been designed so that anyone who has already practised it will not be at any great advantage. The test forms just one small part of the overall assessment of applicants (based on the written application, school and college record, interviews, etc); even if an applicant does not do particularly well at this written test, it is perfectly possible for them still to be offered a place.

Applicants are asked to read a brief passage in English (300-350 words) and then to answer two or three questions about it. They will write their answer in a target language that they are studying at A level (A2) or equivalent and that they are applying to study at the University of Cambridge. The questions will contain an element of comprehension but will also invite applicants to add ideas of their own. In other words, the exercise is a combination of comprehension and free composition. The purpose is to see how applicants write in the foreign language: it assesses their grammar, accuracy, ability to express ideas, and their vocabulary, though they are not expected to know the exact foreign-language term for each English term in the passage. |
Used by (for 2011 entry):	University of Cambridge
Entry method:	Applicants need do nothing special about entering for the test, as colleges will inform applicants of all admissions requirements.
Duration of test:	45 minutes
Other information:	For more information about the test go to www.cam.ac.uk/admissions/undergraduate/courses/mml/tests.html

Sixth Term Examination Papers (STEP)

Used for:	Entry to mathematics
What it is:	STEP is a well-established mathematics university admissions test, which is used to help select very academically able students for courses which are usually oversubscribed. STEP was originally administered by OCR (Oxford, Cambridge and RSA Examinations). However, in 2008 STEP was transferred from OCR to its parent Cambridge Assessment which has a specialist team that manages assessments relating specifically to university entrance. STEP has been designed to test candidates on questions that are similar in style to undergraduate mathematics. It is used by the University of Cambridge as the basis for conditional offers. There are also a number of candidates who sit STEP papers as a challenge. Other universities may ask candidates to take STEP as part of their offer; candidates should consult their university regarding which papers to take. Cambridge Assessment is responsible for producing and marking STEP. It consists of three 3-hour examinations, STEP I, STEP II and STEP III. Candidates are usually required to sit either one or two of the examinations, depending on the requirements of the universities they have applied to. It is not possible to take STEP I and STEP III in the same year. The syllabuses for STEP I and STEP II are based on A level content while the syllabus for STEP III is based on Further Mathematics A level. The questions on STEP II and STEP III are of the same difficulty and harder than those in STEP I. Candidates are only expected to have knowledge of topics within the A level syllabus. Candidates who are not studying further mathematics will not be expected to sit STEP III.
May be used by (for 2011 entry):	University of Cambridge and University of Warwick
Entry method:	Applications to take STEP should go through a school or college, in the same way as your GCE A levels. The papers must be taken at a recognised centre.
Duration of test:	45 minutes
Other information:	See www.stepmathematics.org.uk/

Thinking Skills Assessment (TSA Cambridge)

Used for:	Mainly computer science, natural sciences, engineering and economics
What it is:	The University of Cambridge has been using the TSA (designed, developed and extensively researched by Cambridge Assessment) since 2001. The TSA is a 90-minute multiple-choice test consisting of 50 questions. These measure an applicant's critical thinking and problem-solving skills.
Used by (for 2011 entry):	University of Cambridge
Entry method:	Applicants need do nothing special about entering for the test, as colleges will inform applicants if they need to take it.
Duration of test:	90 minutes
Other information:	For further information go to www.tsa.cambridgeassessment.org.uk

Thinking Skills Assessment (TSA Oxford)

Used for:	Entry to Philosophy, Politics & Economics (PPE) or Economics and Management (E&M)
What it is:	The TSA (University of Oxford) is a pre-interview admissions test for applicants to undergraduate courses in PPE, E&M, Experimental Psycology (EP) and Psychology and Philosophy at the University of Oxford. Admissions decisions are complex because candidates come from a wide variety of subject backgrounds, and the study of PPE, E&M, EP, or Psychology and Philosophy requires a range of abilities. The TSA will help tutors to assess whether candidates have the skills and aptitudes that are required to study these subjects. It is a 2-hour pre-interview test consisting of two sections: • Section 1: Thinking Skills Assessment (TSA) • Section 2: Writing task.
Used by (for 2011 entry):	University of Oxford
Entry method:	Through Cambridge Assessment – see the TSA website www.admissionstests.cambridgeassessment.org.uk/adt/
Duration of test:	2 hours
Other information:	TSA website – www.admissionstests.cambridgeassessment.org.uk/adt/

Thinking Skills Assessment (TSA UCL)

Used for:	European Social and Political Studies
What it is:	The TSA is a 90-minute multiple choice test consisting of 50 questions. These measure an applicant's critical thinking and problem-solving skills.
Used by (for 2011 entry):	University College London (UCL)
Entry method:	The TSA is used as part of the interview process for candidates applying to UCL. Any candidate needing to take the TSA will have their test sitting arranged for them by UCL when they come for their interview.
Duration of test:	90 minutes
Other information:	For further information go to www.tsa.cambridgeassessment.org.uk

UK Clinical Aptitude Test (UKCAT)

Used for:	Entry to medical and dental schools
What it is:	The UKCAT Consortium Ltd is a company limited by guarantee. The members of the company, who also nominate its board of directors, are the 26 universities that have agreed to adopt the UKCAT as part of their selection process for medicine and dentistry. The test helps universities to make more informed choices from among many highly qualified applicants. It ensures that the candidates selected have the most appropriate mental abilities, attitudes and professional behaviour required for new doctors and dentists to be successful in their clinical careers. The UKCAT does not contain any curriculum or science content, nor can it be revised for. It focuses on exploring the cognitive powers of candidates and other attributes considered to be valuable for health care professionals. The test is run by the UKCAT Consortium in partnership with Pearson VUE, a global leader in computer-based testing and part of Pearson plc. It is delivered on computers worldwide through Pearson VUE's high street centres. All test questions are written by assessment experts and must pass detailed trials to ensure their validity and reliability. All questions, test duration, sequencing and style are continually reviewed to ensure that the test is culturally fair and bias is minimised. There is a programme of new item development including the testing of new questions as non-scoring components of the test.

continued overleaf

UK Clinical Aptitude Test (UKCAT) continued

	The test assesses a wide range of mental abilities and behavioural attributes identified by university medical and dental schools as important. The UKCAT currently consists of: ■ Verbal reasoning – assesses candidates' ability to think logically about written information and to arrive at a reasoned conclusion. ■ Quantitative reasoning – assesses candidates' ability to solve numerical problems. ■ Abstract reasoning – assesses candidates' ability to infer relationships from information by convergent and divergent thinking. ■ Decision analysis – assesses candidates' ability to deal with various forms of information, to infer relationships, to make informed judgements, and to decide on an appropriate response, in situations of complexity and ambiguity. ■ Non-cognitive analysis – identifies the attributes and characteristics of robustness, empathy and integrity that may contribute to successful health professional practice. There is no curriculum content as the test examines innate skills. Examples of questions you may be asked can be found in the Preparation section. It is not necessary or possible to practise for these questions but you are advised to familiarise yourself with the format. The test is delivered in 2 hours. Each subtest is in a multiple-choice format and is separately timed. There are two versions of UKCAT: the standard UKCAT and the UKCATSEN (Special Educational Needs). The UKCATSEN is a longer version of the UKCAT intended for candidates who require additional time due to a documented medical condition or disability.
Used by (for 2011 entry):	University of Aberdeen, Brighton and Sussex Medical School, Barts and The London School of Medicine and Dentistry, Cardiff University, University of Dundee, University of Durham, University of East Anglia, University of Edinburgh, University of Glasgow, Hull York Medical School, Keele University, King's College London, Imperial College London, University of Leeds, University of Leicester, University of Manchester, University of Newcastle, University of Nottingham, University of Oxford, Peninsula College of Medicine and Dentistry, Queen's University Belfast, University of Sheffield, University of Southampton, University of St Andrews, St George's University of London, Warwick University
Entry method:	Online registration only, through www.ukcat.ac.uk
Duration of test:	2 hours
Other information:	UKCAT website – www.ukcat.ac.uk

Register for a UCAS Card

If you're in Year 12, S5 or equivalent and thinking about higher education, then the UCAS Card scheme is designed for you. You can sign up for a UCAS Card online, at UCAS higher education conventions or through your school if they are participating in the scheme.

There are many benefits that you can take advantage of:

- discounts in your favourite high street shops

- regular information about the courses and universities you're interested in

- free monthly newsletters providing advice on the application process

- expert help from our UCAS advisers including reminders about important deadlines, hints and tips

- access to **yougofurther.co.uk**, the UCAS student network, where you can chat to other students.

The information you provide us with when you sign up for the UCAS Card means that you'll receive essential information about the courses and universities you are interested in applying for. If you change your mind about those courses and universities, you can update your details at any point so that you are always getting the correct information. You'll also get all the help you need about your application from the experts at UCAS.

You will also receive regular email bulletins which are full of advice, including reminders on key UCAS deadline dates and guidance about filling in those difficult aspects of the application such as the personal statement.

It's important to remember that you're not alone. Thousands of students like you talk about the step up into higher education on **yougofurther.co.uk**. Chat with other students and make new friends on the UCAS student network before you start university.

How do I register?
To register, visit **www.ucas.com/ucascard** and fill in the short application form.

Need some help?
If you get stuck or have a query you can call 0871 468 0 471 for advice or email us at ucascard@ucas.ac.uk.

Online protection
The yougo team at UCAS monitors the **yougofurther.co.uk** site during the day, Monday to Friday. The rest of the time it is monitored by an external moderation agency. In addition, we have a button on every single page of the site that allows users to report suspicious activity direct to a policed organisation.

FAQs on the UCAS Card

What is a UCAS Card?
The UCAS Card can be used as a discount card on the high street. By signing up you will also receive information specifically relevant to you, regarding the courses and institutions you are interested in, and you will also have access to online forums.

Who can have a UCAS Card and when can I sign up?

You are eligible for a UCAS Card if you are in Year 12, S5 or equivalent. You can register online from October through to August each year.

It says on the website that signing up for a UCAS Card comes with unlimited use of yougofurther.co.uk. What is yougo?

yougo is the UCAS student network website where you can meet people doing your course, or going to the same institution as you. You can make friends, and talk directly to UCAS and universities and colleges to help you make big decisions.

I have already signed up. How long until I get my UCAS Card?

Once you have registered online, you can expect your card to arrive within a few weeks. You will be given your card number immediately so make a note of this.

How do I change my contact details?

There is an option to edit your details on the website. You simply need to log in to the UCAS Card area of the site using your UCAS Card number, email address and password. Alternatively, you can call UCAS Card Customer Service Unit on 0871 468 0 471 for assistance.

I've forgotten my password. What should I do?

There is a link on the login page where you can enter your email address and your password will be sent to you.

Chapter checklist

These are the things you should be doing in Step 1 of your applicant journey:

- [ ] Explore different career paths to ensure you choose the right subject and qualification. Research the resources available in careers centres, Connexions and websites.

- [ ] Complete the Stamford test at **www.ucas.ac.uk/students/choosingcourses/choosingcourse/stamfordtest**.

- [ ] Use Course Search on **www.ucas.com**. Check the entry requirements on the Entry Profiles.

- [ ] Look at the case studies on **www.ucas.tv**.

- [ ] Visit the universities or colleges on their open day, or just make an arrangement to visit.

- [ ] Visit a UCAS education convention and start thinking about your personal statement (see Step 2 Applying).

- [ ] Use prospectuses and university websites. Focus on your subject choices and related career prospects.

- [ ] Check the results of the National Student Survey at **www.direct.gov.uk/unistats**.

- [ ] Check if there are any admissions tests you need to register for (eg LNAT, BMAT).

- [ ] Narrow down your choice of institutions – you can only apply to a maximum of five courses.

- [ ] Look for available scholarships.

- [ ] Consider attending a summer school or taster course.

Step 2
Applying

Now you've done lots of research and decided on the course you want to study and where you want to study it, you need to start thinking about making your application to the universities and colleges. This section of the book guides you through the process, from those all-important deadlines, to how to apply for different types of courses, and how to complete your UCAS application. It also includes specific advice for Oxbridge applicants and those of you applying to medicine, dentistry, veterinary science and veterinary medicine.

Applying

Step 2 **Applying**

Step 2 (vertical watermark)

Go to www.ucas.com/students/apply

First visit → Click on Register and complete the details requested. You will need your username and password to finish your application

Second and future visits → Fill in all sections of Apply – this chapter will help you

When do I need to apply by?

Deadlines

15 October – Medicine, dentistry, veterinary science, veterinary medicine and all applications to the universities of Oxford and Cambridge

15 January – all other courses except certain art and design courses using 24 March deadline

24 March – Certain art and design courses (check on Course Search)

After 30 June applications go straight into Clearing

What happens next?

UCAS processes your application into our central system

UCAS sends you a Welcome letter which lists your choices in random order

UCAS sends your application to your chosen universities and colleges for them to consider

Universities and colleges tell UCAS their decisions

When to apply

Different application deadlines you need to know

Applying from the UK

There are three different application deadlines, depending on the course you are applying for. It's important to check the deadline for your chosen course(s) on Course Search at **www.ucas.com**.

- **15 October** – application deadline for the receipt at UCAS of applications for all medicine, dentistry, veterinary medicine and veterinary science courses, and for all courses at the universities of Oxford and Cambridge.

- **15 January** – application deadline for the receipt at UCAS of applications for all courses except those listed above with a 15 October deadline, and art and design courses with a 24 March deadline.

- **24 March** – application deadline for the receipt at UCAS of applications for art and design courses except those listed with a 15 January deadline.

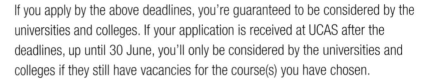

You can only send us one application in each year's application cycle. If you send a second application, it will be cancelled and you will not receive a refund.

If you apply by the above deadlines, you're guaranteed to be considered by the universities and colleges. If your application is received at UCAS after the deadlines, up until 30 June, you'll only be considered by the universities and colleges if they still have vacancies for the course(s) you have chosen.

Art and design courses: if you apply for art and design courses with different deadlines, you can submit your application before 15 January for courses with that deadline, then add further choices before the 24 March deadline using Track (as long as you haven't already used all five choices).

If you're applying through a school or college: they might set an earlier deadline – you need to send your application to them by this date so that they have time to write your reference and send your completed application to us before our deadline.

If you're applying as an individual: it is your responsibility to make your referee aware of any deadlines when asking them to provide you with a reference.

Course start dates
Not all courses start in September or October – some start between January and May. Check the start dates for the courses you are interested in on the Course Search at **www.ucas.com**. For courses that start between January and May, you may need to apply before the three application deadlines above, as the universities and colleges will need time to consider your application.

Student tip:

'I think the most important message to anyone applying to university is get it done quickly! The sooner your application is off the sooner you can stop worrying. Start thinking as early as possible about courses and universities, and the rest is simple.'

Contact the university or college direct for advice about when they need your application. Although some will be happy to receive applications right up to the start of the course, be prepared to send your application early.

Please remember you do not have to apply for all your choices at the same time. You can add further choices, up to 30 June, as long as you have not used up all your choices and have not accepted a place.

International applicants

If you are applying from outside the UK or EU, whatever your nationality, you need to be aware of the three application deadlines, although many universities and colleges will consider your application up until 30 June. This does **not** apply to applications for the universities of Oxford and Cambridge, courses in medicine, dentistry, veterinary medicine or veterinary science. For all of these, you must apply by 15 October.

Universities do not guarantee to consider applications they receive after 15 January, and some popular courses may not have vacancies after that date. Please check with individual universities and colleges if you are not sure. You are advised to apply as early as possible.

Remember to allow enough time for entry clearance or immigration; also travel and accommodation arrangements, which can take longer during the summer when immigration departments are busy.

If you think you may be assessed as a 'home' student (UK or EU) for tuition fees, you should apply by the relevant deadline as shown in the 'Applying from the UK' section on page 121.

Several countries require their citizens to complete mandatory military or national service. If this affects you, check with universities and colleges in advance to discuss when you should apply. You can defer through UCAS for a maximum of one year. It would be useful to include information about your military or national service in your personal statement.

Taking a year out?

If you want to take a year out before starting your course, check with your unis that they will accept a deferred entry application. If you apply for deferred entry, you must still apply by the relevant deadline above, and meet the conditions of any offers by 31 August in the cycle in which you are applying, unless an alternative date is given by the university. If you accept a deferred entry place, you can't reapply through us in the following year's cycle unless your original application is withdrawn.

When to apply – FAQs

Why do universities have application deadlines?

Universities need a certain amount of time to consider the thousands of applicants who apply to them. Deadlines are set so that the universities have time to consider all applications.

How do I know what the application deadline is for my course(s)?

There are three major application deadlines – your deadline will be dependent on the subject you want to study and whether you are applying to an Oxbridge university or not. Deadlines for each course are listed on Course Search at **www.ucas.com**. A university has no obligation to consider a late application, so we would always advise you to check this information to ensure you don't miss your deadline. More information about deadlines is shown on page 121.

I'm applying for a nursing course which starts next spring. Do I have a different deadline?

Most undergraduate courses start in September; however nursing diplomas and nursing degrees are often the exception to this rule. You may find that some universities offer either a January, February, March or April start, as well as an autumn start for these courses. If you wish to apply for a spring start, you must ensure that you submit your application as soon as possible, in order for the university to have time to shortlist and interview their applicants. Contact the university direct for advice about when they need your application. From September 2013, new entrants to the nursing profession will have to study a degree rather than a diploma. Diploma courses will be phased out between September 2011 and early 2013. More information can be found on the NHS Careers website at **www.nhscareers.nhs.uk**.

Can I apply after the deadline?

All applications sent by the required deadline are given equal consideration by the universities. If your application is sent after the deadline, it will only be considered at the discretion of the university. UCAS processes applications and sends them to universities until 30 June; however there is no guarantee that the universities will consider a late application, or offer an interview or place. If you are applying after the deadline for your course(s), contact the unis first to find out if there are any vacancies and if they are happy to consider a late application from you.

How to apply

Full-time undergraduate courses: you apply through UCAS using our online service called Apply at **www.ucas.com**. You can only send us one application in each year's application cycle, but you can choose a maximum of five choices on your application.

Part-time undergraduate courses: we do not recruit for these – you apply direct to the universities and colleges. However, from July until September we provide a part-time course search at **www.ucas.com**.

Music courses: there are two ways to apply for music courses – the route you take depends upon the type of course you'd like to study. For full-time undergraduate music degree courses, you apply through UCAS.

If you'd like to study a practice-based music course, you apply through the Conservatoires UK Admissions Service (CUKAS), an admissions service for seven of the UK conservatoires. The Guildhall School of Music and Drama and the Royal Academy of Music do not recruit through CUKAS: they accept applications direct.

If you can't make up your mind which music courses to apply for, why not apply through UCAS and CUKAS? You can then decide which course to take later in the year.

The courses offered by conservatoires are creative and varied. You can choose to study full- or part-time, take a postgraduate course if you have already completed a degree, and can specialise in one or more instruments.

For more information about CUKAS, please visit the website at **www.cukas.ac.uk** where you'll find a detailed list of available courses and the online application. You can access the courses available by clicking on the Course Search link and searching by various criteria, such as type of study (eg undergraduate, postgraduate) or by instruments and study areas.

Postgraduate courses: with the exception of the subjects detailed below, UCAS does not recruit for postgraduate courses.

If you are applying for a subject listed below, please read through the following information.

- **Medicine and dentistry:** for some postgraduate courses you apply through UCAS.

- **Nursing:** for diploma and degree qualifications (postgraduate and undergraduate) in nursing, you apply through UCAS.

- **Social work:** for degree qualifications (postgraduate and undergraduate) in social work, you apply through UCAS.

- **Teaching:** if you are applying for postgraduate teacher training courses in England, Scotland or Wales, you will usually need to apply through the Graduate Teacher Training Registry (GTTR) at **www.gttr.ac.uk**. If you are applying for postgraduate teaching courses in Northern Ireland, you normally apply direct to the university. Teaching courses at undergraduate level are processed through UCAS.

UKPASS: search for postgraduate programmes through UCAS' postgraduate application service, UKPASS (UK Postgraduate Application and Statistical Service) at **www.ukpass.ac.uk**. You can apply online to universities and colleges using the scheme and there are links to universities and colleges who use other online application systems. Contact details are provided for those without an online system, so that you can check how they would like you to submit an application.

How to apply – FAQs

What is UCAS' role?

We are the organisation responsible for managing applications to higher education courses in the UK. If you want to make an application to a full-time higher education course, you will need to apply through UCAS. Once you have completed your application and sent it to us, we forward it to the universities of your choice. It is then up to the unis to decide if they can offer you a place. UCAS is not involved with the decision-making process.

Which courses can I apply for through UCAS?

You apply through UCAS for all full-time undergraduate courses. You can also use it to apply for nursing diplomas and degrees, for some postgraduate medicine and dentistry courses, and for postgraduate social work courses.

For most postgraduate and part-time courses, you apply direct to the university or college. If you are unsure of how to apply, you should contact the institution for advice.

You may need to use a different admissions service to apply for your course. Use the table below to find out which system you should be using. If you are still unsure, contact the uni to check.

UCAS	GTTR	CUKAS	UKPASS
All undergraduate courses, including medicine courses.	Full-time and part-time postgraduate teaching courses.	Practice-based music courses at seven of the UK conservatoires.	Some postgraduate programmes, including part-time and distance learning, with the exception of those currently in the UCAS scheme.
Postgraduate social work courses.			
Nursing courses (undergraduate and postgraduate).			
Some postgraduate medicine and dentistry courses.			
Undergraduate teacher training courses.			

Can I make more than one application in the same year?

No, you can only submit one UCAS application per academic year. You can apply for a maximum of five choices on your application.

If you contact us to cancel your application within seven days of the date on your Welcome letter, we'll give you a refund. You could then submit a second application for the same academic cycle if you wished, as long as the first application was cancelled within the seven-day period. If you cancel an application after the seven days have passed, you cannot send another application.

Where can I find information about foundation degrees?

The study methods for foundation degrees can be very flexible, which means that they are available to people already in work, to those wishing to embark on a career change, and to those who have recently completed level 3 qualifications (eg A levels, Advanced Apprenticeships or NVQ3). You can research them on the Foundation Degree Course Search at **http://fd.ucas.com/CourseSearch/**, or contact universities for more information.

How to complete your UCAS application

To apply for a university or college place you use our online application service, called Apply. Apply is a secure web-based system, available 24 hours a day. You can use it anywhere that has internet access, so you can complete your application where and when it suits you. You do not have to complete your application in one go – you can start it and come back to it as many times as you like.

At **www.ucas.tv** you can watch our video guide *How to apply* and our frequently asked question videos to find out more. There is also detailed help text throughout Apply and at **www.ucas.com** to help you fill in your application.

We provide an option to apply in Welsh, but only use the Welsh version of Apply if you're applying to Welsh universities and colleges or English universities with the resources to translate your application into English. If you're not sure, check with your universities and colleges before applying.

If you choose to receive correspondence in Welsh, any written communication from us will also be in Welsh.

Student tip:

'Your UCAS application is not as scary as your teachers make out... it is really hard to make a mistake as it takes you through step-by-step. The quicker you embrace it the easier it becomes.'

This section gives you an overview of the different sections you'll need to complete in Apply.

Registration

This is the first step to applying. You'll need to add personal details, such as your name, address and date of birth, and you'll be asked to read and agree to the terms and conditions for using Apply. Once you've registered you'll be given a username and be asked to create your own password. **Keep these in a safe place as you'll need them every time you log in to your application.**

If you're applying as an individual: if you're not applying through a school, college or centre, you'll need to answer a few questions to confirm your eligibility before you can start your application. If you're applying from the UK and don't have access to a computer, you can use one at a local online centre. Search for your nearest centre at **www.ukonlinecentres.com**.

If you're applying through a school, college or centre: you'll need to obtain a 'buzzword' from the centre you're applying through. This buzzword links your application to your centre so that your referee can write and attach their reference.

Personal details

The personal details you entered when you registered will be automatically transferred into this section. Check that your name, address, date of birth and contact details are correct.

International students: It is very important to make sure your postal address is up-to-date to ensure that UCAS and the universities you apply to can get in touch with you. If you're studying in the UK but live in another country and you enter your school as the postal address then you will receive post there. But you must remember to update the address when you leave in the summer. Make sure you add in your home address (or BFPO if your parents are in the armed forces) in your home country. You can update this information in Track.

We ask for further information that the universities require, such as your nationality, residential status and an outline of any disabilities or special needs you may have. The unis can then decide what tuition fees you should be charged and what entitlements you might qualify for.

Fee code: you'll need to choose a code from a drop-down list to show the university how you expect to pay for your tuition fees. Most applicants from the UK, Channel Islands, Isle of Man and the EU will be in category 02. You should use that code if you are eligible for assessment under student support arrangements, even if you think your family income will be too high for you to receive support.

The options available to you are:

- 01 Private finance – entire cost of tuition fees is to be paid by private finance.

- 02 UK, ChI, IoM or EU student finance services – applying for student support assessment by local authority, Student Finance England, Student Finance Wales, Student Awards Agency for Scotland, Student Finance NI (Northern Ireland), Northern Ireland Education and Library Board, SLC EU Team, Channel Island or Isle of Man agency

- 04 Research councils – contribution from a research council.

- 05 DHSS/Regional Health – contribution from the Department of Health and Social Security or from a Regional Health Authority

- 06 UK Govt international award – international student award from the UK Government or the British Council

- 07 Training agency – contribution from a training agency

- 08 Other UK Govt award – contribution from another Government source

- 09 International agency – contribution from an international agency, government, university or industry

- 10 UK Industry/commerce – contribution from UK industry or commerce

- 90 Other source – other source of finance

- 99 Not known.

If you're applying to any of the authorities listed in fee code 02, they may assess your eligibility for any financial support towards tuition fees.

If you are applying for a mixture of courses involving more than one fee code, such as 02 and 05, enter the fee code that applies to most of the courses you have chosen.

Student tip:

'The online application wasn't hard to fill in and I could easily go back and change details as and when I wanted, so don't worry if you are unsure what to put or what UCAS are asking on the form, check with a teacher and then you can go back to it.'

If all or part of your tuition fees will be paid by an award from another organisation (for example, a National Health Service bursary, a company sponsor or a training agency), please choose the appropriate code. Bursaries for nursing courses are usually category 05. If you're applying for sponsorship, give the name of your first choice sponsor in your personal statement section. You can find out more about company sponsorship from a careers adviser. You should say in your personal statement if you plan to defer to the next academic year if your application for sponsorship this year is unsuccessful.

You should only use code 01 if you are paying all of your tuition fees from private finance and you are not eligible for assessment under student support arrangements.

A small number of universities and colleges don't receive public funding and their students may not get help towards tuition fees under the student support arrangements. These institutions are clearly marked in the Course Search section of the UCAS website. Alternatively, please refer to their prospectuses for more information.

You can find out more about student finance on pages 43 to 53.

Watch our UCAStv video guides *Students with disabilities* and *Advice from disability officers* at www.ucas.tv.

Students with disabilities or special needs: it is not compulsory but we would encourage you to enter details of any disabilities or special needs on your application. Universities and colleges welcome students with disabilities, and will try to meet your needs wherever possible. Don't be worried about disclosing your disability or special needs as the earlier the unis and colleges know, the easier it will be for them to get support put in place for you. This might include adapted accommodation, extra equipment, readers or interpreters or extra time to complete your course. If you do not know what facilities or support you need, please contact the disability coordinator at your chosen unis. You can find their contact details on the Skill: National Bureau for Students with Disabilities website at **www.skill.org.uk**, and you could also visit the university to make sure you are happy with their facilities. They may ask you for more details to help them plan for you, as well as explain to you how they will keep any information you give them confidential. You may be able to get extra financial support or help with care from a Disabled Students' Allowance (DSA); see page 50 for more information.

Skill: National Bureau for Students with Disabilities has provided the following pros and cons of disclosing your disability or special needs on your UCAS application:

Pros

- **Getting support set up**

  You may need additional support to attend an interview or sit an admissions test. If you need support on the course, such as a reader or an adapted computer, it is best to set up the support as early as possible. If you need adapted residential accommodation, or if ramps, new signs or other building modifications have to be made, then work needs to start early, not the day you arrive. Staff may also need training, which can take time to arrange.

- **Supporting your application**

  You may have had an unusual academic career, perhaps sitting exams later than other people on your course. Without the knowledge that you have a disability or impairment, tutors might wonder why you took longer over some courses.

- **The information will come from you**

  Disclosing the information yourself, and in a way you feel comfortable, may be preferable. This may be at the application stage or you might want to give this information at an interview. Alternatively, you could think about whether you are happy for the person who fills in your reference to mention your disability or impairment.

Cons

- **Irrelevance**

  You may have a disability or impairment that you do not think will affect your study. However, it is important to remember that studying in higher education may be very different from studying at school, and you may need additional support.

  If you do not disclose your disability on your application, you can still tell the disability coordinator once you've been accepted onto the course. However, if the disability coordinator is not informed before the start of the course, it may take longer to arrange the support or access requirements and these may not be in place as soon as you need them. Whether you disclose does not affect your right to the Disabled Students' Allowance (DSA), although in Scotland the disability coordinator or assessor needs to sign your DSA application form.

- **Discrimination**

  It is unlawful for institutions to discriminate against you because of your disability or impairment. You may still feel, however, that an institution will discriminate against you, even if your disability or impairment will not affect your studies. In this case, you may choose not to tell the college or university. If you need support, you could tell the relevant staff once you have been accepted. However, it can take longer to make access arrangements or set up support if they are told after your course has begun. This is a risk you take if you do not inform someone at an early stage.

International students: if your permanent home is outside the UK, we collect applicants' passport information on behalf of universities and colleges, who need it for purposes of visa application and checks with the UK Border Agency (UKBA). For further details of UKBA please visit their website **www.ukba.homeoffice.gov.uk**. If you plan to change your passport before starting at university, enter the current details but be sure to update any changes direct with your firm and insurance choice universities.

If you are taking, or have taken, Test of English as a Foreign Language (TOEFL) you should enter your registration number in this section; for International English Language Testing System (IELTS), enter your Test Report Form (TRF) number. More information about English language proficiency tests can be found at **www.ucas.com/students/wheretostart/nonukstudents/englangprof**.

Student tip:

'Applying to UK universities was so easy and I did not have to make several applications to different universities.'

Criminal convictions: as part of their duty of care to all applicants and existing students, the universities will also need to know if you have any relevant criminal convictions. If you have a relevant criminal conviction that is not spent, you're required to declare this on your application. If you declare a relevant criminal conviction it does not mean you will be automatically excluded from the application process. More detailed information about the criminal convictions declaration is provided in Apply.

Nominated access: if you want to, you can choose to nominate someone who can discuss your application with us and the universities if you're unavailable. This could be, for example, a parent, grandparent, guardian or adviser.

Additional information (UK applicants only)

This section provides extra information required by the universities and colleges. It is only available in Apply to those applicants who are permanently resident in the UK. You're asked for the following details:

- **Ethnic origin and national identity** – your national identity reflects how you choose to classify yourself. It's different from ethnicity and nationality and can be based on many things, such as culture, language or ancestry/family history. You do not have to provide this information if you'd prefer not to.

- **Activities in preparation for higher education** – you can enter details of up to two activities, such as summer schools or taster courses.

- **Care** – this question is optional. If you have spent any time in local authority care, even for one day (this includes if you have been in public care and have lived in one or more of foster care, semi-independent living or residential care homes), you should select 'yes' from the drop-down list. Universities will treat this information in confidence and may contact you to discuss if you need any extra resources or support to undertake your chosen course. Selecting 'yes' to this question may also enable you to access additional financial support universities provide to young people who have been in care.

- **Parental education** – you'll be asked to indicate whether or not any of your parents, step-parents or guardians have taken a course at higher education level. This question is also optional.

- **Occupational background** – if you're under 21, you are asked to give the job title of your parent, step-parent or guardian who earns the most. If she or he is retired or unemployed, you give their most recent job title. If you are 21 or over, you're asked to give your own job title. If you prefer not to give this information, you can enter 'I prefer not to say' in the text box. This information will not be passed to your chosen institution until they have given you an unconditional offer that you have accepted as your firm choice. This information will be used for statistical monitoring only.

Student tip:

'Filling in the application is simple... with little help boxes next to every piece of information... telling you exactly what they want...'

Choices

- You can choose a maximum of five choices and there's no preference order – Apply will store your choices in alphabetical order.

- Your application is sent to all your chosen unis at the same time.

- Each uni will only see details of its course(s) that you've applied to. They won't see your other choices until you've received the final decision on your application.

Course combinations

You can apply for any combination of unis or colleges and courses that you want, with the following exceptions:

- a maximum of four courses in any one of medicine, dentistry, veterinary medicine or veterinary science courses

- you can only apply for one course at either the University of Oxford or the University of Cambridge (unless you already have a degree or will have gained a degree before September of the cycle in which you're applying, in which case you can apply to both).

You can use your remaining choice(s) for any other subject. For example, if you apply to four medicine courses, you could still make one choice for veterinary medicine. However, be aware that your personal statement will be sent to all the universities and colleges that you've chosen. See page 159 for more information about applying to multiple courses.

More advice about applying to medicine, dentistry, veterinary medicine and veterinary science courses can be found on page 167.

There are different application deadlines for some courses, universities and colleges – see the When to apply section on page 121 for more information.

Did you know?

Choices are not sent in preference order

Your application is sent to your chosen unis at the same time, so it doesn't matter which order you add your choices. They'll be listed in alphabetical order in Apply, then we will generate a random order when we process your application.

Myth buster

You don't have to add five choices

There's space for five choices, but you don't have to use them all up – you can apply for just one if you know exactly where you want to go, or two, three or four if you want – it doesn't have to be five.

Only add choices you're sure about. If you wouldn't be happy going to one of them, see if there's somewhere else, or apply to fewer choices – you don't have to fill up the space for the sake of it.

If you apply to fewer than five choices, you can add more later if you want to (but be aware of the deadlines for adding choices – see page 198). This can be useful if you spot a new course after you've sent us your application. You can add another choice in Track if you have space (Track lets you see the progress of your application once we've processed it) and we'll send it to the university as normal.

Additional requirements

Admissions tests: some courses require an admissions test. It's your responsibility to find out if you need to take one for your course(s), and to register by the deadline. Go to the admissions tests section on pages 101 to 114 for more information.

If you're applying for **medicine, dentistry, nursing, midwifery or certain other health courses**, UK health authorities recommend you should be immunised against Hepatitis B before you start training. Universities and colleges may also ask you for certificates to show that you're not infected. Check the immunisation and certification requirements with your universities and colleges.

International applicants for nursing or midwifery diplomas or degrees: before applying please check the latest information at **www.ucas.com/students/wheretostart/nonukstudents/choosingacourse/ nursing**.

Criminal convictions declaration: you will be required to declare whether you have any relevant unspent criminal convictions. The help text in Apply explains what is classed as a relevant unspent conviction. In addition, some courses have entry requirements which might require you to disclose further information regarding any past criminal activities, and may also require a criminal records check.

University of Cambridge

If you're applying to the University of Cambridge, you may be required to complete one or more application forms in addition to the UCAS application. These forms should be sent to the university, not to UCAS. See the Applying for Oxbridge section on pages 173 to 178 for more information.

Unless asked, don't send any exam certificates or other papers to us or to your unis.

Education

Universities need to know where you've studied and which qualifications you're taking or have taken. You add your schools and colleges, then list your qualifications. You must include all schools, colleges and universities that you have attended since the age of 11, even if you withdrew from your course.

For each school and college, you provide details of:

Student tip:

'..it [the application] was organised in such a manner in which you can easily view, edit or even update information regarding your education or employment. The thing I found most useful was that you could go back to the information at any time.'

- all qualifications for which you have accepted certification from an awarding organisation, even if you're retaking all or part of the qualification

- all qualifications for which you are currently studying or awaiting results.

All qualifications must be entered, even if you received an unsuccessful grade, if you are still waiting to take the final exams or if you are waiting for the results.

Resits: If you're resitting a qualification you need to enter it twice: once as a completed qualification with the grade achieved and once as a qualification with the result 'Pending'.

All qualifications have to be entered manually – you can't copy and paste in transcripts.

More information about entering specific qualifications can be found at
www.ucas.com/students/applying/howtoapply/education/quals

Your highest level of qualification: you'll be asked to select the highest level of qualification you will have before you start your course. This doesn't include the course you're applying to – it's just about the qualifications that you'll complete before starting the course.

Mature students: enter details for all your qualifications. If you don't have any qualifications, you should still enter details for your schools. If you're hoping to enter higher education through the Accreditation of Prior Learning (APL) or the Accreditation of Prior Experiential Learning (APEL), you still apply through us, but you should contact your chosen unis first to discuss whether APL or APEL is acceptable and what evidence they'll need.

International students: check the suitability of your qualifications with the admissions offices at your unis before applying. A lot of schools outside the UK are not listed as a 'centre' in Apply. Don't worry, just enter the school name and country – there will be a warning message on the screen if you don't enter a centre number but this will not affect your application. When you apply, you must give full details of all your qualifications, including exams you took when you left school, exams you took to get into higher education, vocational exams and any other qualifications or awards. You should also include qualifications you are studying currently or planning to complete. Please do not try to give a UK equivalent. If your first language is not English:

- say whether or not your qualifications were completely or partly assessed in English

- enter details for any English language tests you have taken or plan to take.

UCAS has made it easy for international applicants to enter their qualifications. They are listed by country and name. You can also find a listing for many English language exams and degrees (if you have already taken or are currently taking a degree course). If you cannot find your qualification, list as much information as possible under 'Other'. The unis and colleges will then contact you for further information about your qualification if required.

Employment

In this section, you fill in the details of your paid work history and employers. If you've not had any jobs, you can leave this section blank, but you'll still need to mark it as complete to continue with your application.

Personal statement

The personal statement is your opportunity to tell universities and colleges why they should choose you. You need to demonstrate your suitability for the course(s), your enthusiasm and commitment, and above all, make sure you stand out from the crowd. Because this is such an important part of your application there is a separate section to help you with your personal statement, on pages 145 to 165.

Your reference

Your application needs a reference from a tutor, careers adviser or other professional who knows you well enough to write about you and your suitability for the course.

Applying through a school or college or other organisation: this section will be completed by your referee and you won't have access to it. Once you have completed each section, checked your application and marked all sections as complete, you pay for it and send it online to your referee. Your referee will then check and approve your application, write the reference and send your application to us.

Applying as an individual: if you're applying independently you will be asked to provide contact details of your referee. A request will then be sent by email to your referee asking them to complete and submit a reference through our secure website. Your referee can click on the help text links to read advice on what to include in the reference. We check that they are still able to supply your reference and ask them to confirm their identity. If they decline to give you a reference for any reason we will notify you. We notify you by email when the reference is complete and a red tick will be displayed next to the 'Reference' section in the left-hand navigation in Apply. You can then complete and submit your application. **It's up to you to ensure that your chosen referee is aware of any deadline you have and for you to make sure that you request a reference allowing adequate time for them to prepare and submit the reference.**

Student tip:

'I wish I had finished my personal statement earlier along with my application, because the sooner you get them in the more time you have to revise for January exams and less hassle and stress when the deadline creeps up on you.'

If you're applying independently but would like your reference to be written by a registered school, college or other organisation, you can request that the centre completes the reference for you in Apply. This means that the centre can write a reference for you but they won't be involved in the rest of your application. Once they have completed the reference, a red tick will be displayed next to the 'Reference' section in the left-hand navigation.

Who should write the reference?

- Your referee should know you well enough, in an official capacity, to write about you and your suitability for higher education.

- If you're at school or college, or left recently, ask your principal, head teacher, teacher or tutor.

- If you left school or college several years ago, ask your current or previous employer, or in the case of voluntary work your supervisor.

- If you've recently attended any training courses you could ask your training provider.

International students: you will probably need a teacher to write a reference for you, and it may be in a style that differs from the typical style of references in your country. Show this page on the UCAS website to your referee – www.ucas.com/advisers/online/references. References must be entered onto the UCAS application in English, although they can be translated. Make sure you keep a copy of both the original and translated reference, as your chosen institutions may ask to see a copy for verification purposes.

If you're in prison, your application must include a statement from the prison authorities, even if you're asking someone else to write your reference. The prison authority has to say whether you're suitable for a course of study, and whether you'll be able to accept a place for the start date chosen.

Who should not write the reference?

- It is not permitted for family, friends, partners or ex-partners to write your reference. If we find this to be the case, your application may be cancelled.

More information about the reference and a guide to writing references can be found at www.ucas.com/students/applying/howtoapply/reference.

Cost of applying

How much will it cost?

The fee depends on how many courses and universities you apply to. Please check **www.ucas.com** for up-to-date information about the application fee.

How do I pay?

If you're applying through a school, college or other organisation, they'll let you know how to pay. It will be either by credit or debit card online, or by paying your centre who will then pay us. If you apply to one course and pay the reduced application fee, and later add choices to your application after it has been sent to UCAS, you pay the additional fee to UCAS.

If you're applying independently, you pay online using a credit or debit card. The card doesn't have to be in your name, but you will require the consent of the cardholder. If you pay your fee using a credit or debit card that you do not have permission to use, we will cancel your application.

We accept UK and international Visa, Visa Debit, Delta, MasterCard, JCB, Maestro, Solo and Electron credit or debit cards. At the moment we do not accept American Express or Diners Club cards.

When do I pay?

You pay after you have completed your application and are in the process of sending it to us (or to your referee).

If you're paying by card, you'll be asked for your card details once you have agreed to the terms of the declaration and data protection statement.

Please remember that you can only complete one application in each cycle. If you send a second application, it will be cancelled and you will not receive a refund.

How to complete your application – FAQs

How do I apply for more than one subject?

You can apply for a maximum of five choices on your application. This could be five different universities for the same subject, or five different subjects at one university, or any combination. You can select any course you wish (with the exception of those courses detailed in the 'Choices' section on page 136).

However, you can only submit one personal statement with your application. If you are applying for different subjects, you will need to try to write your statement more generally. This will be easier if the subjects are similar. If the subjects are quite different (for example, medicine and law) you can contact the university and ask if it is possible to send an amended version of the statement direct to them. If they agree, you can write the statement on your application specifically about one subject, and then write an amended version about the second subject. More advice about applying for multiple courses is given on page 159.

Will the universities I've chosen be able to see my other choices?

No. UCAS will keep this information private, so the universities will be not be able to see your other choices. However, once you have accepted your firm choice and your insurance choice (if you have one), then both of these universities will be able to see the other. They can also see whether they are the firm or insurance choice.

Can I reapply if I already have a deferred place?

No. If you don't want to attend the course you have accepted, you will need to discuss your options with your university or college. If they agree to withdraw your place and you had applied for the course in the previous application cycle, you can complete a new application.

How do universities and colleges view deferred entry applications?

The value of gap year activities is widely documented and most unis will allow you to apply for deferred entry, but check with them before applying. When you apply, include details of your proposed gap year in your personal statement to support your application.

Student tip:

'...the application on the UCAS website was very easy to complete, partly due to its structure and also because it had tips all over the application, in case I got a little confused about what was asked for.'

A note for international applicants:
Several countries require their citizens to complete mandatory military or national service. If this affects you, check with universities and colleges in advance to discuss when you should apply. You can defer through UCAS for a maximum of one year. It would be useful to include information on your military or national service in your personal statement.

What happens when my application is sent to UCAS?

Once your application is completed and sent to us, we process it. If we have to query anything, we'll contact you for more information. Your application will then be sent to your universities and colleges to consider and we'll send you a Welcome letter. If your postal address is in the UK, allow 14 days for your letter to arrive. If your postal address is outside the UK, please allow 21 days. Find out more about what happens next in the Step 3 Offers section on page 183.

Personal statement

This is your opportunity to tell the unis why they should choose you. In your personal statement you'll need to demonstrate why you're suitable for the course, and show your enthusiasm and commitment. Above all, you'll need to ensure that you stand out from the crowd. Watch our UCAStv video guide at **www.ucas.tv** for help on how to start and what to include in your personal statement.

Look at our timeline overleaf to see when you need to start researching and writing your personal statement.

See when you need to start researching and writing your personal statement.

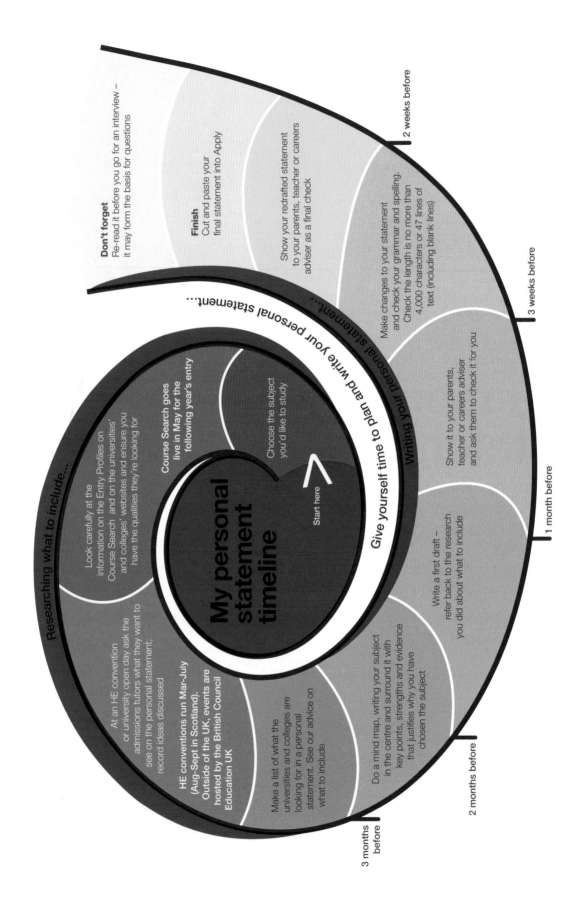

My personal statement timeline

Start here

Choose the subject you'd like to study

Researching what to include...

Look carefully at the information on the Entry Profiles on Course Search and on the universities' and colleges' websites and ensure you have the qualities they're looking for

Course Search goes live in May for the following year's entry

At an HE convention or university open day ask the admissions tutors what they want to see on the personal statement; record ideas discussed

HE conventions run Mar-July (Aug-Sept in Scotland). Outside of the UK, events are hosted by the British Council Education UK

Make a list of what the universities and colleges are looking for in a personal statement. See our advice on what to include

Do a mind map, writing your subject in the centre and surround it with key points, strengths and evidence that justifies why you have chosen the subject

Write a first draft – refer back to the research you did about what to include

Give yourself time to plan and write your personal statement...

Writing your personal statement...

Show it to your parents, teacher or careers adviser and ask them to check it for you

Make changes to your statement and check your grammar and spelling. Check the length is no more than 4,000 characters or 47 lines of text (including blank lines)

Show your redrafted statement to your parents, teacher or careers adviser as a final check

Finish
Cut and paste your final statement into Apply

Don't forget
Re-read it before you go for an interview – it may form the basis for questions

3 months before

2 months before

1 month before

3 weeks before

2 weeks before

Structure and format

Think about the structure of your statement – it needs to look and sound good. A bad statement can say a lot, so make sure your get the grammar, spelling and punctuation right.

A representative from Ulster Business School told us:

'The presentation of the personal statement is of critical importance to demonstrate use of English language and grammar at a standard suitable for entry to higher education.'

How to provide your personal statement

You can enter up to 4,000 characters (this includes spaces) or 47 lines of text (this includes blank lines), whichever comes first. You don't have to use all the space provided. **We strongly recommend that you prepare your personal statement offline using a word-processing package and copy and paste it into the Apply system.**

Please note that you cannot use *italics*, **bold**, <u>underlining</u> or foreign characters (such as á, ë, õ) in your personal statement – the system will automatically remove these when saved. This will not disadvantage your application.

If you are an international student, we know that you may want to give correct titles of some things in your own language but universities and colleges are aware that accent marks and certain foreign characters are not accepted in Apply.

Note: From the 2012 entry application cycle you will be able to enter some accent marks and foreign characters into your personal statement, if you wish to do so. Further details of this will be available nearer the time.

Student tip

'The character limit is tough but try to cram in as much as you can because it is the only image that the universities will have of you – first impressions count!... It may be the first time you are encouraged to "brag" about yourself. Just keep it professional. And absolutely no spelling errors. You want to seem well rounded and also focused on your subject.

A tip that I have... is to type out your personal statement in a word document first, then get it read by anybody who is willing to read it!'

What to include

This section gives you some suggestions of what to include in your personal statement, but these are only guidelines so don't worry if some of them aren't relevant to you. More detailed information and a UCAStv video guide to writing a personal statement are available at **www.ucas.com/students/applying/ howtoapply/personalstatement.**

Firstly, check the Entry Profiles for the courses you're interested in on Course Search at **www.ucas.com**. These explain what the unis are looking for in their students and the qualifications and experience you'll need for the courses. The Entry Profiles will give you some ideas about what to include in your personal statement.

Our mind map shown opposite summarises what you need to know about the personal statement, including preparation, presentation and what to include.

The worksheet overleaf has been designed to help you think about information you could include in your personal statement.

You can photocopy our timeline, mind map and worksheet from this book or download and print off PDF versions from **www.ucas.com/students/applying/ howtoapply/personalstatement.**

Writing about the course

Two of the most important things to think about are:

- **Why you're applying for the courses you've chosen:** this is particularly important when you're applying for a subject that you have not studied before. Tell the university the reasons why that subject interests you, and include evidence that you understand what's required to study the course. For example, if applying for psychology courses, show that you know how scientific the subject is.

- **Why you're suitable for the course:** tell the universities the skills and experience you have that will help you succeed on the course.

Also think about:

- how your current or previous studies relate to the courses that you've chosen

- any activities that demonstrate your interest in the courses

- why you want to go to university.

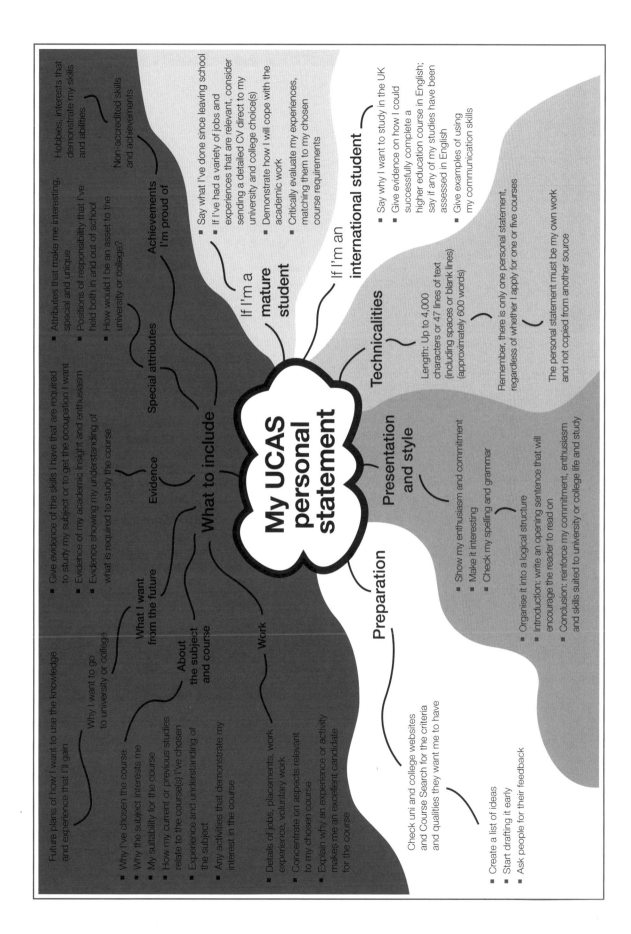

My UCAS personal statement

What to include

About the subject and course

- Why I've chosen the course
- Why the subject interests me
- My suitability for the course
- How my current or previous studies relate to the course(s) I've chosen
- Experience and understanding of the subject
- Any activities that demonstrate my interest in the course

What I want from the future

- Future plans of how I want to use the knowledge and experience that I'll gain
- Why I want to go to university or college

Evidence

- Give evidence of the skills I have that are required to study my subject or to get the occupation I want
- Evidence of my academic insight and enthusiasm
- Evidence showing my understanding of what is required to study the course

Special attributes

- Attributes that make me interesting, special and unique
- Positions of responsibility that I've held both in and out of school
- How would I be an asset to the university or college?

Achievements I'm proud of

- Hobbies, interests that demonstrate my skills and abilities
- Non-accredited skills and achievements

Work

- Details of jobs, placements, work experience, voluntary work
- Concentrate on aspects relevant to my chosen course
- Explain why an experience or activity makes me an excellent candidate for the course

If I'm a mature student

- Say what I've done since leaving school
- If I've had a variety of jobs and experiences that are relevant, consider sending a detailed CV direct to my university and college choice(s)
- Demonstrate how I will cope with the academic work
- Critically evaluate my experiences, matching them to my chosen course requirements

If I'm an international student

- Say why I want to study in the UK
- Give evidence on how I could successfully complete a higher education course in English; say if any of my studies have been assessed in English
- Give examples of using my communication skills

Technicalities

- Length: Up to 4,000 characters or 47 lines of text (including spaces or blank lines) (approximately 600 words)
- Remember, there is only one personal statement, regardless of whether I apply for one or five courses
- The personal statement must be my own work and not copied from another source

Presentation and style

- Show my enthusiasm and commitment
- Make it interesting
- Check my spelling and grammar
- Organise it into a logical structure
- Introduction: write an opening sentence that will encourage the reader to read on
- Conclusion: reinforce my commitment, enthusiasm and skills suited to university or college life and study

Preparation

- Check uni and college websites and Course Search for the criteria and qualities they want me to have
- Create a list of ideas
- Start drafting it early
- Ask people for their feedback

Personal statement worksheet

This worksheet is designed to help you think about information you could include in your personal statement. We've included space for you to write down any thoughts you have as you go along. More detailed advice and guidance about writing your personal statement, including our UCAStv video guide, is available at **www.ucas.com/personalstatement**

Writing about the course

Why are you applying for your chosen course(s)?

Why does this subject interest you? Include evidence that you understand what's required to study the course, eg if applying for psychology courses, show that you know how scientific the subject is.

Why do you think you're suitable for the course(s)? Do you have any particular skills and experience that will help you to succeed on the course(s)?

Personal statement worksheet

2

Do your current or previous studies relate to the course(s) that you have chosen? If so, how?

Have you taken part in any other activities that demonstrate your interest in the course(s)?

Skills and achievements

Universities like to know the skills you have that will help you on the course, or generally with life at university, such as any accredited or non-accredited achievements. Write these down here. Examples can be found at
www.ucas.com/personalstatementskills

Also think about any other achievements you're proud of, positions of responsibility that you hold or have held both in and out of school, and attributes that make you interesting, special or unique.

Personal statement worksheet

3

Hobbies and interests

Make a list of your hobbies, interests and social activities. Then think about how they demonstrate your personality, skills and abilities. Try to link them to the skills and experience required for your course(s).

Work experience

Include details of jobs, placements, work experience or voluntary work, particularly if it's relevant to your chosen course(s). Try to link any experience to skills or qualities related to the course.

Mature students

Explain what you've been doing since leaving education, and provide additional evidence to support your application. If you're not in full-time education, you should give details of any relevant work experience, paid or unpaid, and information about your current or previous employment.

Personal statement worksheet

International students

Tell universities why you want to study in the UK and why you think you can successfully complete a course that is taught in English. Say if some of your studies have been taught or examined in English and if you have taken part in any activities where you have used English outside of your studies.

Future plans

If you know what you'd like to achieve after completing the course, explain how you want to use the knowledge and experience that you gain. How does the course relate to what you want to do in the future?

Dos and don'ts when writing your personal statement

- **Do** use your best English and don't let spelling and grammatical errors spoil your statement.
- **Do** show that you know your strengths and can outline your ideas clearly. Use words you know will be understood by the person reading your statement.
- **Do** be enthusiastic – if you show your interest in the course, it may help you get a place.
- **Do** expect to produce several drafts of your personal statement before being totally happy with it.
- **Do** ask people you trust for their feedback.
- **Don't** exaggerate – if you do you may get caught out at interview when asked to elaborate on an interesting achievement.
- **Don't** rely on a spellchecker as it will not pick up everything – proofread as many times as possible.
- **Don't** leave it to the last minute – your statement will seem rushed and important information could be left out.

How to make your application stand out from the crowd

We asked some universities what they were looking for in a personal statement to make it stand out. These are the answers they gave us:

University of Bristol

'Interest in and commitment to the subject. A sense of the individual is crucial. A personal statement should be just that – a personal reflection on what it is that interests the applicant about the subject and why.'

University of Birmingham

'An engagement with the course they [the applicants] are applying for; and we want to hear their own personal "voice", and approach to the subject.'

De Montfort University

'"Standing out" is definitely the key phrase – students need to bear in mind that applying to university is a competitive process and that their application is not judged in isolation but rather against that of potentially hundreds of other candidates. Getting the basics right is important, therefore the statement needs to clearly explain why the student is applying for the subject and why they would be a strong candidate. All applicants should use positive and enthusiastic language, pay attention to detail and ensure that spelling and grammar are of the highest standard.

'The statement needs to be a balanced document, with a focus on academic life but also talking about work experience, where they see themselves in the future and what they do in their spare time. Applicants should avoid simply listing their accomplishments and should ensure that every point they make links back into the subject they have chosen and highlights skills or knowledge and experience that they have gained. For example a student who works part-time in a leading supermarket would not simply say "I work part-time in a leading supermarket", they would instead talk about the skills gained – which could be anything from time management to communicating with a diverse range of people depending what he/she feels is most beneficial to highlight.'

Your skills and achievements

Universities like to know the types of skills you have that will help you on the course, or more generally while you're at university. They also like to see if you've been involved in any accredited or non-accredited achievements. Include:

- non-accredited skills and achievement which you've gained through activities such as:

  - ASDAN (Award Scheme Development and Accreditation Network) awards, for example, Universities Award

  - CREST awards

  - Diploma of Achievement

  - Duke of Edinburgh Award

  - Millennium Volunteers Scheme

  - OCNW Level 3 Certificate in Personal Development for Progression (previously known as the Liverpool Enrichment Programme)

  - vfifty award

  - WorldWide Volunteering Certificate of Volunteering Achievement

  - Young Enterprise

- accreditation achieved for any activities in preparation for higher education, for example through the ASDAN Aimhigher Certificate of Personal Effectiveness (CoPE qualification)

- any other achievements that you are proud of, eg reaching grade 3 piano or being selected for the county cricket team

- positions of responsibility that you hold, or have held, both in and out of school, for example prefect or representative for a local charity

- attributes that make you interesting, special or unique.

Remember: your personal statement could be used as a basis for an interview, so be prepared to answer questions on it.

Student tip:

'The best piece of advice I can give is to be unique and try to give the person who is reading it a sense of your personality and commitment to the subject. It's not all about grades.'

Hobbies and interests

Think about how your hobbies, interests and social activities demonstrate your skills and abilities. If there's anything that relates to your course or to the skills needed to complete a higher education course, include it – the more evidence the better.

The Assistant Registrar for Undergraduate Admissions from the University of Warwick says:

'The strongest applicants are those who can link their extracurricular activities to their proposed course of study.'

Your statement will be more convincing and personal if you write about why an experience, activity or interest makes you a good candidate for the course. Include enough additional information to make it interesting and to demonstrate your own interest. Rather than making a statement such as:

'I enjoy badminton'

try to provide context and show what you have learnt:

'I play badminton twice a week with a club that plays in local competitions and I play in both singles and doubles matches. Doubles matches require good team working, an ability to support your partner, to devise a game plan but be able to adapt it as required and fast reactions. I enjoy the social side of the club and take responsibility for organising the social activities and fundraising events. This gives me an opportunity to develop my organisational and planning skills. Fitting in all these activities while keeping up with my academic studies demands good time management and I think I do that very well.'

Work experience

Include details of jobs, placements, work experience or voluntary work, particularly if it's relevant to your chosen courses. Try to link any experience to skills or qualities mentioned in the Entry Profiles. For example, rather than just saying:

'I spent two weeks working at a department store. I enjoyed speaking to customers and helping them with their enquiries'

you could say:

'I spent two weeks managing customer enquiries at a department store. I learnt how to interact with customers and handle complaints. The experience highlighted the importance of positive communication between a business and its

Student tip:

'When I started I didn't have a clue what to write. What I found helpful was writing down a list of every activity that I had done in school and outside of school that related to my course. Also why you are passionate about that particular subject and why the uni should choose you.'

customers, and taught me how to manage difficult enquiries effectively. I would like to develop this skill further by studying for a degree in public relations.'

If you are not in full-time education, you should give details of any relevant work experience, paid or unpaid, and information about your current or previous employment.

De Montfort University explained how work experience can enhance an application:

'Work experience is always positive, but for some courses it is absolutely crucial. An applicant wishing to be a teacher, nurse, pharmacist, social worker, midwife etc will have a considerably better chance of obtaining an offer if they have acquired relevant work experience. This is for two reasons:

- *Firstly, it demonstrates motivation for their chosen subject. If a student writes "I am extremely passionate about becoming a teacher", but has not organised any work experience in Years 10, 11, 12 or 13 in a school environment, then an admissions tutor might be cynical as to how genuine that passion really is.*

- *Secondly, relevant work experience reassures the admissions tutor that the applicant really knows the reality of what the course and career involves and isn't just looking at it in a rose-tinted light.*

Students are encouraged to not just state that they have undertaken work experience but to expand by talking about exactly what they did and the skills they acquired.'

Mature students

If you are applying as a mature student, use the personal statement to explain what you have been doing since leaving education, and provide additional evidence to support your application.

A representative from University of Ulster stated:

'A mature student might have valuable experience (perhaps 10 years working in the courts service, or a solicitor's office), and this might form the basis for an APEL (Accreditation of Prior Experiential Learning) offer. So it is worth seeing if your experience could count towards an offer.'

Find out more about APEL at **www.ucas.com/students/wheretostart/maturestudents/courses/apl**.

The University of Bristol offered this advice for mature applicants:

'When we read personal statements we obviously look for a number of things. An important criterion is the demonstration of a real interest in the subject. This may be through work experience or conferences or talks but this may be difficult for mature students to achieve. Evidence of extra reading and perhaps a brief description of which areas of the subject they find interesting is always a good sign.

'With mature students it is nice to see some evidence that they have thought hard about the move to higher education. Clearly there are often difficulties for these students given their possible additional responsibilities, so I would be looking for commitment, enthusiasm and motivation, as well as some understanding of what will be expected of them... ie that university is not an easy option and that they will often have to put in more effort than the 18-year-olds straight from school.'

International students

If you're an international student, use the personal statement to tell universities why you want to study in the UK. Also try to answer these questions in your statement:

- How can you show that you can successfully complete a higher education course that is taught in English? Say if some of your studies have been taught or examined in English.

- Have you taken part in any activities where you have used English outside of your studies?

Personal statements may be in a different style to what you are used to in your own country, or for other countries you may be applying to. Make sure you read more about what should be considered when writing your personal statement at: **www.ucas.com/students/applying/howtoapply/personalstatement**.

Future plans

If you know what you'd like to achieve after completing a university course, explain how you want to use the knowledge and experience that you gain.

Applying to multiple courses

Remember that you only write one personal statement, so it will be used for all your choices. Try not to mention a university by name, even if you're applying to only one – your personal statement cannot be changed if you apply to a different place later.

If you're applying for a joint degree – explain why you are interested in both aspects of this joint programme.

If you're applying for different subjects or courses – identify the common themes and skills that are relevant to your choices. For example, both mathematics and law are subjects where you have to think logically and apply rules. You may like both subjects because you enjoy solving problems, using theory and natural or man-made laws to come to a correct conclusion.

If your chosen courses can't be linked by a common theme – think about your reasons for applying to such varied courses. It might be useful to speak to a careers adviser to get some guidance.

If you mention a subject in your personal statement and are applying to other courses, you may be asked by the university or college for additional information about why you have chosen alternative courses.

Don't be negative in your statement; put a positive slant on everything you can.

Attention-grabbing

Some statements start with quotes, some include jokes, some set out to be unusual or eye-catching. Sometimes it works, but it might have the opposite effect to what you hoped. The admissions decision-maker may not share your sense of humour so be careful when trying to make your statement stand out.

Write what comes naturally

In your personal statement you need to put your meaning across directly and simply. You can do this by keeping your sentences to an average of 12-20 words, and using English (or Welsh) in a way that is natural to you. Avoid sounding either over-familiar or over-formal and write to get yourself and your message across clearly. Check that each sentence adds something new, otherwise it is just adding to the word count rather than adding value.

The quality of your writing reflects the quality of your thinking. Show that you know your strengths and can outline your ideas clearly. Use words you know will be understood by the person reading your statement; you might find it easier if you imagine you are talking to them across their desk. In fact, you can sometimes spot where your statement doesn't work well by reading it aloud!

Dos and don'ts when writing your personal statement

Do create a list of your ideas before attempting to write the real thing.

Do expect to produce several drafts before being totally happy.

Do ask people you trust for their feedback.

Do check university and college prospectuses, websites and Entry Profiles (at **www.ucas.com**), as they usually tell you the criteria and qualities that they want their students to demonstrate.

Do use your best English/Welsh and **don't** let spelling and grammatical errors spoil your statement.

Do be enthusiastic – if you show your interest in the course, it may help you get a place.

Don't feel that you need to use elaborate language. If you try too hard to impress with long words that you are not confident using, the focus of your writing may be lost.

Don't say too much about things that are not relevant – if you think that you are starting to, take a break and come back to your statement when you feel more focused.

Don't lie – if you exaggerate you may get caught out at interview when asked to elaborate on an interesting achievement.

Don't rely on a spellchecker as it will not pick up everything – proofread as many times as possible.

Don't leave it to the last minute – your statement will seem rushed and important information could be left out.

Don't expect to be able to write your personal statement while watching TV or surfing the internet – this is your future, so make the most of the opportunity to succeed.

Student tip:

'I didn't really know where to start, what to write or anything, but after looking on the UCAS website I found some pages that gave me advice on what to include and what not to include. When I actually wrote my personal statement, I found that making a list of the things I wanted to include in it very useful. I then expanded on each of my points in my list, put the most important first and the whole thing slowly fitted together.'

Similarity detection

We put all applications through similarity detection tests, which identify statements that have been copied from another source. The service we use, called Copycatch, finds statements that show similarity, works out how much of the statement may have been copied, and reports the findings. Don't be tempted to copy another person's application materials, or download your personal statement from a website. There could be serious consequences to using other people's work. If any part of your personal statement appears to have been copied, we will inform all the universities and colleges that you have applied to. They will then take the action they consider to be appropriate. We will also contact you by email.

What the Similarity Detection Service does

Each personal statement is checked against:

- a library of personal statements previously submitted to UCAS

- sample statements collected from a variety of websites

- other sources including paper publications.

Each personal statement received at UCAS is added to the library of statements after it has been processed.

What happens if a personal statement has similarities?

- Any statements showing a level of similarity of 10% or more are reviewed by members of the UCAS Similarity Detection Service Team.

- Applicants, universities and colleges are notified at the same time by email when an application has similarities confirmed.

- Admissions tutors at individual universities and colleges decide what action, if any, to take regarding reported cases.

- If you applied through a school, college or other UCAS-registered centre, we and the universities and colleges might, with your consent, communicate direct with the centre to seek further information on it.

Eliminated words: the Copycatch process ignores commonly used words that many applicants use in their statements such as 'and', 'so' and 'with'. Copycatch also ignores a selection of commonly used words and phrases including 'Duke of Edinburgh' and 'football'.

What are the most common opening sentences used in personal statements?

The table below details the most common personal statement opening sentences from the UCAS scheme in the 2010 application cycle:

Rank	Sentence	Number of statements
1	I am currently studying a BTEC National Diploma in ...	464
2	From a young age I have always been interested in ...	309
3	From an early age I have always been interested in ...	292
4	Nursing is a very challenging and demanding career ...	275
5	For as long as I can remember I have been fascinated with ...	196
6	"Fashion is not something that exists in dresses only"...	189
7	Nursing is a profession I have always looked upon with ...	178
8	For as long as I can remember I have been interested in ...	166
9	I am an International Academy student and have been studying since...	141
10	Academically, I have always been a very determined and....	138

Applicants found to have a level of similarity of 10% or above

The figures in **bold** show those detected by the Similarity Detection Service (SDS).

Year of entry	UCAS applicants	GTTR applicants	CUKAS applicants	Total number of applicants	Applicants detected by SDS
2010	687,368	67,278	3,901	758,547	**29,228 (3.85%)***
2009	639,860	63,138	3,841	706,839	**20,086 (2.84%)**
2008	588,689	N/A	N/A	588,689	**17,811 (3.03%)**
2007	In a pilot study of 50,000 UCAS applicants, approximately **5%** were detected by SDS				

*Figures as at 5 October 2010.

You can find further guidance about the UCAS Similarity Detection Service at
**www.ucas.com/students/applying/howtoapply/personalstatement/similarity
detection**.

Personal statement – FAQs

Does the word limit really matter?

Yes, it does. The limit is there for a reason and a key test of the process is to
check whether you are able to explain your reasons for wanting to study in a clear
and succinct way.

I'm not interesting or unique... what should I do?

Everyone has aspects to their personality that make them interesting; it is just a
case of putting them into words. You might find it helpful to ask someone close to
you such as a friend, relative or teacher. The hardest part of the process is getting
started, so at first try not to confine yourself to a word limit or worry too much
about the structure – just get your ideas down.

What balance should I make between my course interests and my extracurricular activities?

There's no clear rule for how much of the personal statement should be allocated
to course-related interests and skills, and how much for hobbies and other
activities. The importance placed on the information varies between universities,
colleges and courses. What is important to remember is that a good personal
statement will usually manage to link most activities back to your chosen degree.

Case study

Name: Olamide Agboola

For me the hardest part [of the application] was writing my personal statement because I wasn't sure whether I needed to make myself sound like the perfect student or not. Over the summer, before starting my A2 year, I had thought about my statement but, like most good college students, hadn't actually put pen to paper. So here's where my first words of wisdom come in – START NOW! It doesn't have to be perfect, but at least writing something over the summer will really help you get organised. If I had done a draft it would definitely have taken a lot of weight off my shoulders. Around October we started preparing for January modules so I really struggled to find the time to write and rewrite my personal statement.

But with help from my personal tutor, careers adviser and older sister I managed to get my application finished and sent off mid-October. Tip 2 – you don't have to go it alone! Although it is a *personal* statement, I found it really useful getting other people to read it and suggest what to put in or take out and so on. My sister had been in my position only a year before, so she passed on a load of advice that she'd been given at sixth form!

When writing my statement I didn't want to dress it up too much – lecturers aren't really fooled by big words and wishy-washy sentences. Instead I highlighted a few of my personal strengths, remembering to always explain why that particular skill would make me a good candidate to study economics. I approached it the same way my history teacher had told me to approach my essays – always link back to the question! I also put in bits about extracurricular activities I had taken part in and books I had been reading about my chosen course. Another word of warning – there's really no point describing every Cadets meeting you've ever been to (if that's what floats your boat!). Just make sure you keep it simple and to the point because 'quality over quantity' has never applied to anything as much as it does to writing personal statements!

That's just my opinion, but it's landed me offers from the universities that I was dying to go to so I guess I must have done something right.

Applying for medicine, dentistry, veterinary science or veterinary medicine

Early deadline: If you're applying for medicine, dentistry, veterinary science or veterinary medicine you'll need to submit your application to UCAS by the early deadline of 15 October.

Admissions tests: For most medicine, dentistry, veterinary science or veterinary medicine courses you'll need to sit an admissions test for the course(s) you are applying for. You can check this on the Entry Profiles for your chosen courses on Course Search at **www.ucas.com**. You can read more about admissions tests on pages 101 to 114 in the Choosing courses section.

Interviews: You'll normally be interviewed by the university before they decide whether to offer you a place or not. If they want to invite you for an interview, this will usually be displayed in UCAS Track. You can accept the invitation in Track, or if you are unable to attend, you can request that the university offers you a different date.

Medicine and dentistry

We asked the Peninsula College of Medicine & Dentistry what guidance they could give to potential medicine and dentistry students. They offered the following advice.

What are you looking for within a student's personal statement which will make them stand out?

'Peninsula College of Medicine & Dentistry does not score personal statements as there is no evidence to prove that they have been written by the applicant. We prefer to assess applicants face-to-face at interview. We do, however, read all personal statements to ensure that the applicant has not said anything that would lead us to believe that they would not make a good doctor or dentist.'

What are your selection criteria when considering applicants?

'Peninsula Medical School selects direct school leavers mainly on achieved GCSE grades and achieved or predicted GCE A/AS grades (or equivalent), together with UKCAT scores. Non-direct school leavers are selected on the basis of GAMSAT scores.

'Peninsula Dental School selects graduates on the basis of degree subjects and classification, plus evidence of voluntary work experience in a dental setting. Health care professional applicants, who do not have qualifications equivalent to a degree, take GAMSAT and provide evidence of past higher education experience plus a high level of work experience.'

Any myth busters which you can share about your uni?

'It is not easy to get into Peninsula College of Medicine & Dentistry. Approximately 10 applications per place are received for medicine and seven applications per place for dentistry. Only one third of applicants are selected to attend an interview.

'Peninsula Medical School will consider applicants who have not achieved all grade A or A* at GCSE.'

Work experience

Most medical schools will expect you to have gained some work experience in a health or social care setting. We asked several universities what work experience they were looking for in their applicants.

Peninsula College of Medicine & Dentistry

'Peninsula Medical School is committed to widening access to medicine and therefore does not insist on work experience in a health care setting, as it favours those applicants who have contacts in the health care profession. However, we do recommend that applicants undertake any work experience that may help them improve some of the personal qualities that we assess at interview, eg communication skills, team work and flexibility.'

University of Bristol

'Whatever is possible for the applicant – for example, volunteering or work in a caring environment, such as an old people's home. We are not prescriptive because we know opportunities vary enormously.'

University of Oxford

'For medicine, some work experience in hospitals is theoretically desirable, but we do appreciate that it can be very difficult to arrange and we therefore have no requirement for it. Some candidates are exposed to more opportunities in this area than others. Any form of voluntary work would be beneficial in the context of applying for medicine (such as helping out in a hospital, at an old people's home, St John's ambulance, or work with a charity or overseas agency).

Veterinary medicine

The Head of Admissions at The Royal Veterinary College offered this advice about work experience requirements for their veterinary medicine courses:

'For our veterinary medicine courses our current minimum work experience requirements are one week in veterinary practice and one week in different animal environment/s. This is going to be increased from September 2012 onwards to two weeks in vet practice and two weeks in different animal environment/s.

'Our minimum requirements are quite low; we understand that it can be difficult for some applicants to gain a lot of relevant work experience and do not want to discourage applicants from different backgrounds from applying.

'We encourage applicants to undertake as much varied work experience as they can so that they can gain a greater understanding of the role of a vet and get useful animal handling experience. This can also help them if they get selected for interview as it is likely that they will need to talk about what they understand the role of a vet to be and also what they have learned from their work experiences. However, we would not disadvantage any applicant who has only completed the minimum work experience requirements.'

Thoughts from two professionals...

Junior doctor

Dr Nina Reeve, who works as a junior doctor in a general hospital, offered this advice to potential medicine students:

'It's a great job with so much variety. You can really find a speciality that suits your personality. You do have to work hard and work lots of nights and weekends. You also still have lots of exams to do after you qualify in order to progress to your chosen speciality. I like it because no two days are the same, you get to meet lots of people, both colleagues and patients, and so it is a very sociable job.

'There is also plenty of opportunity to travel and work abroad for a year. Most people do this after foundation training and before speciality training and usually end up in Australia and New Zealand. There are difficult times, and times where you think is medicine worth it, and these are the times that test you because to do medicine, you need to love it, otherwise you wouldn't be able to do it well.

'I absolutely love it and can't imagine doing a 9-5 and living for the weekends. Of course there is a life outside of medicine, but I think that you should love your job and that way both you and your employer get the most out of the situation. It is a big commitment and you have to miss things such as bank holidays and Christmas occasionally but when a patient and their family thanks you for what you have done for them, I promise it's worth it.'

Small animal vet

Small animal first opinion vet, Caroline Queen, had this to say to anyone thinking of studying veterinary science or veterinary medicine:

'If someone wants to do veterinary science or veterinary medicine then be single-minded and don't be put off! Be persistent, even if you are initially rejected. Get

as much work experience as you can in as many different disciplines as possible, for example dairy farming, lambing, kennel work, small animal practice, equine practice, farm animal practice, abattoir work.

'My advice would be to work hard, play hard, and at the end of the course you'll have a good qualification, and have had the most carefree, fun years of your life!

'If you are sure it is what you want to do, then go for it! Don't do it if the reason is for financial gain as there are lots more higher paid, but less rewarding jobs. Being a veterinary surgeon is a lifestyle, and a profession. There will be times when you are exhausted, but extremely rewarded by the work that you and your colleagues are doing.'

Other websites you may find useful

Medschools online is a free information resource for people who are considering applying to study medicine in the UK: **www.medschoolsonline.co.uk**

Widening Access to Medical School – a resource for potential medical students: **www.wanttobeadoctor.co.uk**

New Media Medicine – an online community of doctors, medical students and applicants to medical school from around the world: **www.newmediamedicine.com**

British Medical Association – includes advice about careers in medicine and a guide to medical student finance: **www.bma.org.uk**

Dental Schools Council provides advice on education and research in UK dental schools: **www.dentalschoolscouncil.ac.uk**

British Dental Association offers advice about careers and education in dentistry: **www.bda.org**

NHS Careers gives information about working within the NHS: **www.nhscareers.nhs.uk**

British Veterinary Association has a 'Student centre' section on its website: **www.bva.co.uk**

'Emma the TV Vet' – this website includes advice about getting into vet school: **www.emmathevet.co.uk**

www.ucas.com

Applying for Oxbridge

Early deadline: the application deadline for all courses at the universities of Oxford and Cambridge is 15 October.

Admissions tests: Depending on the course, you may need to take an admissions test. It's very important to check this so that you don't miss any deadlines. More information about admissions tests is available on pages 101 to 114 and on the universities' websites.

If you're applying to the University of Cambridge, you may be required to complete one or more application forms in addition to the UCAS application. These forms should be sent to the university, not to UCAS.

- **If you're applying from outside the EU**, you must submit a Cambridge Online Preliminary Application (COPA) in addition to a UCAS application by 15 October (for courses starting the following year). This applies to all applicants who are living in a country outside the EU and is regardless of fees status or nationality. If you are studying at a school in the UK you do not need to submit a COPA.

Official figures from the Higher Education Statistics Agency (HESA) show that, for 2008/09 entry, 59.3% of full-time first degree entrants to the University of Cambridge were from state schools; the figure for the University of Oxford was 54.7% (Source: www.hesa.ac.uk).

Student tip:

'Because I had decided to apply to Oxford my application had to be in a lot earlier than everyone else's. But this is no bad thing. Not only is all the pressure of making those life decisions off you, you can also relax over Christmas rather than trying to rush off a personal statement.'

- **If you would like to be considered for an interview in a country outside the EU** where interviews are held, earlier deadlines usually apply for receipt of your COPA. You should consult the University of Cambridge website for details.

- **If you're applying for the Graduate Course in Medicine (UCAS code A101),** you must submit a Graduate Course in Medicine Application Form by 15 October.

- **If you are applying for a Choral or Organ Award**, you must submit a Cambridge Online Preliminary Application. Earlier deadlines also apply.

See the University of Cambridge website at **www.cam.ac.uk/admissions/ undergraduate/** for further details.

The University of Oxford does not require a separate application form, except for students applying for medicine course A101 (fast-track graduate entry only), or those applying for a choral or organ scholarship. For some courses you may need to submit written work to the university. Check the University of Oxford website at **www.admissions.ox.ac.uk** for more details.

In December, the Universities of Oxford and Cambridge hold their interviews for undergraduate applicants. See pages 207 to 215 for examples of interview questions you may be asked by the University of Oxford or the University of Cambridge.

University of Cambridge

We spoke to the University of Cambridge, who gave this useful information for those of you who are thinking of applying to them:

How important is the applicant's personal statement when applying to Cambridge?

'An applicant's personal statement is one of the many sources of information the University of Cambridge uses to assess an application. A personal statement should reflect why you want to study the course you have applied for and indicate any additional independent work you have done that further illustrates your interest and understanding of the subject.'

Did you know ...

- More than 1 in 5 applicants are successful in gaining a place at Cambridge.

- The Cambridge Admissions Office runs a number of summer schools and residential events – 724 people took part in 2010.

- There are over 600 student societies run by students at the university.

- Cambridge has one of the lowest drop-out rates in the UK: just 1.2% of students leave their studies after one year, compared to a UK average of 8.6%.

- After six months, 97% of the students who graduated in 2009 were in employment, further study or were not available for either (eg they were travelling).

- Cambridge students are some of the most satisfied in the country. Cambridge is consistently awarded a top ten place following the annual Student Satisfaction Survey.

There are still misconceptions about the University of Cambridge. Here are some myth busters, provided by the university itself:

Myth 1: Cambridge is not for people like me, I won't fit in there.

There is no typical personality type at Cambridge and students come from all sorts of backgrounds. Cambridge is no different from any other university – you will always find plenty of like-minded people.

Myth 2: So many people apply, I have no chance of getting in.

The odds of getting a place at Cambridge are better than 1 in 5. Many other universities have far more applicants per place. There is no 'secret' to making a successful application. We are looking for students who have academic potential, are best suited to the course in question, and who will most benefit from what we have to offer, whatever their background.

> **Myth 3: Cambridge selects applicants who are good at everything.**
> We select on academic ability alone: enthusiasm, knowledge and interest in your subject is much more important than extracurricular participation.
>
> **Myth 4: There's so much work you don't have time for any fun.**
> Cambridge students participate in a huge range of activities outside their studies. Cambridge has more than 600 student societies, which is more than any other UK university.

University of Oxford

We also asked the University of Oxford some questions, and they provided us with the following helpful advice for potential applicants:

What are you looking for within a student's personal statement which will make them stand out?

'We are looking for students who demonstrate passion and commitment to their course, so we're interested to know what inspires them about the subject, and why they have chosen to study it. It's not about extracurricular activities! We are happy for students to mention these, but please bear in mind that they won't be taken into account in admissions unless they are supporting a student's interest in their chosen subject.'

What work experience are you looking for?

'Our tutors select students using our agreed selection criteria. All candidates are free to make reference to skills or experience acquired in any context when trying to address our selection criteria; sometimes candidates refer to voluntary work and other extracurricular activity, but many forms of evidence can help demonstrate to tutors that a candidate has tried to make an informed decision regarding his/her own suitability to study a particular course.' (If you are applying for medicine at the University of Oxford, read what they said about work experience specifically for medicine applicants on page 169.)

Any myth busters which you can share about your uni?

'Many people seem to think Oxford's admissions process is designed to be as intimidating and confusing as possible but nothing could be further from the truth. We go to huge efforts to be as open and transparent as possible, including offering videos of admissions interviews, putting sample interview questions on the web, and providing podcasts with further information. We even have a dedicated team of staff here specifically to answer questions from applicants, their parents, teachers and other advisers.'

'The university itself is also very different from the image sometimes presented in the media. Oxford students are very diverse, from all different backgrounds, from all parts of the UK and around the world.'

In other sections of this book, you can find more information and advice from the Universities of Oxford and Cambridge (including specific guidance for disabled, international and mature applicants) about their admissions tests, selection process, interviews, bursaries, and what to expect if you start studying at the university.

Applying for Oxbridge – FAQs

Which college should I choose?

For admission to Oxford or Cambridge, it is necessary to be accepted by a college. Under 'Campus code' in the Choices section of your application, select the appropriate campus code (a single letter or number) to denote your choice of college. Applications may be submitted without a nominated college by selecting the 'Open application' option.

You can contact the universities direct for information about all of their colleges. Try to visit the college if possible, or arrange to attend an open day. This will help you decide if you feel comfortable with the college and with the university.

Can I apply to both Oxford AND Cambridge?

You can only apply to both universities if you already have a degree or will have completed a degree by the September of the application cycle in which you are applying (for example, if you are applying in the 2012 entry application cycle you must have completed your degree by September 2012). Otherwise, you can only apply to one of them, not both.

Chapter checklist

These are the things you should be doing in Step 2 of your applicant journey:

☐ Check the deadline for your chosen course(s) on Course Search at **www.ucas.com**.

☐ Watch the UCAStv video guide *How to apply* at **www.ucas.tv**.

☐ Register on Apply at **www.ucas.com** and **keep your username and password in a safe place**.

☐ If you have a disability or special needs watch our UCAStv video guides *Students with disabilities* and *Advice from disability officers* at **www.ucas.tv**.

☐ Check if you need to take an admissions test for the course(s) you've chosen.

☐ If you're applying to the University of Cambridge check with them if you need to complete an additional application form.

☐ If you're applying for medicine, dentistry, nursing, midwifery or certain other health courses, check the immunisation and certification requirements with your unis.

☐ Look at our personal statement timeline and plan when you need to start researching and writing it.

☐ Check uni prospectuses and websites, and the Entry Profiles at **www.ucas.com** – you'll find info about the criteria and qualities they're looking for in personal statements.

☐ Use our personal statement mind map and worksheet to help you think about what to include.

☐ Watch the UCAStv video guide to writing a personal statement at **www.ucas.tv**.

☐ Check the spelling and grammar in your personal statement. Don't rely on a spellchecker as it will not pick up everything – proofread as many times as possible and ask other people to read it for you.

www.ucas.com

Step 3
Offers

This section explains what happens after you've sent your application to us and it's been processed. It provides advice on preparing for and attending interviews and auditions. It describes the different decisions unis can make and explains the difference between conditional and unconditional offers. You'll also find out about replying to offers and when you can accept a second offer as an insurance.

In this section you'll discover all the things you can do using our online Track service at ucas.com, including making changes to your application, finding out your unis' decisions, replying to offers and starting your student finance application.

If you don't receive any offers, you'll find out how you can apply for further courses.

Step 3 **Offers**

No change?

Remember universities and colleges can take several months to make their decisions

UCAS emails you whenever there's a change on your application that needs your attention

Go to www.ucas.com/students/track

A university has responded

Universities and colleges may offer you an interview/audition or a place, or you may be unsuccessful

Invitation for interview, audition or to do a piece of work

Check whether the date suits you and respond. Start preparing! See page 219 and **www.ucas.com**

Unsuccessful

Offer

Wait for further responses

Try Extra if you are left holding no offers

Feedback may be shown on Track, or you may ask for it

Unconditional offer or conditional offer
See page 220 for an explanation of the different types of offer you may receive

When you have received all your decisions you must reply to your offers to tell the universities which you would like to accept

Step 3

After you apply

What happens next?

After we've received your completed application, the following things happen:

- We process all the information you've provided and if we need to query anything, we contact you for more details.

- After processing your application, we send you a Welcome letter that lists your choices. We ask you to check your personal details and choices carefully and let us know immediately if anything is not correct. We also ask you to contact us if you don't receive your Welcome letter within 14 days of sending your application to us.

- You will have researched your chosen unis and courses thoroughly before you applied, so there should be no need to change your choices. However, you may make changes in Track for seven days from the date on your Welcome letter, provided it's before 30 June.

- You can view your application in our online Track service using your Personal ID and the same username and password you used to apply. We print your Personal ID and username on your Welcome letter. To find out about our Track service see page 187.

- Once your application is processed, unis can access it online. They can view your application, but they will not see where else you have applied. They'll only see any other choices after you have replied to your offers. Unis may contact you to tell you that they are considering your application. Not all of them do this, so don't worry if you don't hear from some of your choices.

- The unis consider your application against their own admissions requirements. Each has their own way of working, so you can expect to hear from them at different times. You may be contacted quite quickly or it may be some months before you hear anything.

- They decide whether or not to offer you a place and send their decision to us. Decisions are displayed in Track as soon as we receive them. For information about decisions, see page 219.

- If you have one or more offers and you've received decisions from all your unis, we'll ask you to reply to your offers. See page 229 for information about replying to offers.

Messages from UCAS

Throughout the application cycle, you'll receive messages from us about changes to the status of your application. After we have processed your application and sent it to your unis, we send you a Welcome letter and an *Applicant Welcome Guide*, which explains the next stages of the application process. We ask you to check all the information on this letter and let us know if anything is wrong.

Each time we receive a decision from one of your unis we send you an email asking you to log in to Track to look at the change and read our online letters. When the last uni makes a decision, it's time to reply to any offers you've received.

After you've replied to your offers, we send you a Status Check letter to confirm that we've recorded your offer replies correctly. You need to contact us if any replies on the letter are wrong.

We send you a Confirmation letter when you accept an unconditional offer or when a uni confirms your place after your exam results are published. This letter will tell you whether or not you need to take any further action.

If you've received no offers or you don't have a confirmed place from the offers you accepted, we send you a New Options letter, which explains what you might do next.

If you or the unis tell us that you want to withdraw your whole application, we send you a Complete Withdrawal letter.

You can view your letters online in Track. These will be in Welsh if you requested correspondence from UCAS in Welsh when you applied.

Applicants with disabilities

You may have discussed your disability and requirements with unis before deciding where to apply. However, if you still have any doubts about how your unis will meet your needs or you want to see the facilities for yourself, contact the admissions officer or the head of department for your course. They will be used to arranging visits and will welcome enquiries from disabled students.

During your visit ask tutors about different course options and the number of assignments, lectures and seminars. Talk to them about how your individual needs can be met. Find out what kinds of adjustments the uni will make so you can complete your course. If you'll need flexible exam arrangements, discuss these as well. If a uni agrees to adapt buildings and/or elements of your course, ask them to put this in writing.

Most unis have a disability coordinator who should be able to help with disability-related questions and tell you about the uni's services for disabled students, including accommodation and support arrangements. You may also be able to meet accommodation staff and try out the facilities in halls.

The disability coordinator may be able to arrange for you to speak to students who are on the course you are interested in and other disabled students at the uni. Students will be able to tell you about the level of work expected and any difficulties they have had. Disabled students can tell you how good they find the support arrangements and what life is like there.

If the people you meet are not able to answer your questions, ask to speak to someone who can or ask for information to be sent to you. If you have further questions after your visit, don't be afraid to ask.

After you apply – FAQs

What happens to my application after I've sent it to UCAS?

When we receive your application we validate the information you have provided. We check whether or not you have already applied in the current application cycle and whether any of your personal statement has been copied from another source. We then send the application to your chosen unis for consideration.

When will I receive my Welcome letter?

We send you a Welcome letter after we've processed your application and sent it to your chosen unis. If you haven't received this letter within 14 days of sending your application to us, call our Customer Service Unit.

I've sent my application to you. Why can't I get into Track?

You will only be able to log in to Track after we have fully processed your application and you've received your Welcome letter.

When will I hear from my unis?

If we receive your application by 15 January, unis must make their decisions by early May, but you could hear from them much earlier.

Why are the unis on my Welcome letter in a different order to my application?

The order of your universities was changed when we processed your application. The order does not indicate any preference because your application is sent to all your unis at the same time.

Why is my Welcome letter in Welsh?

When you applied you must have ticked the box to receive correspondence in Welsh. You need to call our Customer Service Unit to amend your application.

Track

When you receive your Welcome letter, you can follow the progress of your application using the online Track service on the UCAS website. You log in to Track with your Personal ID and the username and password that you used when you made your application. We print your Personal ID and username on your Welcome letter. For security reasons your password is not printed on this letter. Don't worry if you can't remember your login details; Track has a 'Forgotten login details?' service.

When you look at your choices on Track, they may be displayed in a different order to what you expected because we generate a random order when we process your application. Don't panic – the displayed order doesn't indicate any preference order; we send your application to all your chosen unis at the same time.

Whenever a uni makes a decision about your application, the details will be shown on Track. If you supply a valid email address on your application, we'll email you each time a decision has been made. To protect confidential information, the email doesn't contain the actual decision; you still need to go to Track to check the details.

You can also use Track to:

- change your postal address, telephone numbers and email address
- add and remove choices (depending on your circumstances)
- reply to interview invitations
- reply to your offers of a place
- send your application to a uni in Extra (see page 237)
- register for Adjustment (see page 269)
- send your application to a uni in Clearing (see page 273).

Track is normally available 24 hours a day, seven days a week.

Here's what some of our applicants said about Track...

'The Track feature was something that I found especially valuable. It set a lot of my nerves at rest to be able to see the progress of my application, and it was very easy to use.'

'I sometimes logged on [to Track] 3 or 4 times a day because I was so excited. The choices page is set out clearly to show exactly where you stand with your universities of choice, so it only took a quick flash to see if anything had changed.'

'The next thing I wanted to know was how my application to the different universities was going. This was effortless with the tracking feature that UCAS provides.'

'UCAS Track was really useful in the process. I love the fact that they email you when your application has been updated.'

'UCAS Track has been incredibly useful.'

Starting your student finance application in Track

If you wish to apply for student finance, you can make the process easier by sharing some of your application details with Student Finance England, Student Finance Wales or Student Finance Northern Ireland. When you agree to share your details, your student finance application will be pre-populated with the personal and course information from your UCAS application. Unfortunately, we don't share data with the Student Awards Agency for Scotland.

We transfer your application details to the student finance service using a secure network, so the information is safe. The student finance services will only use your data for your finance application. They won't give your details to anyone else. If you agree to share your application details, you will automatically be transferred to the student finance service's registration form on their website and logged out of Track.

You can use Track to opt out of sharing your data at any time.

Track on your iPhone

After we have processed your application you can download our Track app on to your iPhone from the iTunes store. This app is a read-only version of our Track service that provides a summary screen for your application record and the facility to view choice information in more detail. You can also use the app to view key dates in the UCAS calendar and to read the top FAQs. Your login details for accessing the app or entering Track from our website are the same.

Look out for the latest news about our iPhone app at **www.ucas.com**.

Tips for using Track

- Use Internet Explorer version 5 or higher, or Mozilla Firefox version 2.0 or higher to access the service. Older versions of browsers can cause problems with secure websites.

- Don't save your password using a facility within your internet browser. This prevents anyone else from logging in to Track and viewing your details.

- When you've finished using Track, log out by clicking on the 'log out' button and then close down your browser. This prevents anyone else from accessing your details. For security reasons, Track times out after five minutes of user inactivity.

UCAStv

Watch our video about how to use Track on UCAStv at **www.ucas.com** for more information.

Here's what the Track choices screen looks like just after we've processed your application...

UC∧S

track

main menu   choices   personal

> LOG OUT

> HELP

: choices

you**go** further

university / college	course	starting	decision	your reply	updated	preference
University of Cambridge campus: 4 entry point: 1	A100	08-Oct-2012			10-Oct-2011	-
University of Birmingham campus: - entry point: 1	C100	24-Sep-2012			10-Oct-2011	-
Keele University campus: - entry point: 1	A100	24-Sep-2012			10-Oct-2011	-
The University of Nottingham campus: - entry point: 1	A100	08-Oct-2012			10-Oct-2011	-
The University of Sheffield campus: - entry point: 1	A100	08-Oct-2012			10-Oct-2011	-

Add choice   Reply to offers   Payment

Please make sure you have checked the details of your choices **before** making replies. Click on the course code in red above to access the choice details.

application processed by UCAS : 10-Oct-2011

last log in : 11-Oct-2011

ucas.com

terms & conditions | contact us

Track – FAQs

Why can't I log in to Track? My details aren't accepted.

You cannot use Track until we've received and processed your application. If your application has been processed, you must make sure that you enter your Personal ID exactly as it appears on your Welcome letter, and enter the username and password you used to apply. Your username and password are case sensitive.

If the fields are reset after you click on the 'log in' button, this usually means that incorrect details have been entered.

If you have five failed attempts to log in to the service in one day, you'll be 'locked out' of the system for 24 hours. If this happens, you need to contact our Customer Service Unit and we'll unlock your account.

I've forgotten my Track username and password. What should I do?

You can find out your Personal ID, Track username and password by using our 'Forgotten login details?' service. You can access this service from the Track page on our website or from the Track login screen. If you've entered and verified an email address on your application, you just need to enter it in the 'Forgotten login details?' service and we'll email the requested details to you.

I've been locked out of Track. What can I do?

You need to contact our Customer Service Unit and, if you can answer the security questions on your application correctly, we'll unlock your account.

Track has timed out. What should I do?

Track automatically times out after five minutes of inactivity, for security reasons. You need to go back to the Track gateway page on our website and log in again.

How quickly is information updated on Track?

When you or universities provide updates, the changes are shown on Track almost immediately.

Money: apply for student finance

Don't wait until your exams, or (worse still) your results, before applying for your student funding. Making an early application will ensure your funding will be sorted before your course starts. If for any reason you change your course or uni, you can update your information, so there's no need to delay.

If you live in England, you can apply for your funding online by going to **www.direct.gov.uk/studentfinance**.

If you live in Wales, you should visit www.studentfinancewales.co.uk or **www.cyllidmyfyrwyrcymru.co.uk**.

If you live in Scotland, you should visit **www.saas.gov.uk**.

If you live in Northern Ireland, you should visit **www.studentfinanceni.co.uk**.

If you live in Guernsey, Jersey or the Isle of Man, you should visit **www.education.gg**, **www.gov.je** or **www.gov.im**.

The way you apply and the deadline dates to guarantee your money will be in place for the start of term will depend on in which country in the United Kingdom you normally live. All of this information is available from the Directgov website. Read it and commit it to memory!

To complete the student finance application successfully you will need:

- information about your parents' income – such as their P60s

- your National Insurance number – don't guess it or you won't be paid

- your bank details – the money will be paid into your bank account

- your passport if you have one – make sure it hasn't expired.

Get all this together before you start to complete the application and it will be much easier and quicker to do.

Did you know?

If you live in England, Northern Ireland or Wales you can start your application for student finance through UCAS using a service within Track at **www.ucas.com**. You can opt to share your personal details and course choices with the Student Loans Company.

Although you can share your data with the Student Loans Company after we've processed your UCAS application, the student finance service in Track only becomes available when the services in the different countries go live. Student Finance NI, Student Finance Wales and Cyllid Myfyrwyr Cymru usually go live in November, with Student Finance England on the Directgov website following in February. Look out for instructions in Track on how to use the service.

After you submit your application you will be assessed and receive written confirmation of what you can expect (your entitlement). It is really important that you understand this, as it sets out exactly how much money you will have to live on for the whole year. You should also keep this document safe because you will need it when you enrol at uni. You may also need to show your bank or Jobcentre Plus a copy if you wish to apply for a student account or any benefits.

Funding for students on health-related courses

Students on health-related courses, such as medicine, physiotherapy, nursing, midwifery and occupational therapy, are funded differently from other students. At the time of writing the NHS was reviewing the financial support that it offers to its students and these changes are likely to come into effect in 2011 or 2012. The NHS is also looking to phase out diploma courses, so that all NHS students will be studying at degree level.

Information about NHS funding can be found at **www.nhsbsa.nhs.uk**.

Tuition fees

As long as you meet the residency requirements and have not been funded by the NHS previously, you will not have to pay the tuition fees yourself. The NHS will pay these fees direct to your uni.

Living costs

If you are starting a health-related degree, you will be eligible to apply for a means-tested NHS bursary and a reduced rate student loan. This means that the NHS will look at your parents' or partner's income when they assess your living costs. In addition, you may be eligible to claim means-tested support for children or other dependants.

To apply for a reduced rate student loan, visit **www.direct.gov.uk**. The reduced rate loan is not means tested for NHS students; it is repaid at the end of the course once you are earning more than a certain amount.

How do I apply for an NHS bursary?

When your uni offers you a provisional training place, they will advise the NHS Student Grants Unit. The NHS will then send you a letter of confirmation, which will give you your unique student reference number. This letter will also tell you how to download the form from their website. You should return your completed form and supporting documentation to them. They will assess your application and let you know if you qualify for an award.

Unlike student loans that are paid in three termly instalments, NHS bursaries are paid to students monthly. If you are going to move into student accommodation, you should check the payment dates on your accommodation contract before you sign it. In some cases, it may be possible for you to pay this in line with your bursary payments.

International students

If you live outside the European Union, you cannot currently apply for a loan but your chosen universities may offer bursaries or scholarships that are worth applying for – check the finance section on their websites. If you live in the EU, see **www.direct.gov.uk/en/EducationAndLearning/UniversityAndHigherEducation/StudentFinance/index.htm** for up-to-date student finance information.

Making changes

After you've sent us your application you may need to change some of the details you've provided or supply additional information. This section summarises the changes or additions you can make to your application when you receive your Welcome letter. Unfortunately, you can't make any changes to your personal statement or reference.

You're happy with the uni, but not the course, start date or point of entry

You need to contact the uni and not us if you still want to apply to them but want to change:

- your course

- your start date, for example to the next year if you decide to have a gap year

- your point of entry. You may have applied to start the course in the first year (year 1 entry) but later decide that you need to do a foundation year (year 0 entry) or find out that you have the qualifications to start the course in the second year (year 2 entry).

If the uni agrees, they will tell us about the change. If we have already sent you an offer for your original choice, we will change it and the new offer will be displayed in Track.

You want to change a choice of uni

You can change a uni choice in Track within seven days from the date on your Welcome letter, as long as it's before 30 June. You cannot normally change your uni choices after seven days. If there are exceptional reasons, like a change in your family circumstances or any personal problems, you need to ask your referee to write to us, explaining the situation and recommending that you are allowed to make the change. Your referee should include details of the proposed change(s) in the letter.

You've applied to one uni only and want to apply to others

If you only apply for one course and pay the reduced application fee, you can add up to four more if you pay an additional fee, as long as you have not already accepted or declined an offer. You can add choices and pay the additional fee in Track until 30 June.

You've made fewer than five choices and you want to make more

If you initially applied to fewer than five choices, you can add more choices as long as you have not accepted or declined your offers. You can add further choices in Track until 30 June.

Cancelling a choice

You can cancel an individual choice as long as the uni has not sent us a decision. You do this in Track.

Address and phone number changes

You can change your postal address, home and mobile phone numbers in Track and we let your chosen unis know. If you change your postal address and you're expecting any urgent letters from your unis, you should also tell them yourself. Remember to get your mail redirected so that you receive any letters that have already been sent.

If you're using a different address during term time, make sure that you change your postal address to your home or your new address at the end of the summer term.

Email address change

You can change your email address in Track. We send an email containing a verification code to the new address. You then enter this code into Track to confirm that the email address is correct.

Changes in exams and course arrangements

You must write to us immediately if your exam subjects, modules or units, exam board, centre number or any other details change. You must also tell the unis where you have offers or those that are still considering your application.

Unis usually base their conditional offers on your exam details. If your details change, they may change their offers or decisions.

If a uni cannot confirm your exam results because they do not have enough information, they may not be able to offer you a place. You need to tell us and the unis immediately if anything changes.

Accident, illness or personal problems that affect your exam results

If you suffer an accident, illness or personal problems that affect your exam results, write to each uni that is considering your application to explain. You need to include a supporting letter from your school or other authority and, in medical cases, from your doctor. You should send the details as soon as possible after the problem has arisen. Do not wait until you receive your exam results.

Cancelling your application

If you want to cancel your application and receive a refund of your application fee you must call our Customer Service Unit within seven days from the date on the

Welcome letter, which we send to you when we have processed your application. You cannot cancel your application in Track.

Withdrawing your application

If you decide you don't want to go to uni this year, you can withdraw completely from the UCAS scheme. You should tell us as soon as possible, preferably by mid-September before courses start, so that the places can be offered to someone else. We will let your chosen unis know that you have withdrawn. If you want, you can reapply in the following year.

If you have withdrawn from the scheme but, for exceptional reasons, you want to re-enter it, you need to contact our Customer Service Unit for advice.

Making changes – FAQs

How do I change my address, phone number or email address?

You can change your postal address, email address and phone number using Track. We will then send your new details to your unis. If you are expecting correspondence from a particular uni you may wish to contact them direct to give them your new details.

Can I change my personal statement?

You cannot update your personal statement through UCAS. If you have additional information relevant to your application which you think your unis would find useful, you should contact them direct.

How can I change my year of entry?

You need to contact your unis direct. If they agree to change your year of entry, they will tell us and we'll show the change in Track.

Can I change my choice of uni?

You can change your choice of university or college within seven days from the date on your Welcome letter, depending on the time of year. After that, you can only make choice changes if your chosen course is no longer running or you have exceptional circumstances. To change a choice due to exceptional circumstances, we will need a letter of support from your referee, detailing the change you want and your reasons for requesting the change.

If you wish to change the course details at your chosen uni, you should contact them direct. In this situation, you do not need to contact us. If they are happy to change your course, they will tell us and we'll show the change in Track.

I haven't used all my five choices. Can I use the others now?
You can add further choices to your application using Track up to 30 June as long as you have not replied to any offers that you've received.

If you only had a single choice and paid the reduced application fee, you will also have to pay an additional amount. You can do this in Track.

Can I cancel my application and reapply?
You can cancel your application for seven days from the date on your Welcome letter by calling our Customer Service Unit. After we have cancelled your application, you will be able to register on Apply again to make a new application.

After seven days from the date on your Welcome letter you can withdraw your application at any time, but you cannot reapply in the same application cycle.

www.ucas.com

Interviews, portfolios and auditions

Interviews

Many unis (particularly popular ones, running competitive courses) want to meet you and find out whether you'd cope with the demands of your chosen course before making you an offer. More and more are inviting potential students for interview before making a conditional or unconditional offer of a place.

Policies vary greatly and some unis interview only selected or borderline applicants and some do not interview at all. If you're invited for interview, there are lots of things you can do before, during and after interviews to get the most from the experience.

Some unis will contact you direct to invite you for interview and others will send online invitations to you in Track. If the interview invitation is made in Track, you can accept the invitation, turn it down or ask for another day online. The Unis' decisions section on page 219 gives more information about interview invitations.

Preparation

There's lots you can do to prepare for the big day – from having a mock interview to arming yourself with information about the uni and the course.

Top tips

The whens and wheres: Make sure you know where you need to be and when, and make any necessary travel and accommodation arrangements in advance. Visit the uni's website for maps and directions and make sure you know exactly where on campus you need to be. If you need more information, get in touch with the uni.

Knowledge is power: Be sure to read the prospectus and look on the uni website – the more you know about the uni and the course you have applied for, the keener you'll seem. Make a list of questions you'd like to ask, perhaps the kind of things the prospectus doesn't tell you.

Know your application: Make sure you're familiar with what you put in your application – this is all your interviewer knows about you, so he or she will probably ask you about some of the things you've mentioned.

Be familiar with 'hot topics' in your subject area: You may well be asked about them, and don't forget to read the newspapers too. Interviewers commonly ask for your views on the issues of the day.

Practice makes perfect: A mock interview might be a good idea. Typical things you might be asked are:

- Why did you choose this course?

- What do you enjoy most on the course you are currently studying?

- Why did you choose this uni?

Ask a teacher or careers adviser to run through a mock interview with you.

Get a good night's sleep: You won't perform your best without one!

At interview

Interviews are always nerve-wracking as you don't know what you're going to be asked. Just be yourself, be enthusiastic and be sure to 'sell' what you have to offer as a student on your chosen course.

Interviewers are looking for students who show an interest, who can think independently and consider new ideas. They are looking for students who will thrive well on their course and enjoy a varied academic life alongside their outside interests.

Top tips

Dress appropriately: Although you probably won't need to wear a suit to interview, show your interviewer you are taking things seriously by dressing smartly.

Arrive in good time: Take any contact numbers just in case the worst happens and you get delayed on the way to your interview.

Body language: Be aware of your body language in the interview room – don't slouch or yawn; sit up and look alert. Make sure you are giving out all the right signals.

Stumped?: If you don't understand a question ask for it to be repeated or rephrased. Make good guesses or relate your answer to something you do know something about.

Expect the unexpected: While interviewers aren't trying to trick you, some will want to see how you react under pressure. A surprise test or exercise isn't unheard of, so stay calm and think clearly.

Ask questions: While your interviewer needs to find out about you by asking lots of questions, you'll come across as enthusiastic if you ask appropriate questions too. Use the interview as a chance to find out answers to your questions that weren't answered on the website or in the prospectus.

Next steps

An interview is as much a chance for you to check out a uni, as it is for them to check you out, so take some time to reflect and consider how things could have gone better.

Top tips

Make notes: While the questions and your answers are still fresh in your mind, make some notes. If you're going to other interviews similar questions may crop up and it will be useful to compare responses.

Self-appraise: Think about what went well and what you can improve on. Start thinking about what you felt comfortable answering and what left you struggling. Come up with some answers that you are confident in, should similar topics crop up next time.

Sit back and wait: Once we've heard from the uni, we'll let you know in Track if you were successful or not. If you receive an offer, it may be conditional on you achieving certain exam grades.

Applicants with disabilities

Think about how you're going to get to the uni and the room where the interview will take place. You may want to arrange for help from your parents or other people such as a personal assistant or an interpreter.

Even though you may have provided information about your disability and requirements on your application, talking about your impairment at interview will enable tutors to ask questions about the effect of your disability on studying. Staff may need to adapt their teaching materials or methods to suit you.

Be prepared to speak about potential problems and solutions. If you've managed well at school, you've good reason to say you'll do well in higher education. Say what support you expect from the uni to help you succeed. Discussions about your disability in the interview are not part of the admissions process. Your application should only be judged on your academic ability and experience. Ideally, you will have already discussed this with the disability coordinator.

What will they ask me at interview?

If you receive an interview invitation, you'll almost certainly ask yourself this question. Here are some example interview questions that the Universities of Oxford and Cambridge have asked applicants and what interviewers were looking for in the answers.

University of Oxford's interview questions

Subject: English literature
Interviewer: Lynn Robson, Regent's Park College

Q: Why do you think an English student might be interested in the fact that Coronation Street has been running for 50 years?
A: First and foremost this brings popular culture into the mix and also shows that techniques of literary analysis can be applied to other media. It could also open up discussion about things such as techniques of storytelling; mixing humorous and serious storylines and characters; how a writer might keep viewers or readers engaged; collaborative writing; the use of serialisation; and how writers and their texts might move from being perceived as 'popular' (like Dickens, say) to be 'canonical'.

Subject: Music
Interviewer: Dan Grimley, Merton College

Q: If you could invent a new musical instrument, what kind of sound would it make?
A: This question is really very open-ended, and I'm interested in answers which demonstrate a critical imagination at work – what kinds of sounds do instruments and voices make now, and how might these be imaginatively extended or developed? Are there new ways of producing sound (digital media) which have transformed the way we listen or understand sound? Is the idea of an 'instrument' somehow outdated these days, and can we imagine more symbiotic or hybrid ways of generating or experiencing musical sound? It's by no means limited to classical music – I'd welcome answers which deal with musical styles and tastes of all kinds (and which are produced or consumed in all places).

Subject: Biological sciences
Interviewer: Martin Speight, St Anne's College

Q: Here's a cactus. Tell me about it.

A: We wouldn't actually phrase the question this way – we give the student a cactus in a pot and a close-up photo of the cactus's surface structure and ask them to describe the object in as much detail as possible using the plant and the photo. We are looking for observation, attention to detail, both at the large and micro scale. We ask them to account for what they see – this means they don't have to use memory or knowledge about cacti (even if they have it) but to deduce the uses and functions of the shapes, sizes, structures that they have just described. So for example, why be fat and bulbous, why have large sharp spines, surrounded by lots of very small hair-like spines? Why does it have small cacti budding off the main body? There will frequently be more than one logical answer to these questions, and we are likely to follow one answer with another question – for example: 'the big spines are to stop the cactus being eaten, yes, but by what sort of animals?' We would also bring in more general questions at the end of the cactus discussion, such as what are the problems faced by plants and animals living in very dry habitats such as deserts.

Subject: Theology
Interviewer: Andrew Teal, Pembroke College

Q: Is someone who risks their own life (and those of others) in extreme sports or endurance activities a hero or a fool?

A: Theology doesn't require A level Religious Studies, so we always want to find issues that enable us to see how a student is able to handle and unpick a question, relating the particular to more general concepts. The question appeared to work well because there really isn't a single answer – it's open not least because we could state the opposite case and observe how flexible, reasoned and committed each student was. The question is properly approached from many perspectives and opens up many topics – is there something distinctively human about going beyond boundaries? Is this impulse selfish, or does it contribute to the whole of humanity's attainment? Is the heroism of those who respond to the need of the sportsperson more heroic still? What debts do individuals owe to society, and society owe to individuals? What is a hero, and is that category in opposition to folly? What we found with this question is that it did manage to open what is a stressful occasion into a real discussion, and we want to offer places to gifted candidates who are willing to think out loud with us in tutorials, and in a college community, whilst they are still explorers into truths.

Subject: Psychology
Interviewer: Dave Leal, Brasenose College

Q: What is 'normal' for humans?

A: We're keen to point out to potential psychology applicants that primarily psychology is the study of normal human beings and behaviour; in part this is because of a suspicion that potential undergraduates are attracted to psychology to help them study forms of human life they find strange (neuroses, psychoses, parents). There were various ways that this question might be approached, but some approach that distinguished the normal from the statistical average was a good start. Issues such as whether normality is to be judged by 'biological' factors that might be held to be common to humans, or whether it's normal within a particular culture or at a particular period of history, might also be worth addressing. We are mainly looking for a line of thinking which could be developed and challenged. Once candidates show a defensible position regarding what might serve as the basis of normality we extend the discussion to (for example) the relation between abnormality and eccentricity.

Subject: Biomedical sciences
Interviewer: Jan Schnupp, St Peter's College

Q: Why do a cat's eyes appear to 'glow' in the dark?

A: This question builds on commonly held knowledge and on material covered in biology at school about visual processes. The question assesses criteria such as scientific curiosity (has the applicant ever wondered this themselves? Have they formulated any theories?) and scientific reasoning, based on information provided by the interviewer as the interview progresses. After establishing that the applicant understands that light is detected by photoreceptors in the eye (and exploring and explaining this concept if it is a new one), the discussion would consider how the glow might be advantageous to the cat, seeing whether the applicant can appreciate that it may help the animal to see in the dark. Possible explanations for the glow would be discussed with an expectation that applicants might recognise that the light could be generated within the eye or alternatively that light entering the eye is in some way reflected back out. Having established the second possibility as being more plausible, the interviewer would probe to see whether the candidate recognises the significance of giving photoreceptors two chances to capture light as rays pass into and then out of the eye and why at night this might enhance vision.

University of Cambridge's interview questions

Subject: English

Q: Which of the literary works on your A level (or equivalent) syllabus have you most enjoyed studying? Can you tell me what qualities in it you most enjoyed, and analyse in a bit more detail why you think they work so well?
A: The purpose of this question is to measure how far applicants can reflect on what it is they find pleasurable in a literary work and explore the criteria which they use to assess literary works. An interviewer will want to know whether this pleasure is gained from the applicant's appreciation of the ways in which the writer has composed the work or if they just enjoy the subject matter. Further to this, can the applicant identify what specifically in a text creates that pleasure – is it a matter of style, of fidelity to reality, of psychological truth?

(After reading a previously unseen literary text)
Q: Are there any formal qualities to this poem/prose extract/dramatic excerpt which support or enhance its meaning? If so, show me where and how they work.

A: Questions like this enable assessment of the applicant's understanding of what is going on in the text being considered, and their willingness to engage in analytical thinking. Applicants should acknowledge that there might be an issue of plain sense, but also recognise nuances of meaning that need further exploration beyond the dictionary definition of words. An interviewer is looking to see if the applicant can understand why certain texts are written in certain ways. Further questions may emerge about the function of rhyme and metre in verse, or sentence structure and vocabulary in prose, or use of colloquialism in a dramatic extract, or any of these elements.

Subject: History

(About a piece of work submitted before the interview)
Q: If you were doing this piece of work over again, what, if anything, would you do differently? Please explain why.

A: This is an introductory question which is designed to gain an insight into whether the applicant has the capacity to reflect on what they have done, to move their thinking along in the light of new material, and to connect material in some work to other aspects of their studies. This question can also provide a starting point for further prolonged discussion as a result of the applicant's response.

(About a text read just before the interview)
Q: What are the main arguments within the piece you have just read?

A: Here we are looking to test an applicant's ability to read critically and to offer analytical criticism of what has been read. The question also provides evidence of how flexibly an applicant thinks. Interviewers are looking for applicants to identify evidence which supports their view and ability to recognise alternative interpretations.

Subjects: Engineering or physics

Q: From what height H must a roller-coaster car be released if it is to successfully travel around a loop of radius R without falling off at the top of the loop?

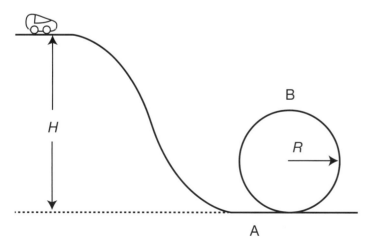

A: This question seeks to discover how well an applicant can link various concepts from physics and mechanics to solve a problem. It also tests some basic mathematical skills.

The discussion at interview breaks this down into a sequence of questions: having satisfactorily resolved one, perhaps with some help and prompting from the interviewer, we move on to the next.

1. *Assuming frictional forces can be neglected, if the car is released from rest at height H, how fast will it be moving when it reaches point A?*

   This can, perhaps with a hint from the interviewer, be answered using the principle of the conservation of energy – potential energy is converted into kinetic energy as the car descends the track:$V_A = \sqrt{2gH}$ where g is the acceleration due to gravity.

2. *If the car follows the track to the top of the loop at B what then is its speed?*

   This too can be answered using the principle of the conservation of energy. A very alert applicant will realise they can use the previous result but replacing H with the net change of height from the start to B (H – 2R): $V_B = \sqrt{2g(H - 2R)}$

3. *When the car is at B what forces are acting on it and in what directions?*

   Here we are looking to see how well the applicant understands the physical origin of forces. If frictional forces are still neglected, the only forces acting are the car's weight and the reaction from the track on the car – both of which act straight downwards.

4. *What is the acceleration of the car at B and in what direction?*

   The applicant will hopefully recognise that this is an example of circular motion. If they cannot remember the expression for centripetal acceleration (V^2/R) we would tell them this result (without penalty). If the applicant has not yet covered circular motion (rare) we would briefly explain the key points needed to make progress on the question.

5. *How are the forces acting on the car at B and its acceleration linked?*

   This requires the applicant to recognise that Newton's Second Law (F = Ma) can be applied to this situation. If all goes well, they will reach the result:

$M \dfrac{V_B^2}{R} = N + Mg$ in which N is the reaction from the track on the car and M is the car's mass.

6. Under what circumstances will the car lose contact with the track at B?

    Here we hope the applicant will recognise that the car will lose contact if the reaction N falls to zero, which will happen if the car is not going fast enough at that point.

7. So, from what height must the car be released if this is not to happen?

    Pulling together the preceding analysis the applicant can show that $H > \frac{5}{2}R$ if the car is not to lose contact with the track at B.

    If an applicant does all of the above well and quickly then the question can be extended further by asking them to think qualitatively about how the situation changes if the object on the roller-coaster track is a ball bearing rather than a car, so it gains both translational and rotational kinetic energy as it descends the track.

Subject: Chemistry

Q: How does the structure of salt (sodium chloride) influence its properties?
A: The discussion breaks down into a series of questions of increasing difficulty: having satisfactorily resolved one, perhaps with some help and prompting from the interviewer, we move on to the next. The order of the individual questions might vary somewhat, and the number that might be completed depends on how fluently the applicant is responding.

1. What is the formula of sodium chloride?

    Everybody knows the answer to this, and so this is just to get things going.

2. What is the structure of solid NaCl?

    A regular arrangement of cations (Na^+) and anions (Cl^-), in a six coordinate structure. Perhaps a sketch of the three-dimensional structure might be given.

3. NaCl has a high melting point solid, why is this?

Here we are looking for statements about the high lattice energy, which prompts supplementary questions about the nature of the interactions which lead to the high lattice energy. Some discussion of the interaction between charges would follow, and perhaps on how this varies with distance and charge.

4. *In the structure a given positive ion is surrounded by six negative ions, but if you move further out the next ions you encounter are positive, and there are more than six of them. Comment?*

   What we are looking for here is a realisation that although the interactions with these positive ions are unfavourable, they are further away than the first set of negative ions. This leads to a discussion of how successive shells of positive and negative ions, at different distances, gives an overall favourable interaction.

5. *If the applicant is taking physics as well, they might be asked whether or not there is a force on each of the ions.*

   The point here is that although there are interactions between the ions, these are in balance so there is no net force. This leads to a discussion of what these balancing forces might be – repulsions at short distances.

6. *Does solid NaCl dissolve in water?*

   Of course, yes, easily.

7. *Given that the lattice energy is so large, why does NaCl dissolve in water?*

   Here we are looking for an understanding that the interactions between the ions and the solvent water are strong enough to overcome the interaction between the ions. There are many directions this discussion can then take depending on the ideas put forward by the applicant: we might discuss dielectric constants, entropy effects or solvation energies, for example.

8. *Why doesn't NaCl dissolve in organic solvents, such as hexane?*

   Here we are looking for a discussion of the fact that the interactions between the ions and hexane are rather different to, and weaker than, those between the ions and water. Again, the discussion can taken many directions at this point.

9. Now a change of direction: why do greases and oils dissolve easily in hexane, but not in water?

   With some help, it should be possible to tease out the idea that the inability of water to dissolve oils is a result of the strong interactions between water molecules – but this is a difficult point to get straight away.

Subject: Biology

Q: How does DNA interact with proteins?
A: Discussion builds through a series of questions. The aim is to start with a simple question that everyone can answer and then develop discussion from there. The question can develop in a variety of ways, depending on the response of an applicant. Knowledge base should not be a problem, as we are looking for the applicant to develop ideas based on their basic knowledge of the structure of macromolecules. How far we get will depend on the applicant.

1. *What is the structure of DNA?*

   A simple question that all biologists can answer, often drawing a diagram as part of their answer. Discussion about the linear molecule follows.

2. *How does DNA fit into a nucleus?*

   Applicants give various replies about packaging. This leads to discussion of the other molecules present in a nucleus and thus to proteins, either directly or indirectly.

3. *With reference to a chart of amino acid side chains: which amino acids might the proteins involved be rich in? Or what properties would you expect of amino acid side chains in these proteins?*

   This leads to discussion about which part of the DNA molecule is interacting with the proteins (the negatively charged backbone). So, we are looking for positively charged amino acid side chains.

What applicants say

Here are some comments from our applicants about interviews.

> 'In order to prepare for university, besides doing tons of background information on the university, you need to research yourself. Know what you love and have a passion for and let it show at interview. That's most important.'

> 'Interviews! Everyone is scared of interviews… Just prepare. All the processes are based on self-preparation, and everyone can do this! Just be calm, have a clear knowledge of your subject and try to act mature enough to get through it.'

Portfolios

If you've applied for courses in art or design subjects and you're invited for interview, unis will usually ask you to present a portfolio of your work as part of their selection process.

Top tips

Here are some top tips from Central Saint Martins College of Art and Design, University of the Arts London about putting together your portfolio.

- **Preparation** – be prepared to adapt the portfolio according to the course you are applying to (just like you would a CV or personal statement).

- **Sequence** – the portfolio should be well organised, so that whoever looks through it understands how you move from one idea to the next.

- **Scope** – show the range of what you can do, concentrating on recent work. Include visual and other background research, sketches, models and prototypes – not just the finished work.

- **Culture-wise** – your portfolio should show whatever interests you and influences your work: fashion, music, sport, environment, whatever.

- **Selection** – be choosy. Pick work that shows ideas, skills and media, which you want to explore further in the course that you would like to do. Don't include too much and avoid repetition of one kind of work just because you think you're good at it. Generally 15-20 items for a portfolio should be enough.

- **Identify yourself** – if you include work that was generated as a group project, highlight what your role was in the collaboration. If you are applying from a college or school, include a signed confirmation that the work included is your own.

Auditions

If you've applied for courses in performing arts, such as music, drama and dance, the unis may ask you to give an audition as part of the interview. They'll tell you in advance what you'll need to do for the audition, but you may be able to choose the piece or pieces you perform.

Top tips

Here are a few tips to help you get ready for your audition.

- Take advantage of any opportunities to perform in public or in front of other actors, musicians or dancers.

- Stage a practice audition with friends and family.

- If you're playing music, practise with an accompanist as often as possible.

- Practise your set or chosen pieces until you can perform them with confidence.

- Research the pieces you'll be performing so that you can talk about them and answer questions at interview.

- Practise relaxation and breathing exercises to help you handle nerves on the audition day.

Other things you may have to do

As part of the interview unis may ask you to:

- bring some pieces of written work with you

- write something on the day

- give a presentation

- take their own admissions test

- carry out a task on your own or in a group

- take part in a group discussion with other applicants.

The unis will tell you what you'll be asked to do at interview before the big day!

Whatever it is – be prepared and stay calm!

Interviews, portfolios and auditions – FAQs

How will I know if I have been invited for interview or audition?

Some universities will send all the interview or audition arrangements direct to you. Others will send an invitation to us and 'Invitation' will be shown alongside the choice in Track. These unis should also send full details direct to you.

If an interview invitation is shown in Track, you can accept or decline it online.

May I request a different interview or audition date?

If there is an invitation decision in Track, you can decline the interview or audition and request an alternative date online. You should contact the uni before you do this. If the interview or audition invitation is not shown in Track, you need to contact the uni direct to request a different date. Try to make the initial interview or audition date because unis may not be able to offer an alternative.

Unis' decisions

After a uni has considered your application, they decide whether or not to offer you a place. Some unis may be able to make a final decision using the information on your application, but others might ask you to attend an interview or audition, or to provide a portfolio of work, an essay or other piece of work. They can send this request direct to you or send it through us as an invitation.

Did you know?

Unis send their decisions at different times

Each uni considers your application against their own admissions criteria, so you'll hear from them at different times: it could be days, weeks or months before you hear anything, depending on where and when you apply and what you apply for. So don't worry if people you know have heard from a uni and you haven't – unis have years of experience and will contact you if they need information before they make a decision.

Invitations can be sent for any course. When a uni sends you an invitation, it will show in Track. If the invitation is for an interview or audition, you need to accept or decline it, or request an alternative time or date in Track.

If you need to change the time or date for an interview or audition, you also need to contact the uni. They can then update the invitation so that the revised details are shown in Track. You should try to attend on the date requested as it may be difficult for them to offer an alternative day. See pages 203 to 218 for tips and advice about preparing for and attending interviews.

If you need to attend an interview or audition, or send off a piece of work, after you've done this the uni will tell us if you've been offered a place or not, and we'll show its decision in Track.

You provide an email address and verify it when you apply so we can tell you when each uni makes a decision about your application. These emails do not provide details of the decision; they ask you to log in to Track to find out this information.

If you've a question about a decision, you should contact the uni and not us for advice.

We give unis the following deadlines for making decisions, but you may hear from them much earlier.

Application received at UCAS	Unis' deadline for making a decision
By 15 January	Early May
From 16 January to 30 June	Mid-July
From 1 July to mid-September (Clearing applications – see page 273)	Late October

Here are the decisions that unis can make.

Decision types

Conditional offer
A conditional offer means that the uni will offer you a place if you meet certain conditions, which are usually based on your exams.

You may be asked to achieve particular grades or results in qualifications, for example:

- grades ABB in three A levels, including an A in biology

- AABB in SQA Higher grades to include an A in maths

- pass an Access course with 60 credits, including at least 45 at level 3 and the remainder at level 2.

You could also be asked to gain certain grades in the units that make up qualifications.

Sometimes unis will ask you to achieve a certain number or UCAS Tariff points, for example:

- 280 Tariff points from a BTEC National Diploma

- 200 Tariff points from 3 A levels.

You must meet the conditions of your offer by 31 August, unless otherwise agreed by the uni. If you're taking a winter exam, the offer might ask you to meet the conditions by an earlier date.

One or more of your offers may be a joint conditional offer. It could include different conditions for a degree and an HND course. When your exam results are published, the uni will decide which part of the offer is most suitable for you.

Each offer is specific to your qualifications and circumstances.

Here are some examples of conditional offers from letters in Track.

This offer is subject to you obtaining

    GCE A level
        Grades ABB in any order in
            Classical Civilisation
            English Literature
            Religious Studies

    Pass in a fourth subject to at least AS level.

This offer is subject to you obtaining

AABB in SQA Higher Grades to include A in Maths. This offer
is based on information provided in your application. All subjects
must be university approved subjects and taken in 2010/11
examination year.

This offer is subject to you obtaining

A minimum of 240 UCAS Tariff points

240 points must be obtained from a minimum of 2 GCE A level qualifications
or equivalent

(Equivalent qualifications can include GCE Single or Double Award,
BTEC and OCR Nationals, Scottish Highers and Advanced Highers but
exclude AS awards.)

Please send non-GCE or VCE results to this institution.

If you chose to study at Leeds Met, please see
www.leedsmet.ac.uk/accommodation for details
of Leeds Met accommodation and for information about how to
apply. You can apply online for accommodation from February 2011.

For details on visiting Leeds Met, please see www.experience.leedsmet.ac.uk

See www.ucas.com/students/ucas_tariff for Tariff notes.

This offer is subject to you obtaining

Access to Engineering Course with a minimum of 36
credits at level 3 and 18 credits at level 2 and GCSE
at grade C or higher in English language.

This offer is subject to you obtaining

An English language qualification approved by this institution, for example IELTS overall 6 with at least 5 in each component.

Unconditional offer

An unconditional offer means that you have met all the academic requirements and the university or college is happy to accept you. They will contact you if they need proof of your qualifications. They might have other requirements, such as financial or medical conditions, that you need to meet before you can start the course.

If the offer is for a place on a course that involves working with children or vulnerable adults, such as medicine, dentistry, nursing, teaching or social work, the uni will ask you to have a criminal record check before you start the course. These checks are done through the Criminal Records Bureau in England or Wales or the Scottish Criminal Record Disclosure Service in Scotland. The uni will explain the procedure to you.

If you are not a national from an EU country, the uni may ask you to provide evidence that you can pay your tuition fees and living expenses while you are studying.

These sorts of conditions can also be included in conditional offers.

Please remember – conditional and unconditional offers are only official when our offer letter is shown in Track, even if you receive an offer direct from a uni.

Here are some examples of unconditional offers from offer letters in Track.

Unconditional Offer

This offer is subject to you obtaining a satisfactory
Criminal Records Bureau – Enhanced Disclosure
(Police Check), Medical Questionnaire and State Primary School
Experience between January and July 2011.

Unconditional Offer

Early application for government student support advised.
Details of accommodation available from 020 7815 6417.

If you have a disability, please contact Disability & Dyslexia Support on 020 7865 5432 to discuss your needs.

Unconditional Offer

Your student information pack will follow shortly.
Early application for Tuition Fee Loan and Student Support is advised.
Term dates and/or further course details will follow.

Accept your offer online @ www.ucas.com (app enquiries)

Unconditional Offer

Provide a copy of your passport
Pay tuition fee deposit

This institution regards you as overseas for fees purposes and the offer has been made on this basis.

UCAStv

Watch our video 'Make sense of your offers' on UCAStv at **www.ucas.tv** for more information.

Withdrawn application

A uni can withdraw your application to them if:

- you tell them that you don't want to be considered for a place

- you don't respond to their letters or emails or you don't attend an interview or audition.

A uni cannot withdraw your whole application.

Unsuccessful application

This means that the uni has decided not to offer you a place on their course.

Unis can decide not to offer you a place for many reasons, one of which could be that the course is full, so the decision may not be based on the quality of your application. The uni may provide a reason for their decision either when they send the decision through, or at a later date. If no reason is shown in Track, you can contact the uni to see if they will discuss why you were unsuccessful.

An example of how a university selects their students

The University of Bristol provided the following information about how they select students for their drama degree course.

Things they look for in the application

- Evidence of a commitment to the study and appreciation of film and theatre, including an indication that applicants have read and viewed widely, beyond the requirements of an A level syllabus. Perhaps they have explored films from earlier periods and from different regions of the world, or developed an interest in experimental performance.

- Motivation and achievement in the fields of performance or media-related arts beyond the syllabus. This could be shown, for example, by participation in school or community drama productions, involvement in video production, or by attending summer schools or other courses. Applicants should show that they've made the most of any opportunities available to them and that they have initiative. The uni looks for evidence of potential, passion, maturity and focus rather than sheer quantity of extracurricular activity.

- Appropriateness of the programme to the applicant's declared interests and ambitions. The programme is suitable if applicants are interested in both practice and theory. Applicants need to be interested in film, media and related arts, as the degree involves as much emphasis on film and television as on theatre.

- Does the applicant have any other relevant skills and passions, for example, in language, music, sports, or creative writing? What other experiences have shaped them? Applicants should show that they have reflected on these experiences, rather than simply enumerating them. What skills have they gained? The uni is looking for people with self-motivation, determination and breadth of knowledge, but also an ability to process their experience.

- Experience of having held positions of responsibility, especially where this provides evidence of maturity and of collaborative engagement with a wider community. It is essential that applicants are able to work with others, as the programme is taught primarily in groups, and some of the assessment involves working as part of a team.

- Clarity of expression, both written and oral. Applicants need to demonstrate this in their personal statement. They should avoid clichés, superlatives and generalisations. It would be useful if the reference indicates that they have good essay-writing skills.

- Evidence of intellectual rigour. Applicants need to be able to take a critical attitude to creative practice. The uni will be looking for evidence of independent thinking, curiosity and critical engagement in the applicant's personal statement.

The selection day

After assessing applications the uni chooses candidates to attend a selection day, so that the admissions team can gain further information on which to base decisions, and distinguish between candidates presenting similar profiles on the UCAS application.

The selection day consists of two assessed elements: a creative workshop (60 minutes) and a seminar (45 minutes). It also includes a tour of the department and the opportunity to meet current students.

In the workshop, assessors look not just for practical skills but for imagination and sensitivity, and the ability to work constructively in a group. In the seminar, candidates are asked to respond to and discuss a brief film clip, television sequence, written text or piece of performance footage, as guided by the seminar leader.

The final decision is based on assessment of the UCAS application and the selection day.

Unis' decisions – FAQs

An offer I received direct from a university is not shown on Track. What shall I do?

This means your university has not told us about your offer. As soon as we receive it, you will be able to see it on Track. If two or three weeks have passed since you were given the offer and it is still not shown on Track, you should contact the uni to discuss the matter.

My university says I'm on a waiting list. What does this mean?

Waiting lists are not part of our application procedures, so we cannot advise you on this. You should contact the university to discuss the effect this may have on your application.

My chosen course is not running. What can I do?

The university should offer you another course. If nothing is available that you want, you can apply to another uni in its place. Your university should have sent you a form offering these options. If you have not received this form, contact them immediately for further advice. If you do not receive any advice from the uni, our Customer Service Unit can help.

A decision on Track is different from what the uni told me. What should I do?

The information we send you is exactly what the university sends to us. If a uni has given you different information, you should contact them direct, not us. They may send changes to us and we'll show them on Track.

I don't understand my offer conditions. What should I do?

You need to ask the uni for an explanation. If they change your offer conditions, we'll show the revised conditions in Track.

Can you tell me why my application was unsuccessful?

If the university has provided a reason, we will show it in Track. If there is no reason in Track or you have already replied to your offers, you will need to ask the uni why you were unsuccessful.

Replying to your offers

> ### Did you know?
> **You can wait to hear from all your unis before you reply**
>
> You don't have to accept any offers until you've heard back from all your universities. All your offers are safe until we've had a decision from each one, so don't worry about losing any of them. But, if you receive the offers you want, you can cancel all your choices with no decisions and reply (as long as you're absolutely sure that you won't change your mind – we can't reverse this later).

If we have received decisions from all of your choices and you have at least one offer, we will email you to let you know there has been a change to your application, and ask you to look at Track. If you didn't provide a valid email address when you applied, we send you a letter which asks you to reply to your offers.

Points to remember when replying to your offers

- Try to attend open days or visits before you decide, but remember to reply by the deadline. See the table on page 233 for the reply deadline dates. If you are visiting a uni after your reply date, please contact the uni for advice.

- Think carefully before you decide which offers to accept because once you accept an offer, including an insurance offer, you are committed to that course (or courses).

- You can reply to offers without waiting to hear back from all your unis. You can cancel any choices that have not made decisions and reply to the offers that you have received using Track. But you must be certain that you want to accept these offers, as once you have made your replies you will not be able to reinstate any cancelled choices.

- If you are replying to a joint conditional offer, eg for a degree and HND, you are replying to the whole joint offer – when your exam results are published, the uni will decide which part of the offer is most suitable for you.

Types of reply

You reply to each of your offers in one of the following ways:

- firm acceptance

- insurance acceptance

- decline.

Myth buster

You don't have to accept an insurance choice

The main rule in replying to your offers is to only accept an offer if you'd be happy to study there. When you choose where to accept, decide based on what you want, not what anyone else wants you to do. This is really important – you'd be surprised at how many people accept an offer then change their minds later.

This is apparent more than ever with insurance choices. If we had a pound for every person who calls us to ask if they can cancel their insurance choice, we'd be rich. We want to help you to make the right decision straight away, and not wish you could go back and change it later.

So – only accept an insurance choice if you really do want it as a back-up to your firm choice. If you're not sure it's right for you, just have a firm choice – there are other options later in the year, such as Clearing, if your firm choice can't offer you the place.

Firm acceptance

Your firm acceptance is your first choice – this is your preferred choice out of all the offers you have received. You can only have one firm acceptance.

If you accept an unconditional offer, you are agreeing that you will attend the course at that uni, so you cannot make an insurance acceptance and you must decline any other offers. We send you a letter which explains whether there is anything else you need to do.

If you accept a conditional offer, you are agreeing that you will attend the course at that university or college if you meet the conditions of the offer. You can accept another offer as an insurance choice.

See the 'Unis' decisions' section on pages 219 to 224 for more information about conditional and unconditional offers.

Insurance acceptance

If your firm choice is a conditional offer, you can accept another offer as an insurance choice. Your insurance choice can be conditional or unconditional and acts as a back-up, so if you don't meet the conditions for your firm choice but meet the conditions for your insurance, you will be committed to the insurance choice. You can only have one insurance choice.

The conditions for your insurance choice should normally be lower than for your firm choice. If they are higher than your firm choice, and if you're not accepted by your firm choice, it's very unlikely that you will be accepted for your insurance choice.

You don't have to accept an insurance choice – if you're not sure about any of your other choices once you have accepted a firm choice, you're not obliged to accept one as an insurance option. **Only accept an insurance choice if you're definitely happy to take that course and that uni.**

Decline

Once you have decided which offer to accept firmly, and which (if any) to accept as an insurance, you must decline all other offers. If you don't want to accept any of your offers, you can decline them all. You will then be eligible to use Extra or Clearing, depending upon your circumstances. See page 237 for information about Extra and page 273 to find out about Clearing.

There are four combinations of offers and replies:

- **Unconditional firm only** – you've firmly accepted an unconditional offer. You cannot have an insurance choice. You are committed to take up the place on that course at that uni. The choice shows as 'Unconditional Firm' in Track.

- **Conditional firm only** – you've firmly accepted a conditional offer. The choice shows as 'Conditional Firm' in Track.

- **Conditional firm + conditional insurance** – you've firmly accepted one conditional offer and accepted another conditional offer as an insurance. The choices show as 'Conditional Firm' and 'Conditional Insurance' in Track.

- **Conditional firm + unconditional insurance** – you've firmly accepted a conditional offer and accepted an unconditional offer as an insurance. The choices show as 'Conditional Firm' and 'Unconditional Insurance' in Track.

How and when to reply to your offers

You use Track to view the decisions from all your choices and reply to your offers. Your reply date will be shown in Track. Your reply date is based on when we receive the last decision from your choices, so it might be different to other people's dates. If you don't reply by the date given, your offers will be declined. If this happens, you need to call our Customer Service Unit to find out what you can do.

UCAStv

Watch our video about replying to your offers on UCAStv at **www.ucas.tv** for more information.

Reply dates are based on when we receive the last decision from your choices:

Last decision received at UCAS by	Your reply date is
End March	Early May
Early May	Early June
Mid-June	End June
Mid-July	Late July

The exact reply dates may vary slightly in different application years. See the Important dates page on **www.ucas.com** for the current dates.

Here's what your Track choices screen could look like after you've replied to your offers:

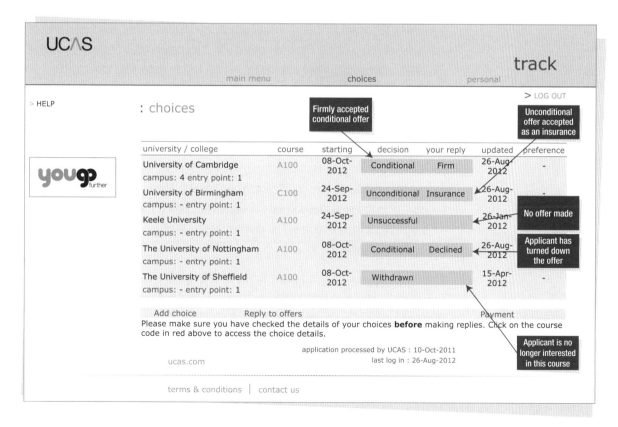

Replying to offers – FAQs

How do I reply to my offers?

You reply to your offers on Track. You do not need to reply to your offers until you have received decisions from all your universities. When they have all sent their decisions to us, we automatically ask you to reply to offers.

If you are no longer interested in receiving offers from the unis that have not made decisions, you can cancel these choices in Track and then reply to the offers you have already received. It may sound obvious, but check you have received the offers you wish to accept from us before doing this.

I want to reply to my offers but there is no reply button on Track. What can I do?

The reply button only appears on Track when you've received decisions from all the universities to which you have applied.

If you want to accept an offer, you can cancel the choices for all unis that have not made decisions on Track. The reply option will then be available. Please check that you have received the offers you wish to accept before cancelling any choices.

If Track shows decisions from all your universities, but there is no reply option, you need to call our Customer Service Unit.

When do I reply to my offers?

We will ask you to reply when all of your universities have sent us decisions on your application. Your reply deadline will be shown in Track. This date will vary depending on the date that you receive your final decision. Your reply date may be different to your friends' dates. The different reply dates are listed on the Important dates page on **www.ucas.com**.

What will happen if I don't reply to my offers by my deadline?

If you don't reply by your deadline, we'll assume that you don't want any of your offers and will decline them on your behalf. We'll write to you and tell you what has happened. In most cases, we can reinstate and accept offers if you contact us within seven days from when your offers were declined. If you are happy that your offers were declined, we will tell you about Extra or Clearing depending on the stage of the application cycle. See page 237 for information about Extra and page 273 to find out about Clearing.

How many offers can I accept?

If your offers are conditional, you can accept one firmly and another as insurance. Your insurance acceptance acts as a back-up in case you don't meet the conditions for your firm offer.

If your offers are unconditional, you only accept one, as you do not need to hold another. It will be your firm acceptance. At that point, the place will be yours.

If you have a mixture of conditional and unconditional offers, you can hold an unconditional offer as insurance if you firmly accept a conditional offer.

Can I accept an offer as an insurance if it asks for the same grades as my firm choice?

Yes, your insurance acceptance can be whichever offer you prefer. It can even ask for higher grades, but remember that if you do not meet the conditions of your firm offer and your insurance offer asks for the same grades or higher, you may find that you cannot be accepted by either uni. You will then go into Clearing. See page 273 for information about Clearing.

Can I choose between my firm and insurance choices if I get the grades for both?

No. If you meet the grades for your firm acceptance, your insurance acceptance is automatically declined and the place is offered to someone else. If you cannot take up the place at the uni where you have a firm acceptance, you should contact them direct to discuss your options.

Can I change my replies?

You can change your replies within seven days of making them by contacting our Customer Service Unit.

If you wish to change your replies after seven days, you should contact your chosen universities direct for advice.

Will I get confirmation of my offer replies?

Yes, you should receive a letter from UCAS within five working days of making your replies.

If you do not receive this letter, you need to call our Customer Service Unit.

www.ucas.com

If you've no offers, Extra could be for you

If you've applied through UCAS and you've:

- already made five choices

- received decisions from all these choices, and

- either had no offers or declined any offers you've received

you might be able to apply through Extra for another course. In Extra, you can apply for any course with vacancies. Extra is open between the end of February and the end of June. You apply for one course at a time using Track.

If you decline your offers and add an Extra choice, you will not be able to accept any of your original offers later.

How does Extra work?

If you are eligible for Extra, a button will appear on your Track screen which you can use to apply for a course in Extra.

Before you apply for an Extra choice, you should:

UCAStv

Watch our video about applying through Extra on UCAStv at **www.ucas.tv** for more information.

- check if the course has vacancies in Extra on Course Search at **www.ucas.com** – courses with vacancies are marked with an 'x'

- read the course Entry Profile on Course Search, if there is one. It will tell you what the uni looks for in their students and may have case studies from students who have taken the course.

- contact the uni to make sure that they can consider you.

When you have decided on your Extra choice, you need to enter the details in Track. We'll then send your application to the uni.

Choosing a course

Research the courses before deciding which to apply for in Extra. If you applied for high-demand courses originally and were unsuccessful, you could consider related or alternative subjects. Your teachers or careers advisers, or the unis themselves, can provide useful guidance.

What happens next?

If you are offered a place, you can choose whether or not to accept it. If you accept an offer, you are committed to it, which means that you cannot apply anywhere else. You will need to reply to your offer by the date shown in Track.

If you decline an offer, or the uni turns you down, you can apply for a different course through Extra (time permitting). Your Extra button in Track will be reactivated.

If a uni has had your application in Extra for more than 21 days and not made a decision, you can choose to let this uni continue to consider you or apply to another uni in Extra. Your Extra button in Track will be reactivated. Before you apply to another uni in Extra, you should tell the uni that currently has your application to stop considering you.

If you don't get an offer in Extra, don't worry! From mid-July you can use our Clearing process which gives you another opportunity to apply for courses with vacancies. See page 273 for information about our Clearing service.

Here's what two of our applicants said about Extra:

'I now know that going through Extra is nothing to be ashamed of. With the current places versus the amount of people going to uni, it is inevitable that some will not get into their choices, but at least we have Extra and Clearing, so there is still an option for us.'

'Now with UCAS Extra you can 'reapply' if you are not satisfied. That's so good!'

Extra – FAQs

Why can't I apply to a uni in Extra?
To apply for a course in Extra you must have already made five choices, received decisions for all these choices and had no offers or declined any offers received.

When can I apply in Extra?
Extra operates from late February to the end of June.

How do I find out which courses are available in Extra?
You need to use Course Search on our website. Courses with vacancies in Extra have an 'x' next to the course title.

How many courses can I apply for in Extra?
While Extra is operating you can apply for as many courses as you like in Track, but you may only apply for one course at a time. If you accept an offer through Extra, you cannot apply for any other courses.

How long does the university have to consider my Extra application?
Universities have 21 days from receiving your Extra application to give us their decision. After 21 days if they have not make a decision, you can choose to give them more time or apply to another university in Extra.

I've applied for a course in Extra but I want to change it. What can I do?
You should tell the uni where you've applied that you are no longer interested in a place and ask them to send a withdrawn decision to us. When we receive this decision you will be able to apply for another course in Extra, time permitting.

Case study

Name: Kevin Minors

Kevin started a mathematics degree
at the University of Oxford in October 2010.

I had mixed emotions when I received my offer. I was extremely excited because the university decided to give me an offer and not to decline my application, but on the other hand, I was filled with shock because the grades my offer required were better than any grades ever achieved at my high school (I did IB in Bermuda) so I was very nervous. But I did not let that stop me and you cannot let it stop you.

If your university gives you an offer that seems out of your reach, or even if you believe that it is within your reach, continue to give 110% to your studies and you will amaze yourself. Use the offer as a personal goal that you have and create a plan to achieve that goal, whether it is making a review schedule for your exams, forecasting the grades that you will need on certain tests that will allow you to reach the offer conditions in the final exams or things like that. My offer was ridiculous but with hard work, not only did I meet the conditions, I exceeded them. And if I can do it, so can you!

For Oxford's admission process, I had to take a mathematics entrance exam before I would even be considered for an interview. I did it and I'm guessing it was OK because they then offered me an invitation for an interview. While researching Oxford interviews, I heard many rumours like people setting themselves on fire just to get attention from the Selection Committee and crazy things like that but none of them are really true.

While I was in Oxford checking the notice board for when my interview would be, I was extremely nervous. More nervous than when I got my offer, but one of the best things about the whole interview process was that I was able to meet other students who applied to Oxford and were there for interviews as well. It was a great way to make new friends and to meet possible classmates in the year to come. And everyone was nervous together! We could talk to each other for support, which made it that much more bearable.

My interview was not a normal interview. It was academic based. There was no 'Why mathematics?' or 'Why Oxford?' We just went through a few maths problems and that was it. Nothing else. But, bear in mind, this may not be true for all universities. In order to prepare for university, besides doing tons of background information on the university, you need to research yourself. Know what you love and have a passion for and let it show in the interview. That's most important.

Once my exams were finished, the wait started for results day. It seemed that time had stood still. Days were lasting weeks, weeks took months. It was painful both mentally and emotionally. But once school had finished and I started my summer job, my mind was not thinking about the grades. I slowly started to think about summer and all the fun things I could do. I temporarily forgot about UCAS, university, grades and all the other things that were out of my control. If you think about it too much, you will drive yourself crazy. No, I'm serious. You will literally become crazy so don't do it. Keep busy and get your mind off grades and you will be fine.

However, once the results day is only a few days away, you will naturally get nervous and start to worry about everything that could happen. Whether you get the grades and everything is perfect or if you need to reconsider where you want to go. No matter what, just remember that there is nothing more that you can do. Whatever happens will happen. You just have to be mature about it and deal with the situation. I collected my results at 12:30pm and at 10:30am the following day I received an email from Oxford saying that I had met the offer so that was really helpful for me because I was thinking about it all morning. The best advice I can give you is to keep busy during results day until the grades are officially released because you will also go crazy if you continuously check the website or your school office.

Chapter checklist

These are the things you should be doing in Step 3 of your applicant journey:

☐ Contact us if you don't receive your Welcome letter and *Applicant Welcome Guide* within 14 days of sending your application to us.

☐ Check the information on your Welcome letter and tell us if anything is wrong.

☐ If your postal address, email address or phone numbers change, enter the new details in Track. If you're at boarding school, don't forget to change your postal address to your home address at the end of the school year.

☐ Tell us and your chosen unis about changes to your course or exam arrangements and anything that could affect your exam results.

☐ Apply for student finance. Agree to share the personal details and choices information on your UCAS application with the Student Loans Company in Track to make the process easier.

☐ If you have a disability, make sure your chosen unis will be able to meet all your requirements before you start your course.

☐ Prepare fully for interviews and auditions.

☐ Whenever we tell you your application status has changed, log in to Track to look at your unis' decisions.

☐ When all of your unis have made decisions, make sure that you reply to any offers received by the deadline shown in Track.

☐ Consider applying for other courses in Extra if you don't receive any offers.

Step 4
Results

Now you've taken your exams you can't just relax and forget about university until August. This section provides advice on what you need to do while waiting for your exam results.

In this section you'll find out whether or not you need to send your results to universities where you're holding offers. If you've asked for any exams to be re-marked or your school has not certificated your A level results, we tell you what you need to do. We clearly describe all the possible situations that could apply to you after your unis have received your exam results. You'll find out what you can do if you don't meet all your offer conditions, but a uni makes you a changed offer.

You'll also discover what happens if you don't have any offers or your unis cannot confirm your place.

Step 4 **Results**

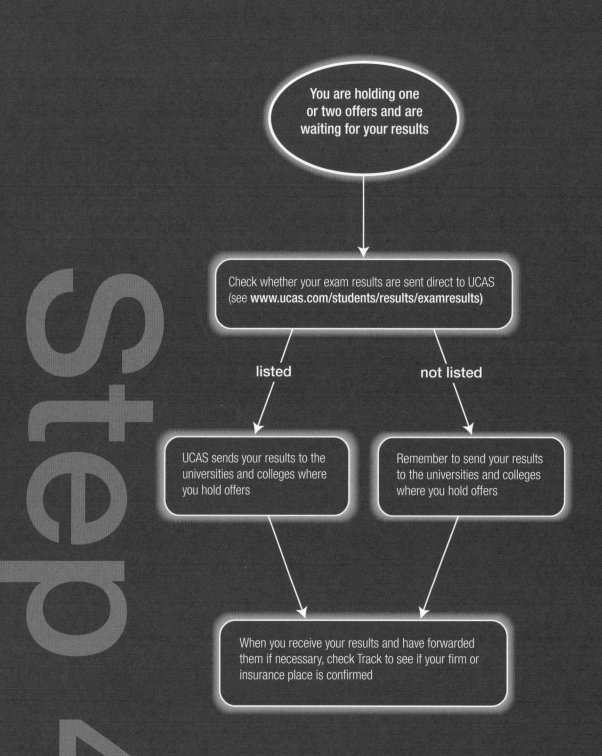

You are holding one
or two offers and are
waiting for your results

Check whether your exam results are sent direct to UCAS
(see **www.ucas.com/students/results/examresults**)

listed

not listed

UCAS sends your results to the
universities and colleges where
you hold offers

Remember to send your results
to the universities and colleges
where you hold offers

When you receive your results and have forwarded
them if necessary, check Track to see if your firm or
insurance place is confirmed

Step 4

Preparing for exam results

After you've replied to your offers, there are several things you should do while you're waiting for exam results.

Know your login details for Track

You'll need access to Track to see if you've been accepted, so make sure you know your Personal ID, username and password for logging in. If you can't remember your login details, use the 'Forgotten login details?' service on the Track login page.

Be available

You need to be available when your exam results are published. You might have to make quick and perhaps difficult decisions about your future. You need to be available to contact unis yourself; they'll want to speak to you and not your friends and relatives.

Check your contact details are up-to-date

You should check that your personal details are correct in Track – we and the unis contact you by email, letter and sometimes by phone, so make sure that we have your up-to-date details.

If you're at boarding school, make sure you change your postal address to your home address when school finishes for the summer.

When you change your postal address, you should arrange for your mail to be redirected in case letters have already been sent.

Making changes

You must contact the uni where you're holding an offer if:

- you're unable to take up a place and you need to withdraw your application

- you want to change the conditions of your offer, such as

    - **the course itself:** you may prefer to take a related course or do an HND course rather than a degree course

    - **the year you start the course:** a uni may have offered you a place for this year's entry, but you now want to take a gap year and start a year later

    - **the point you join the course:** your offer could be to start the course in the first year (year 1), but you've decided that you would rather take a foundation year and start in year 0.

You may need to send your results to your unis

The exam results we currently receive from exam boards and send to the unis are listed on pages 252 to 254. If your qualification is not listed, you need to send your exam results to the unis where you have accepted offers. When the unis have received your results from us or from you, they will decide whether or not to confirm your place.

As soon as one of your unis tells us whether or not you have a place, we will show their decision in Track.

Read the 'What happens after the unis have your exam results' section on page 255 to find out what happens if you do or don't have a confirmed place.

International students

Remember to find out from your school or college how and when your exam results will be given to the universities where you're holding offers. Some exam boards, such as the International Baccalaureate Organisation, may send your results direct to the universities if your school gives them your UCAS Personal ID. If your results are not sent direct to the universities where you're holding offers, you should arrange for a copy of your final results or transcripts to be sent to them.

What applicants have said

Here's what some of our applicants have said about exam results.

'If you think about it [exam results] too much, you will drive yourself crazy… so don't do it. Keep busy and get your mind off grades and you will be fine.'

'Whether you get the grades and everything is perfect or if you need to reconsider where you want to go, no matter what, just remember that there's nothing more that you can do. Whatever happens will happen. You just have to be mature about it and deal with the situation.'

'I did well, but not as well as I wanted… I went to college and boosted my UCAS points up within a year and here I am now. There's always a way to get into uni.'

UCAStv

Watch our video about preparing for exam results on UCAStv at **www.ucas.tv** for more information.

'Fear on results day is rational. Even if you have done superbly, there's still a part of you that thinks 'WHAT IF'… so take it from me, an underachiever; anything is possible if you set your mind to it.'

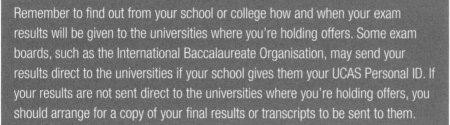

Exam results

You're taking exams for qualifications not listed in this section

We list the qualifications for which we currently receive exam results on pages 252 to 254. If you're taking exams for qualifications not listed, you must send the results to the unis where you're holding offers.

You're taking exams for qualifications listed in this section

If you're taking exams for any qualifications in the list on pages 252 to 254, the exam boards will send us a record of the exams you have entered. We then match this record with the qualifications information on your application.

If there are differences between your exam registration details provided by the exam boards and the information on your application, we will send you a letter in June. You must enter any information requested on the letter and return it to us. This will help us to match your exam results with your application.

If we cannot match the qualification details on your application with the results received, it may take longer for your unis to confirm whether or not you have a place. Applications containing qualifications that cannot be checked against exam results may be considered fraudulent, and may be cancelled.

When the exam boards send us your exam results we match them with your application details. We then send your results automatically to the unis where you are holding offers.

For some of the exam results we receive, we only process the overall result and pass it on to your unis. In some cases if you've taken exams in a modular set of subjects, such as for the BTEC, International Baccalaureate or Irish Leaving Certificate, we pass on the grade for each subject. For A levels we process the unit grades that go towards your overall grade.

If your unis tell you that they've not received your exam results, you must contact your school or college and, if needed, our Customer Service Unit for advice.

Did you know?

We can't tell you your exam results

We receive some exam results and send them to the universities, but this is managed through a dedicated team who keep the details confidential. Some people contact us to find out what their results are, but we can't provide this information.

We see the same as what's displayed in Track – we can see if you have been offered a place at your chosen uni, not specific results for qualifications, so speak to your school or college to find out when you'll receive your results.

Track during results processing

Track is 'frozen' the week before Scottish Qualifications Authority (SQA) and A level results are published so that universities can give us their decisions. While Track is frozen we don't update your application.

On SQA results day we publish a Clearing vacancy list for universities and colleges in Scotland at **www.ucas.com**. Then on A level results day we also publish Clearing vacancies for the whole UK. Applicants who are already eligible for

Clearing or who become eligible after they receive their results can then contact institutions about vacancies.

We open Track mid-morning on SQA and A level results days, so that you can see if your university has confirmed your place.

> **Myth buster**
>
> **Track is not updated at midnight on A level results day**
>
> Each year lots of applicants try to log in to Track to view whether they've been accepted. We don't update Track at midnight, and we never have! It's only the Clearing vacancy search which goes live at midnight. So don't lose sleep by trying to log in – it won't be available.

Re-marked exams

If you ask for any of your exams to be re-marked, you must tell the unis where you're holding offers. If a uni cannot confirm your place based on the initial results, you should ask them if they would be able to reconsider their decision after the re-mark. Unis don't have to reconsider their position if your re-mark results in higher grades. Don't forget that re-marks may also result in lower grades.

The exam boards tell us about any re-marks that result in grade changes. We then send the revised grades to the unis where you're holding offers. As soon as you know about grade changes, you should also tell your unis.

'Cashing in' A level results

If you have taken A levels, your school or college must certificate or 'cash in' all your unit scores before the exam board can award final grades. If when you collect your A level results you have to add up your unit scores to find out your final grades, it means your school or college has not 'cashed in' your results.

We only receive cashed in results from the exam boards, so if your results have not been cashed in, you must contact your school or college and ask them to send a 'cash in' request to the exam board. You also need to tell the unis where you're holding offers that there'll be a delay in receiving your results and call our Customer Service Unit to find out when your results have been received.

When we receive your 'cashed in' results from the exam board we'll send them to the unis where you're holding offers straight away.

International students

If you don't achieve the required English language score in your offer conditions, find out if the universities where you're holding offers:

- will accept other online tests or offer their own test as an alternative

- run 'pre-sessional' English courses

- will accept you on to an International Foundation Programme. These are normally one academic year in length and are designed to give international students extra English language tuition and academic skills for successful entry on to a degree course.

Exam results we receive

We currently receive exam results for the following qualifications, match them with application details and send them to the unis where applicants are holding offers.

- AAT NVQ Level 3 in Accounting

- AQA Baccalaureate

- Asset Languages

- British Horse Society – Horse Knowledge and Care Stage 3, Riding Stage 3, Preliminary Teacher's Certificate

- BTEC

  - HNC/HND

  - National Award, Certificate and Diploma

  - National Certificate and National Diploma in Early Years – Theory/Practical

- CACHE Diploma in Childcare and Education

- Cambridge International Examinations (CIE)

  - Advanced Level, Advanced Subsidiary

  - Advanced International Certificate of Education (AICE) Diploma

- Higher 1, Higher 2 and Higher 3

- Pre-U Diploma, Pre-U Certificate, Pre-U Short Course

- Special Papers (overseas applicants only, winter results only)

- Certificate of Personal Effectiveness CoPE awards (ASDAN)

- Diplomas (Advanced, Progression)

- Diploma in Fashion Retail (ABC)

- Diploma in Foundation Studies (Art and Design) (ABC, Edexcel, WJEC)

- EDI Level 3 Certificates in Accounting and Accounting (IAS)

- Extended Project

- Free Standing Mathematics (AQA and OCR Level 3)

- Functional Skills

- GCE Advanced and Advanced Subsidiary (Single and Double Awards), 9 Unit Awards and Advanced Extension Award

- Higher Sports Leader Award

- *ifs* School of Finance Certificate and Diploma in Financial Studies (DipFS)

- International Baccalaureate (Diploma and Certificate) (if you have agreed)

- Irish Leaving Certificate

- Key Skills (Levels 2, 3 and 4)

- Music examinations grades 6-8 (ABRSM, LCM, Trinity)

- OCR

  - iPRO Certificate and Diploma

  - Mathematics STEP Papers I, II and III

  - National Certificates, Diplomas and Extended Diplomas (all at National Qualifications Framework level 3 only)

  - Principal Learning

- Speech and Drama – grades 6, 7 and 8 (ESB, LAMDA, LCM and Trinity Guildhall)

- SQA

    - Baccalaureate

    - Core Skills

    - Highers, Advanced Highers

    - HNC/HND

    - Interdisciplinary Project

    - Intermediate 2

    - PC Passport

    - Skills for Work

- Welsh Baccalaureate

The above list was accurate at the time this book was published, but further qualifications may have been added since publication. The latest list can be found at **www.ucas.com/students/results/examresults**.

What happens after the unis have your exam results

After we've sent your exam results to the uni or unis where you're holding an offer, they tell us whether or not they can accept you and we show their decisions in Track. This process is called 'Confirmation'. If you meet all the conditions of your offer, the uni will confirm your place. Even if you've not quite met all the offer conditions, the uni may still be able to accept you. You need to look at Track to find out if you have a confirmed place.

We update information on the Track 'choices' screen exactly as it is provided by the unis. If you have any queries about changes to choice details, you need to contact the unis and not us.

The sections below describe the different scenarios that could apply to you after the unis have given us their final decisions and what happens next.

You're accepted by your firm choice

If you're accepted by your firm choice, we send you a Confirmation letter in the post. This letter confirms that you have a definite place at the uni and lets you know if there is anything you need to do. You may still need to tell the uni whether or not you will be taking up your place. When you receive this letter, you have officially gained a place. The uni will contact you with any further information.

You're accepted by your firm choice and you meet and exceed the conditions of the offer

If you meet and exceed the conditions of the offer from your firm choice, you can apply through Adjustment. In Adjustment you can apply to other unis with vacancies for a limited period while still keeping your place at your firm choice. See page 269 for more information about Adjustment.

You receive a 'changed course' offer

If you receive a 'changed course' offer, it means that the uni is unable to confirm your place on the course you accepted because you have not met the original offer conditions. They have, however, been able to offer you a place on a different course. For example, you may have applied for a degree course, but the uni now offers you a place on an HND course in the same or a similar subject. You could have applied for medicine and the uni now offers you a place on a related course such as biomedical sciences.

A 'changed course' offer may also cover a change of:

- **start date** – you may have applied to start a course in one year but the uni offers you a place to start in the following year

- **the point you join the course** – you may have applied to start the course in the first year (year 1), but the uni wants you to take a foundation year and start in year 0.

The procedure for replying to 'changed course' offers depends on the status of your application. Here are the different scenarios.

You've only applied for one course

You must accept or decline a 'changed course' offer in Track within five days of the offer being made. If you don't make your reply within five days, the offer will automatically be declined.

If you decline the offer and you've paid the reduced fee for a single choice, you must pay an additional amount in Track if you want to apply for courses with vacancies in Clearing. See page 273 for information about Clearing.

When you've made your additional payment, your Clearing Number will be shown in Track.

You've applied for more than one course, but you've only accepted one offer

You must accept or decline the 'changed course' offer in Track within five days of the offer being made. If you decline the offer you will automatically go into Clearing. See page 274 for information about applying for courses with vacancies in Clearing.

You've applied for more than one course and you've accepted firm and insurance choice offers

There are three possible scenarios.

- **Your firm choice makes a changed course offer** – you must accept or decline the revised firm offer in Track. If you decline it, you will either be accepted by your insurance choice or, if they cannot confirm your place, you will automatically go into Clearing.

- **Your insurance choice makes you a changed course offer** – you will only be able to accept this revised insurance offer in Track if your firm choice does not accept you. It is possible to decline a changed insurance offer immediately. If you are then not accepted by your firm choice, you will be automatically entered into Clearing.

- **Both your firm and insurance choices make changed course offers** – you may accept either revised offer in Track, or decline both and move automatically into Clearing.

Your exam results don't meet the conditions of your firm choice offer, but they meet the conditions of your insurance choice offer

If you don't meet the conditions of your firm choice offer and the uni doesn't confirm your place, but you do meet the conditions of your insurance choice offer, your place at your insurance choice will be confirmed. When the uni confirms your place, the choice will show as 'Unconditional Firm' in Track. We will send you a Confirmation letter by post. This letter confirms that you have a definite place at the uni and lets you know if there is anything you need to do. You may still need to tell the uni whether or not you'll be taking up your place. When you receive this letter, you've officially gained a place. The uni will contact you with any further information.

Your exam results don't meet the conditions of your firm or insurance choice offers

If you don't meet the conditions for the offers you've accepted and the unis can't offer you a place, you'll be automatically entered into Clearing. Your Clearing Number will be shown in Track. See page 274 for information about applying for courses with vacancies in Clearing.

What if you're not holding any offers?

You may not have any offers because:

- none of your choices was able to offer you a place

- you declined any offers received, or

- you applied after 30 June.

If you're not holding any offers and you have paid the full application fee, you'll be entered into Clearing automatically. Your Clearing Number will be shown in Track. See page 274 for information about applying for courses with vacancies in Clearing.

Applicants with disabilities

If the uni where you have a confirmed place has agreed to adapt buildings or the course provision to meet your requirements, check with them that work is under way and that everything will be in place before you start the course. You may want to visit the uni to make sure the changes will meet your needs.

Case study

Exam results day at Bournside School in Cheltenham

You will probably have seen exam results day in the media or may have experienced it second hand either through a sibling or other family member. So what is your impression of the day? Chaos, excitement, terror? If you are applying to university from school, you are inevitably going to experience results day yourself.

All schools offer advice and support in different ways on the 'big day', but here's what happens at Bournside School in Cheltenham.

Results day at Bournside actually starts the previous day, when the Head of Sixth Form and exams officer check that all the results are accessible. With the help of the UCAS Applicant Status Report we are then able to identify which students may need extra help and support.

Students start arriving at the centre at 9.00am, some individually, others in groups. It's a very big operation as AS results are out on the same day. We split the results into two separate venues for AS and A2 students. About three administrative staff are on hand to give out the results to students as they arrive, enabling the sixth form staff to concentrate on offering help, support and congratulations.

Results day can have a unique atmosphere as so much can be at stake. I have known students cry uncontrollably and when asked 'What's up?', the reply may be 'I got three As'. The atmosphere around results day has changed in recent years. Students have come to realise that if they access UCAS Track on the morning of results day they will learn, not their results, but whether their application to university has been successful or not.

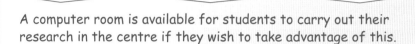

A computer room is available for students to carry out their research in the centre if they wish to take advantage of this.

The day isn't always straightforward and there can be issues with expected marks and students wishing to have re-marks done, but thankfully this is rare. Students are made aware in advance that they can ask the exam board for a 'Priority' re-mark, but also that grades can go down as well as up. If students want a paper re-marked, we always encourage them to 'sleep on it' and come back on the Friday. In the calm light of day, we can explain the process and rationally analyse the likelihood of a successful appeal through the exam boards' priority re-mark scheme.

The problem we sometimes face is that there can be a discrepancy between universities in how quickly they deal with students who are just short of their offers. Some universities have kept students waiting for days before finally deciding not to confirm their places. This can mean that these students have now missed the opportunity to take a meaningful part in Clearing.

In the period from A level results to the start of term there are nearly always sixth form staff available to help, either with queries over AS or A level results or university entrance. These days many students seek advice by email.

Top tip

If you do want to speak to sixth form staff for support and guidance, arrive fairly early in the day. Many students arrive late morning, sometimes at the same time and then have to wait to speak to someone. The 'early bird' will often walk straight in!

FAQs

I've met the offer conditions, but my uni has not confirmed my place. What should I do?

Don't worry – if you have met all the offer conditions the uni will confirm your place in due course. As soon as we receive confirmation the choice will show as 'Unconditional Firm' in Track.

If you are really concerned, you can contact the university, but don't forget that phone lines will be very busy.

I haven't heard from my uni. What should I do?

If you haven't heard from your firm choice uni, read through the conditions of the offer to check that they are not waiting for further details from you, such as exam certificates or the results of health or criminal record checks.

If you haven't met the offer conditions, the uni may still be considering your application. They may still be able to confirm your place if other applicants have not met their offer conditions. Not all applicants receive their exam results at the same time as you so the uni may have to wait a few days to see if they have available places.

If you have met the conditions and the university has received everything they need, you can contact them direct to find out what's happening.

I've met the grades for my firm offer but I now want to go to my insurance choice. What should I do?

When you firmly accept a conditional offer you are making a commitment to go to that uni if they confirm your place. If you no longer want to take up your place, you should contact the university to discuss your situation.

As soon as you were accepted at your firm choice uni, we would have told your insurance choice uni. This means that they will no longer be holding a place for you, even if you have met the offer conditions, so you'll need to contact them to see if they can still offer you the place. If your firm choice agrees to withdraw your offer, you will be entered into Clearing. If your insurance choice can still offer you a place, they can make you an offer in Clearing. See page 273 for information about Clearing.

My firm choice cannot give me a place, but I don't want to go to my insurance choice – can I apply elsewhere?

When you accept an insurance offer you are making a commitment to go to that uni if they confirm your place. If you no longer want to take up your place, you should contact the uni to discuss your position. If they agree to withdraw your offer, you can then apply for another course in Clearing. See page 273 for information about Clearing.

What is my AS12 letter? My local authority and bank have asked for a copy.

We send you an AS12 Confirmation letter when a uni confirms your place. If you have not received this letter within three days of seeing a decision in Track, call our Customer Service Unit to ask for a copy.

Chapter checklist

These are the things you should be doing in Step 4 of your applicant journey:

☐ Make sure we and the unis can contact you. Check all your contact details in Track are up-to-date.

☐ Be available to manage things when your exam results are published.

☐ Tell the uni if you cannot take up a place or you need to change your offer conditions.

☐ Find out if you need to send your exam results to the unis where you're holding offers at **www.ucas.com/students/results/examresults**.

☐ After you've received your exam results, log in to Track regularly to find out if your place has been confirmed.

☐ If you've met and exceeded all the conditions for your firm offer and the uni has confirmed your place, you could consider applying for other courses through Adjustment. See page 269 for information about Adjustment.

☐ Make sure you accept or decline 'changed course' offers in Track. There may be a deadline shown in Track depending on the status of your application.

☐ Tell your unis if any of your exams are being re-marked. If they cannot confirm your place based on your initial results, ask them if they will be able to reconsider their decision after the re-mark.

☐ If your school or college has not certificated your A level results, ask them to send a 'cash in' request to the exam board and tell the universities where you're holding offers that there'll be a delay in receiving your results.

☐ If you do not receive a Confirmation letter within five days of your place being confirmed in Track, ask our Customer Service Unit to send you a copy.

☐ If you don't have a confirmed place, consider applying for other courses in Clearing. See page 273 for information about Clearing.

Step 5
Next steps

The waiting is over and your results are through. It is time to act on the plans you have made, adapting them to the known circumstances you now face. You might be right on course to carry out your plans to the letter, or you might find yourself almost back at square one, or anywhere in between... The video *Next steps after results* on **UCAStv** gives you a flavour of what this step entails.

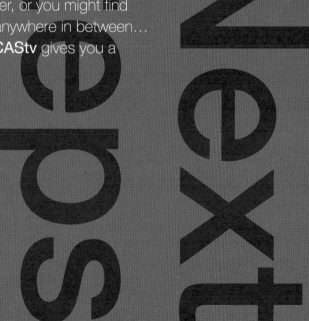

Step 5 **Next steps**

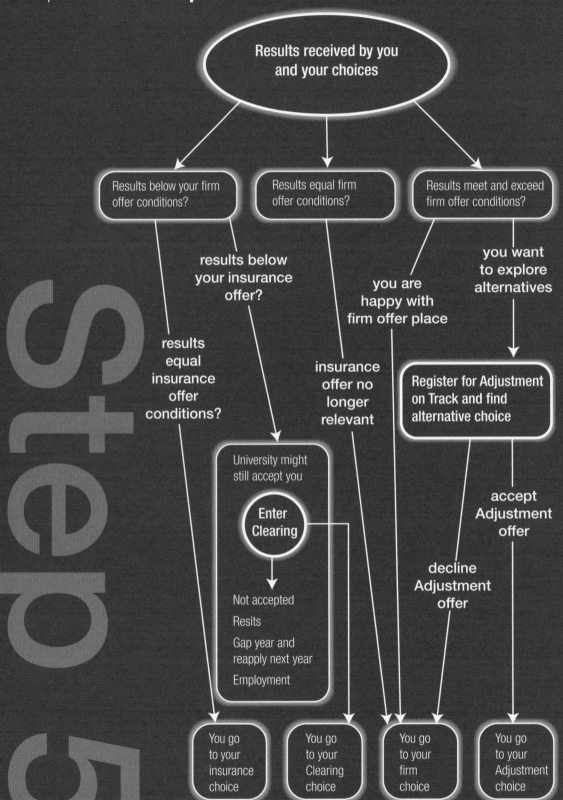

Step 5

Results received by you and your choices

Results below your firm offer conditions?

Results equal firm offer conditions?

Results meet and exceed firm offer conditions?

results below your insurance offer?

results equal insurance offer conditions?

you are happy with firm offer place

you want to explore alternatives

insurance offer no longer relevant

University might still accept you

Enter Clearing

Not accepted

Resits

Gap year and reapply next year

Employment

Register for Adjustment on Track and find alternative choice

accept Adjustment offer

decline Adjustment offer

You go to your insurance choice

You go to your Clearing choice

You go to your firm choice

You go to your Adjustment choice

What next?

What you do next after getting your results depends both on how you got on and what you want. You'll always have options, and sometimes the choice will be obvious and sometimes the choice will be agonising. Preparation and thinking in advance can only help, and this chapter introduces you to the possibilities and challenges of Step 5.

If you met the conditions of your offer, you have a commitment to go to the university that made you the offer, so you can start planning your freshers' fair activities and get on yougo to get to know other people on your course. If however you think you might like to change your mind, remember that when you accepted your offer you took a place that they would have offered to someone else if it hadn't been you. No-one wants you to be unhappy but you have to take your commitment seriously and see it from the university's point of view too. One way to back out of the situation is to withdraw from the UCAS scheme completely, which leaves you free to reapply next year if you wish. If you want to do anything else, the first step is to contact the university which is expecting you to turn up to their course and discuss your options with them.

If you have met and exceeded the conditions of your firm choice's offer, you may want to consider Adjustment, which gives you the chance to raise your aspirations to a course with higher entry requirements. Bear in mind that there was a lot more than entry requirements in your mind when making your original choices and you may have to rearrange such matters as accommodation if you change institutions at this late stage.

If your results mean that you will have to go through Clearing in order to enter higher education this year, then you should probably start researching courses as soon as possible. The list of courses with vacancies is available in newspapers and on **www.ucas.com**. Bear in mind that the list changes as places are taken up or released, so be prepared to keep checking and act speedily once you see a course that you like the sound of and have the entry qualifications for. Alternative approaches are to reapply next year (having re-sat your exams or not), or after taking a gap year, which incidentally can be a great experience in its own right over and above giving you relevant experience or a better bank balance or both, or even studying abroad.

Disappointing results are really not the end of the world, although they can feel like it. You could consider a foundation degree – have a look at **www.ucas.com** to find out more. Another good option is part-time study. UCAS offers a part-time course search from July until September but you can also search in the websites of universities and colleges to see what they have on offer. Other ways of studying include distance learning or online learning – have a look at the website of the Open University to get some ideas of the range of subjects and ways of learning.

Another option is employment, or maybe an apprenticeship. Find out more at the end of this chapter.

Disability – start talking to your university now

If you have a disability and need the university to prepare facilities to suit you, it can be advantageous if you contact them as early as you can. Tutors can discuss with you different course options and the number of assignments, lectures and seminars. Speak with them about how your individual needs can be met; after all, you know more about your condition than they do. Ask what kinds of adjustments the university or college will make so you can access the course. If you will need flexible exam arrangements, it will be useful to talk about these as well.

The disability coordinator should be able to tell you about the institution's services for disabled students, including accommodation and support arrangements. If the institution agrees to adapt buildings and elements of your course, ask them to put this in writing. Once your place is confirmed, check that preparation and activity is under way and, if necessary, visit again to make sure the changes meet your needs and are as you expect. Disabled students who are already at the institution can tell you how good they find the support arrangements and what life is like there. Students who are already on the course will also be able to tell you about the level of work expected and any difficulties they have had. If the people you meet are not able to answer your questions, ask to speak with someone who can or ask for information to be sent to you. If you have further questions after your visit, do not be afraid to ask.

Adjustment

Some people get such a pleasant surprise when they receive their exam results that it seems to open up undreamt-of possibilities and propel them onto a new path before they can take breath. If this is the case with you, then you do in fact have a few days in which to consider what to do for the best.

Don't forget to look at Adjustment on UCAStv *how-to* guides

It might be that such applicants:

- played safe and applied for courses below their real capabilities

- discovered their real passion rather late and their choices now seem as if they were made in a former life or by another person

- were extremely lucky in their exams and now find a whole new world at their feet potentially.

In any event, if your grades meet and exceed all the conditions of your conditional firm offer, you can register for Adjustment and spend up to five days researching alternative courses more commensurate with your exam performance. But only if you want to – there is absolutely no necessity to throw out all your well-laid plans.

You have up to five days to do this research and commit yourself to an alternative place, and the Adjustment period ends on 31 August in any event.

Adjustment affects relatively few applicants: fewer than 400 in both 2009, its first year of operation, and 2010. But for those it helps, it enables them to think about raising their aspirations while keeping the security of their confirmed place at their firm choice. For a quick guide, have a look at the short video about Adjustment on **UCAStv**.

If you find yourself in the happy position of having your results meet and exceed your needs and expectations, you should also start by talking to your careers or HE adviser. You need to check that you really are eligible for Adjustment, and then start checking on Course Search what courses are available that match your interests and results. Universities and colleges might have places available for Adjustment applicants that they will not offer to Clearing applicants, so make sure you look in the correct list and you make it clear to any admissions tutors that you are applying through Adjustment not Clearing.

If you register for Adjustment, the university where you hold a firm place will keep that place for you, but they will be able to see that you are researching your options elsewhere. If you do not find or do not accept an Adjustment place you will still hold your original confirmed place. If you decline an Adjustment place you can research an alternative, but your Adjustment period is still the original five days – it will not be extended for a subsequent search.

Applicants who use Adjustment have a lot of extra work to do, which might include rearranging their student finance, their accommodation, their travel arrangements, and even their career plans. You need to be quite sure that this is what you want to do before throwing overboard all the planning you have been committed to all year so far. But sometimes, as in the case of the student who used Adjustment to change from a course in Diagnostic Radiography to one in Law with French, it can enable applicants to make an off-the-wall switch that makes total sense to them.

Adjustment flowchart

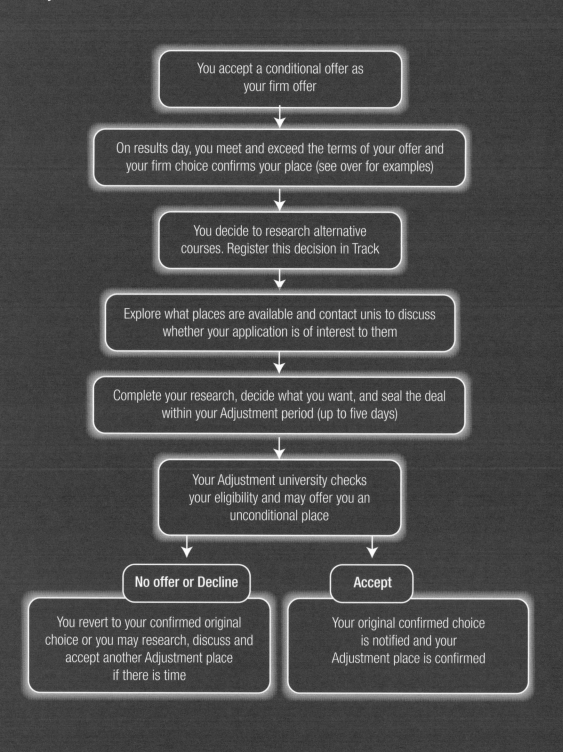

You accept a conditional offer as your firm offer

↓

On results day, you meet and exceed the terms of your offer and your firm choice confirms your place (see over for examples)

↓

You decide to research alternative courses. Register this decision in Track

↓

Explore what places are available and contact unis to discuss whether your application is of interest to them

↓

Complete your research, decide what you want, and seal the deal within your Adjustment period (up to five days)

↓

Your Adjustment university checks your eligibility and may offer you an unconditional place

No offer or Decline

You revert to your confirmed original choice or you may research, discuss and accept another Adjustment place if there is time

Accept

Your original confirmed choice is notified and your Adjustment place is confirmed

Examples of meeting and exceeding offer conditions – you are eligible for Adjustment

Offer	Actual grades achieved
You must get A level grades of AAB	You get A level grades AAA
You need A level grades of CCD (with grade C in chemistry)	You get A level grades of ACD (including grade A in chemistry)
You must get a minimum of 280 UCAS Tariff points including grade B in A level French	You achieve 280 UCAS Tariff points with grade A in A level French
You must get SQA Higher grades BBC (with grade C in geography)	You get SQA Higher grades ABC (with grade B in geography)
Your uni wants you to get International Baccalaureate results of 30 points in total to include at least 5 in English and 5 in physics	Your result in IB is 30 points including a 6 in English and a 5 in physics
You must get Irish Leaving Certificate (Higher level) grade B in mathematics and grades BCC overall	You achieve Irish Leaving Certificate (Higher level) grade B in mathematics and grades ABC overall

Examples of not meeting and exceeding offer conditions – you are not eligible for Adjustment

Offer	Actual grades achieved
Your conditional offer stipulates A level grades CCD (grade C in psychology)	You get A level grades ACD (with grade D in psychology)
You must get A level grades ABB (with grade A in history)	Your results are A level grades A*ABB (including grade B in history)
Your offer requires a minimum of 280 UCAS Tariff points including grade B in A level French	You achieve 290 UCAS Tariff points overall but with grade C in A level French
You must get SQA Higher grades BBC (with grade B in chemistry)	You get SQA Higher grades ABC (including grade C in chemistry)
Your uni wants your International Baccalaureate results to total 30 points and include a 5 in mathematics and a 5 in chemistry	Your IB results turn out to be a total of 32 points with a 4 in mathematics and a 5 in chemistry
You need Irish Leaving Certificate (Higher level) grade B in art and grades BBC overall	You achieve Irish Leaving Certificate (Higher level) grade A in art and grades ACC overall

Clearing

Myth buster

Clearing is not just for people with lower exam results

It's a big myth that Clearing's only used by people who didn't get the results needed for their uni choices. Clearing is for anyone who finds themself without a place at university or college after their exam results have been received, for whatever reason. It could be because they found a new course in Clearing which didn't have vacancies when they applied, or they decided only after 30 June that they wanted to go university or college.

Who is Clearing for?

You might not expect to find yourself in Clearing, but this is what happened to over 200,000 applicants in 2010, and about 160,000 in 2009. They arrived in Clearing by various routes.

Don't forget to look at Clearing on UCAStv *how-to* guides

- Some did not hold any offers (either because they were not made any or because they have declined them, including changed course offers) and so entered Clearing automatically. Remember you can contact universities and colleges direct as soon as your results come through.

- Some entered Clearing because they did not meet the terms of their conditional offers. Perhaps they did not meet the required grades or Tariff points.

- Some were late in filling in Apply. If you apply after 30 June you will be advised that you are automatically entered into Clearing, and you fill in all the sections of Apply except for choices. You then approach the universities and colleges direct, after receiving the results of any exams you have taken, and they look at your application online.

Of the 160,000 Clearing applicants in 2009, about 47,000 or 29% were successful in finding an HE course through Clearing, and of the 200,000 in 2010, about 46,000 or 23% are now at university or college through Clearing. If you are hoping to join them, have a look at the Clearing video on **UCAStv** and the Clearing flowchart on page 276 which will also help you navigate your way through.

How do I get a Clearing place?

First, if you think you may need to use Clearing, it is a good idea to talk again to the people who have been advising you so far. They know you and they know your priorities and wishes, and they know what people like you have done in the past. You should discuss with them what you feel about your new situation and what you want to achieve, and they will help you to get there if they can.

You cannot approach a university for a Clearing place until you have received your exam results, but you can meanwhile start thinking about what courses you would like to consider and how you want to present yourself when you discuss the matter with admissions staff. Prepare for that phone call as if it were a kind of mini-interview.

As soon as you become eligible for Clearing, Track will give you your Clearing Number, which you will need to quote to the universities that you contact so that they can see your UCAS application online.

Course vacancies in Clearing are a moving target as people turn down offers and universities fill places, so keep looking at the list of vacancies on our website **www.ucas.com** and in newspapers. When you have found a course that looks interesting and after checking you fit the Entry Profile, you should contact the admissions office to confirm that places are still available and ask any further questions.

Your list of questions will be similar to any such list you made if you applied earlier on in the cycle, and may include for instance:

- How is the course taught – through lectures, tutorials, seminars, laboratory work, field work, other?

- What is the assessment model – final year exams, interim exams, continual assessment?

- What materials or equipment will I be expected to supply?

- What support is available to disabled students?

- What are the accommodation options and how do I apply for accommodation?

- What are the computing and library facilities like?

Other questions will be very course-specific, regarding for instance options to access hi-tech equipment for sports or science courses, options to include study abroad for language courses, or periods in industry for business or engineering courses.

If the admissions tutor provisionally offers you a place, you need to think about whether you want to accept it. If you're sure you want to accept it, enter the course details in Track. The university will normally confirm your place and you will receive a Confirmation letter from UCAS. If you're not accepted you can apply to another choice in Clearing.

There's help all the way along although the final decision must be yours – after all it is you who will be studying for the next three or so years! If your results look like they're leading you into uncharted waters, you might find it helpful to talk things through with the professional careers advisers on the Exam Results Helpline, who are used to helping applicants work out and evaluate their options at this stage. The number will be available on **www.ucas.com**.

Clearing flowchart

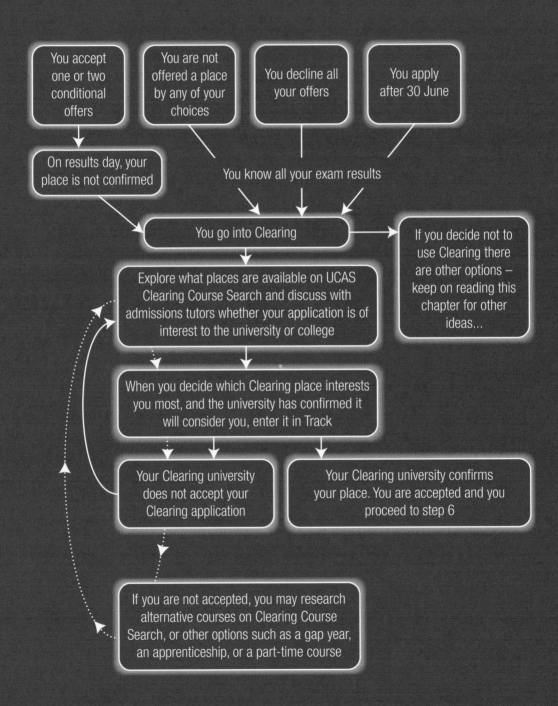

Studying in another country

Sometimes your plans don't work out as expected and then you somehow start thinking very radically. Some people in this situation extend their horizons by researching and considering applying to study in other parts of the world.

Though international study is normal for language students, it can be a real benefit for almost any student, particularly if you are thinking of a career which has international dimensions. Your personal growth may well be accelerated by studying abroad with its extra demands of cultural and educational adaptation. If you want a head start in dealing with people from other cultures, studying abroad is a good way to begin. And that's besides developing a more objective view of your own society and the possible bonus of increased language skills including, paradoxically, better precision in your own language.

Though for you the idea of studying abroad might not be your initial idea or plan, when you go you'll be joining a whole range of students whose choice to learn overseas might be prompted by many situations and aspirations. For some, the unavailability of their course at home, in content or perhaps in terms of methodology, moves them to widen their search. Sometimes the prestige of an internationally respected and renowned centre is irresistible, and by considering going abroad you'll increase the number of top institutions you put within your range. And sometimes the opportunity to change systems is too attractive to forego, even when your own country has so far served you very well.

Practical points that you need to consider are very like those applicable to studying in the UK, though with some extras:

- Entry requirements – you will need to check carefully and you should establish these using the websites of each university you are thinking of applying to. There are no standardised tables for making easy comparisons.

- Visit – if you're thinking of going very far away from home then it makes even more sense to check it out before you commit yourself to a long period away. Try and meet current students as well as the tutors and other staff.

- Research what courses are available and how they are taught and assessed. This might take extra care as some terms might not mean the same things in an international context. For instance, you might want to check whether exams are written or oral, though they would normally be written in the UK. You need to know if you are letting yourself in for the unexpected!

- If you are in receipt of benefits such as Disability Living Allowance, you should investigate how this will be affected by going abroad to study. You should also enquire whether you are eligible for the higher rate of student loan to help with extra expenses.

- Disabled students will have to be extra-rigorous in checking that their needs can be catered for. The law and culture might be different and complicated. Skill (visit **www.skill.org.uk**, then search on "study abroad", "abroad" or "overseas") has useful information, including lists of equipment and various kinds of support which may give you ideas on what could be most helpful to you. Remember that studying at a higher level will probably bring extra challenges and the earlier you think about this the earlier you can start arranging your support. That means you'll have a better chance of your support being there from day one, and the more your experience will be on the same level as that of the other students around you.

And there are some points to consider that might apply only to international study:

- You'll definitely need to understand procedural matters such as immigration and visas.

- There may be cultural differences, often a foreign language, and you may miss some of the things you take for granted at home. You'll almost certainly return home with changed views on your country of origin: you'll have new insights into things you'd never questioned before and you'll appreciate some things you'd taken for granted but now realise are anything but universal. Even where language isn't an issue – for instance English may be the local language or the course may be taught in English even when it is not the local language, or you may already be fluent in the language of your studies – you'll still be doing some cultural acclimatising. You may get help with this through cultural liaison organisations; contact the British Council for ideas (**www.britishcouncil.org**) or research whether there are friendship societies between the country or region and the UK.

But the benefits can be huge:

- Many employers consider that international students develop a greater maturity and breadth of experience than domestic students.

- Employers with a global profile will be particularly interested in students with more varied affiliations.

- You will have already proved you're flexible and mobile, and employers will recognise that you will probably have the means to adapt to new circumstances. After all, you'll have built up your confidence in your ability to rise to the challenge and cross boundaries successfully and that will come across.

- Provided you can explain how the experience of studying abroad gives you added value, you will have an important extra dimension that could make the difference for employers choosing between two otherwise similar candidates, particularly if there is an international or diplomatic dimension to the role.

You do not apply to an overseas university through UCAS. Contact the university or universities where you are thinking of applying and ask for details of the application procedure. Application may involve a mixture of factual information about yourself and your educational background (with certificates in support), references, a statement about yourself and your reason for applying, and possibly an interview, either in the UK or in the host country. You might well also have to provide a portfolio of some sort, or send in some work, say an essay on a given subject relevant to the course you have applied for. Broadly, universities make their decisions on a fairly standard set of facts, but detail here is important and you should make sure you understand their requirements fully before submitting your application.

Funding your studies abroad will need to be thought about at an early stage – your first contact will be the institution you are hoping to attend, but you may also find the following helpful:

- For study in the EU, you need to explore EU-wide funding programmes as well as those particular to the state you are planning to visit. Some information about the former can be found at **http://ec.europa.eu/comm/europeaid** and **www.eu-student.eu/category/study-abroad/**.

- For study in the US, **www.salliemae.com**, **www.FedMoney.org** and **www.fulbright.co.uk** give general information.

- For study in Australia, have a look at **www.deewr.gov.au**.

- For study in Asia, look at **www.moe.sg/aseanscholarships/** for Singapore; at **www.malaysia-scholarship.com** for Malaysia; at **www.koica.go.kr** or **www.kafsa.or.kr** for Korea; at **www.au.emb-japan.go.jp/e_web/ education/Monbukagakusho.htm** for Japan and for China at **http://en.csc.edu.cn**. Information about Thailand may be found at **http://studyinthailand.org** and about India at **www.highereducationin india.com**.

- Some general hints may be found at **www.studyoverseas.com**, **www.acu.ac.uk** (website of the Association of Commonwealth Universities), **www.ukcisa.org.uk** (the UK Council for International Student Affairs) and **www.unesco.org/education/studyingabroad**, the website of the United Nations Educational, Scientific and Cultural Organization.

Please note this is not an exhaustive or authoritative guide to helpful websites, but just a few leads to get you started.

The information about taking a gap year in this chapter has been contributed by the author of *the gap-year guidebook*.

A gap year is a unique opportunity and requires detailed planning and research. For 19 years *the gap-year guidebook* has been an invaluable source of advice for those considering time spent working, volunteering or learning at home or abroad before going to university or college. Visit **www.gap-year.com**.

Taking a gap year

Why a gap year is great for your CV

With the job market still tight, many school-leavers will consider taking a gap year after finishing their A levels in order to boost their UCAS applications before applying to start university.

The good news is that an unexpected gap year could turn out to be a life-changing experience.

Refreshed and ready to learn

Some may take a little time to readjust to academic life but former gappers are generally more focused, responsible and socially conscious, which allows them to take a more mature outlook on their studies and make a greater contribution to their course. Students who have taken a gap year are generally reckoned to be less likely to drop out half way through their course.

Once your studies are completed you will also find your CV is more appealing to graduate employers, who appreciate that those with a gap year experience are more likely to adjust quickly to the working environment and deliver results.

Employers admit that they actively seek to recruit those who have taken a structured gap year because they are more likely to have developed key skills such as teamwork, project management, risk assessment, languages and communication skills.

What you can do

The beauty of the modern gap year is the amount of choice and variety on offer: each gap year is as unique as you are, and each is an opportunity to create a tailored programme to meet your own personal ambitions. Knowing your own personality, your interests, your strengths and weaknesses will help you. Are you someone who likes to get stuck into something for a while or do you want to be on the move a lot? If you're not confident about coping alone with unfamiliar situations you might want a more structured, group setting. On the other hand if you know you need time away from the crowds, you'll be keen to build in some independent activity.

The most popular choice of activity for a gap year is volunteering, with teaching placements in particular having risen sharply in the last few years.

Or perhaps you want to explore things you've always wanted to pursue but never had time. It could be anything from a spiritual retreat to meditation and yoga, art, photography, to a new language or particular places and cultures.

Maybe you're particularly concerned about the state of the world and would like to do your bit environmentally or contribute to helping disadvantaged people? The possibilities are endless and many gappers end up constructing a programme that combines several elements.

Those with a full year at their disposal will perhaps have time for more than one activity, and might want to combine a structured element with some travel. The increase in cheap flights and wider access to previously unreachable destinations have made this even more possible.

Choosing the activity, destination and organisation most suited to you as an individual can be a difficult and time-consuming task. However, proper planning and research are crucial and will help ensure you get the most out of your time; a gap year or career break can easily be wasted without planning ahead.

But don't worry if all this sounds a bit heavy – the planning and preparation stage adds to the excitement and can be almost as much fun as the trip itself. And of course, this is where gap year guidebooks come into their own...

Structure and planning

A gap year is not for everyone, and it should certainly not be considered as a kind of holiday. You should understand that you will only get the most out of the trip if you embark on it with commitment, a sense of responsibility and an open mind. If undertaken lightly, a gap year is a good opportunity which is easily wasted.

You should not drift into a gap year and expect it automatically to be a positive, worthwhile experience: the key is detailed research and careful planning, to enable you both to make an informed decision and to chose an opportunity that best suits your individual needs and interests.

It doesn't matter where you are going or what you plan to do, there are some basics that everyone needs help to organise. Some of those basics, such as passports, visas, medical kits and insurance cover, simply can't be glossed over if the trip is to go smoothly.

This is where the internet and reference books such as *the gap-year guidebook* are so valuable in providing useful, informative and unbiased advice. It will of course be something of a step into the unknown, but with proper planning the chances are high that you will be rewarded with an exciting, challenging, valuable and enjoyable set of experiences that could, and probably will, change your life forever.

It is also important that you are aware of your responsibilities. Dropping out of a placement or programme before it has finished can be disruptive not only to you but also to others directly and indirectly involved.

Case study

Name: Alice Hancock

Alice Hancock took a gap year between her A levels and studying English at Cambridge University; she told us that adding some structured work experience to her time abroad helped her get more out of her travels.

I decided in my Lower Sixth year to take a gap year between school and university as I felt that I needed a break before plunging myself into university life. I also think it was important in terms of maturity – having to look after yourself, your money, travel, health, insurance and so on.

I spent three months in Chennai in India, working on a newspaper in order to get experience in the media and also because I was intrigued to experience India.

I considered charity work and volunteer placements but ideally I wanted some solid, usable experience. I had always wanted to travel so it was never a question of not going abroad but more to do with finding a placement that I wanted to do and felt would be relevant and interesting.

Experience is the main benefit of taking a gap year. For me, it has been more specific in that I got the experience of working on a newspaper. I also developed my interpersonal skills. Travelling does mean you have to be confident in yourself. It also definitely demands that you improve your negotiating ability.

More options...

> ### Did you know?
> #### You can also study part-time
>
> It's not just about full-time degree courses – there are part-time courses, foundation degrees, distance learning options, and plenty more. Although we don't process applications for most of these options, we have some information about them in the 'Next steps' section of our website – take a look at what's available and how to apply.

Part-time study

Another alternative to consider if for any reason your plans change at this stage is part-time study. The benefits are obvious: you can undertake your study at the same time as being employed and often your employer will contribute study time or even help towards your fees if your study will enhance your relevant skills and understanding. Part-time study tends to attract a higher proportion of mature students, so you'll be meeting a huge range of people who have taken different career paths which will perhaps widen your ideas about your own future and give you some useful insights into how career development works.

You apply direct to institutions offering part-time courses so look on university and college websites to find out what is on offer and how to apply. A visit to a local place is just as important as to a place you're moving away from home to join – after all you're likely to be involved with the facilities and teachers for even longer than for a full-time course. Check the dates of open days on websites and if none of them suits you, still contact the part-time admissions office to check whether you can arrange a visit.

One of the main benefits of part-time study is the flexibility it gives you. You're not going for total immersion in the way that full-time study demands, so the rest of your life gets more of a look-in. But part-time students are an integral part of the student community and tutors will give you the back-up you need academically and you will normally have access to the same range of pastoral support.

Part-time degrees tend to be modular in structure, which means they are made up of smaller parts each of which stands alone to some extent. The size of each module is measured in credits which tend to equate to a certain number of hours of study time. This gives you some idea of the practical commitments you would be entering into and the importance of each section of the course to the final result.

Make sure you check entry requirements not only on websites but also in direct communication with admissions tutors as arrangements can often be tweaked and advice given which can show you what the university needs to see in applications. Many institutions offer informal interviews for part-time courses where you can discuss the best route forward from the range on offer.

Apprenticeships

If part-time study appeals to you but you want even more emphasis on the employment side of combining study and working, you could think about starting an apprenticeship. The first websites to visit if this is something you would like to consider are **www.apprenticeships.org.uk** and **www.direct.gov.uk** which give you lots of background information, case studies, and pages of information for parents too. At those sites you can learn about how apprenticeships work and how they fit into the government's vision of opportunities and training for young people, and you can also find lists of vacancies and explore the online support available to apprentices.

Apprenticeships are schemes whereby young people take on employment and gain qualifications at the same time. (The qualifications gained by apprentices range from GCSE equivalents to NVQ level 4 or a foundation degree.) Your skills and knowledge are put into practice as you develop them and you learn about the reality of applying your ideas in the workplace. You also get paid for your work as you progress towards your qualification.

Chapter checklist

These are the things you should be doing in Step 5 of your applicant journey:

☐ Check Track to see whether your choices have accepted you.

☐ If your results are below your firm and insurance offers, look for a place in Clearing on **www.ucas.com**

  - ring the unis to find out if they'll accept you

  - if a uni wants you and you're sure you want to go there, enter it in Track.

☐ If your results are better than expected and meet and exceed your firm offer, read the section on Adjustment to see if it's something you want to consider, but remember, there's a five day limit.

☐ Consider taking a gap year. Ask your university if you can defer your entry.

☐ If things haven't worked out as planned, consider:

  - resits or taking a gap year and reapplying next year

  - studying in another country

  - finding employment

  - part-time study.

☐ If you have a disability talk about your needs with the university disability coordinator.

Step 6
Starting university and college

You've researched, chosen, applied, responded, waited, confirmed and worked and studied until you almost feel you can work and study no more. And now you're off to start your higher education career!

Scary! But thousands if not millions have succeeded in having a great time at university with rewarding study, fascinating opportunities and a terrific flowering of their minds and aspirations – and the same can be true for you too. Have a quick look at the 'Starting university' video on UCAStv, which will give you some pointers about what you'll have to deal with and what help is available.

Step 6 **Starting at university or college**

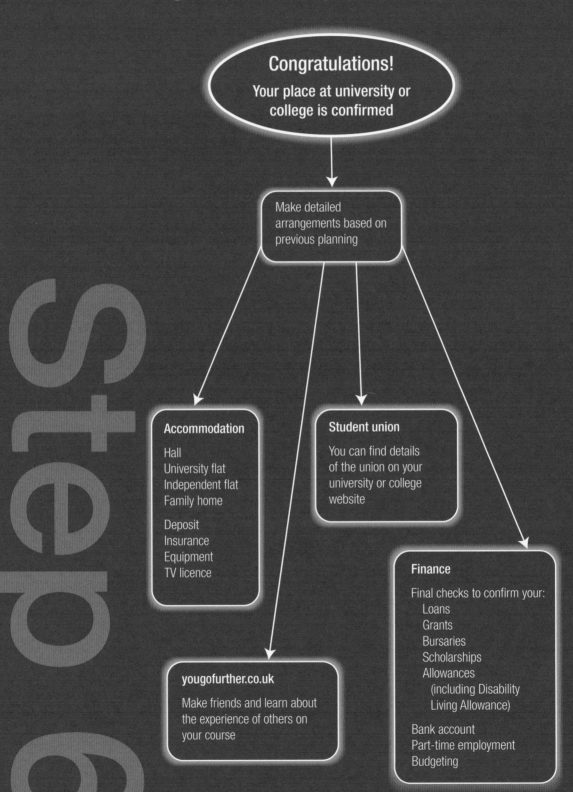

Congratulations!
Your place at university or college is confirmed

Make detailed arrangements based on previous planning

Accommodation

Hall
University flat
Independent flat
Family home

Deposit
Insurance
Equipment
TV licence

Student union

You can find details of the union on your university or college website

yougofurther.co.uk

Make friends and learn about the experience of others on your course

Finance

Final checks to confirm your:
    Loans
    Grants
    Bursaries
    Scholarships
    Allowances
      (including Disability
      Living Allowance)

Bank account
Part-time employment
Budgeting

Step 6

Preparing to study and getting support

One of the first things you'll notice once your course starts is that you won't be told what to do – you'll be much more on your own and will probably need to ask for direction and help at first. You will have a course director and tutors and the university or college will also have counsellors available to give you support as you get used to this new mode of self-directed learning. The courses at uni are more in-depth than at school and you'll soon learn that you have to set some of the boundaries yourself. The change can be quite difficult as you won't get any spoon-feeding now.

The thing to remember is that you are not alone. Everybody is experiencing the same as you (or they did last year or the year before) and there is plenty of help if you go and look for it.

- Your tutors are crucial in helping you to make the change but it is down to you to think about what you are learning and what it all means. The bonus is that you get a sense of independence and credit about your work right from the start.

Student tip:

'Uni is great but it usually takes a little while to settle in.'

First year students are often known as "freshers", especially in their first term at university.

- There are also likely to be some second-year students who will have volunteered to act as mentors to freshers like you. Your tutors may be able to direct you to a central panel or put you in touch with someone in the same faculty but a bit further on than you.

Student tips

Here are some things students say they wish they'd known before starting:

'how many hours of lectures I was going to have, and the amount of time I would need to give to studying on my own'

'how much higher the academic standard is'

- You'll learn in a mixture of ways which might include:

  - lectures (large groups, listening and note-taking; there might be question and answer sections, electronic response technology or quizzes)

  - seminars (small groups, active discussion led by assigned individuals who may be staff or students)

  - tutorials (may be groups of two or more or may – rarely – be individual, when you discuss your own work)

  - individual lessons (if you are studying a musical instrument for example)

  - crits (when you and others each take turns to present your finished or unfinished work within a group of students and tutors and sometimes visiting critics who all question you and discuss it)

  - show and tell (similar to crits but more informal, more of a feedback-gathering exercise)

  - laboratory sessions (which are usually practical and hands-on, but may be demonstrations)

  - fieldwork (practical and experiential learning under guidance)

  - work placement (simulated or real work environments where you apply and refine your more theoretical learning).

Exactly how teaching happens depends on many things, such as whether you're on a really popular course or you are one of just a very few students in your subject, and the traditions and policies of your particular university and course. The lower level of direct contact can be strange at first and you will almost certainly need to exercise some rigorous time management to get those first assignments done in time. University study can seem very unstructured after the rigid school timetable you may be used to. Make use of the opportunities you have to get to know staff in tutorials and seminars and fieldwork sessions, and remember that discussing your ideas can take them to a new level besides helping you identify and resolve any misconceptions you may have.

Student tip:

'You have lots of freedom compared to school – no parents or teachers there to tell you what to do. You must make your own decisions.'

- Welfare officers and student counsellors will also be familiar with the problems of settling in to the new academic world you have entered. Ask your tutor, flatmates or fellow students; or look in your student handbook for student services and the student union – they will have a wealth of experience which will give you ideas and support and will probably offer a range of services through various outlets, for instance a medical centre, student advice and advocacy centre or representation centre, counselling service, nightline and various chaplaincies.

- Make sure you know which way your Disability Support Allowance is going to be paid – it might be paid direct to your institution to administer on your behalf; or direct to the supplier of your support; or it may be paid to you so that you can pay your expenses as they arise. If this is the case you may have to show receipts (for instance for taxi fares) for the amounts you have claimed so make sure you keep these carefully. Also check to see that your home Social Services Department or equivalent is liaising with the equivalent body where you are going to study and with the university or college itself. The university's disability coordinator should be able to help you keep all the right people informed. Again, the Skill website (**www.skill.org.uk**) has useful information, and also publishes a booklet *Funding from Charitable Trusts* which might help if some of your expenses are not recoverable from the above sources.

- International students should familiarise themselves with **www.ukcisa.org.uk**, the website of the UK Council for International Student Affairs, and find the international office at their own uni.

- The new approach to your subject may well contain surprises, and realistically you have to realise that for some new students this will not be all good news. If you're finding the course is too different from what you expected, then it is really important that you check things out with your tutor. Things might be about to change, or you might be just in time to change to a course more like you wanted – so don't be shy about discussing how you're finding it with people who are there to help.

- Your motivation will grow and develop as you understand more of what is expected of you. Your initial enthusiasm will take you through the first stage, but will need to be renewed gradually as your awareness grows. Don't get too immersed in the day-to-day so that you forget either to enjoy yourself or what you're ultimately there for.

You may be sent an enrolment pack when your place is confirmed. This will include full joining instructions and various other information, such as any reading list you need to start looking at before you start college. If this is very long it may be best to wait before spending huge amounts of money. Or even if the reading list is short, the following points may also apply to you.

- It may be a generic reading list which is only partially relevant to you. Or it may relate to one module only so you need to pace your purchasing and reading.

- It may cover the whole year and some texts may not be needed for months yet.

- Don't forget many if not all of the titles will be available in the university library. Be aware though that many university libraries charge hefty fines for late returns, especially on short-term loan items in greatest demand.

- Second-hand books may be on sale from second and third year students.

When you start your course, you may be introduced to new ways of doing familiar things as well as many new things. It won't stay like this forever! You'll be learning many things concurrently – and this will be even more the case if you are relying on the support of interpreters or note-takers as you'll have to get used to each other's ways of working – but you will gradually get the hang of it.

University tip

Oxford University says: 'Our colleges have chaplains, doctors and nurses; and there are also university and student union resources to call on if you need to. We believe our welfare provision is effective, as Oxford has one of the lowest drop-out rates in the UK: figures published in Spring 2010 by the Higher Education Statistics Agency (HESA) show that only one per cent of Oxford students dropped out, compared with the national average of 7.2 per cent.'

www.ucas.com

Making friends

There are many ways of getting to know people at university. We have a look at the main ones below, but don't forget you've also got your family and friends from school or work, as well as the specialist and general advisers at your uni. Your friends know you well but won't necessarily have much idea about what you're dealing with and what your options are, and you may feel that the university advisers don't know you yet but don't forget that they will have vast experience of helping new arrivals settle in.

Meeting people before you go

Many people will have already signed up for yougo when they're in the process of applying to university. It makes sense to join a specialist forum and community where you can ask UCAS, the universities and other experts all the questions you need to have answered as you progress.

If you're already used to yougo, you'll know how friendly and easy it is to use. A lot of the people you'll meet in your lectures will also have joined yougo so why not get talking now? They might have visited your uni on a different day and seen different things; they might have read up on something that has passed you by; or they might be really interested in something your teacher advised you of when making your choices. You can compare your reactions to the freshers' week programme and arrange to go to some of the events together or as a group.

If you haven't yet found yougo – have a look at **www.yougofurther.co.uk** now and sign up using your Personal ID from UCAS. You can make a profile with your personal and educational details and have the chance to sign up for information alerts from different agencies.

One of the most daunting things about going to university for the first time is the feeling of being alone and knowing nobody – but with yougo you can get to know who is in your accommodation block, who is on your course or in your faculty, and who might be joining the Cycling Club or the Einstein Society or whatever it is that you want to explore.

There are various forums covering UCAS, universities, non-UK students, course subjects and application matters, besides live web chats and 19 general forums covering:

Student tip:

'It's amazing how liberating it is, mixing with people from all over the world. You need to be really open to new friends; people with different backgrounds and interests can turn out to be the best mates.'

- Art
- Careers
- Exams & Assessments
- Fashion
- Film
- Gaming
- General discussion

- Health
- Housing
- Life choices
- Literature
- Money
- Music

- Part-time jobs
- Politics
- Religion
- Sport
- Travel
- TV & Radio

Some universities and colleges operate buddy programmes by which current students volunteer to make contact with new students in order to answer any questions about studying, about the university or about student life. If your university has such a scheme and you receive a letter, email or phone call from your buddy, do respond to it as it is well known to be a great way to find out more about what's about to happen.

The students' unions of many universities and colleges have a Facebook page which is yet another way you can compare notes and get to know friends before you arrive.

Meeting people when you're there

> ### Student tip
>
> *'The people you meet in the first week of term are not necessarily your friends for life. The beauty of uni is that you continue to meet new people throughout, especially if you join societies etc.'*

It is true that you'll meet people all the time, and they're all in the same boat – that is a cliché but only because it is true! You'll see new people where you live, where you study, in the library, in the laundry, in the cafeteria – and you'll have different things in common with lots of them. Just be yourself, friendships which start on the basis of a pretence usually go nowhere, and remember that the university selected you because they knew you'd fit in.

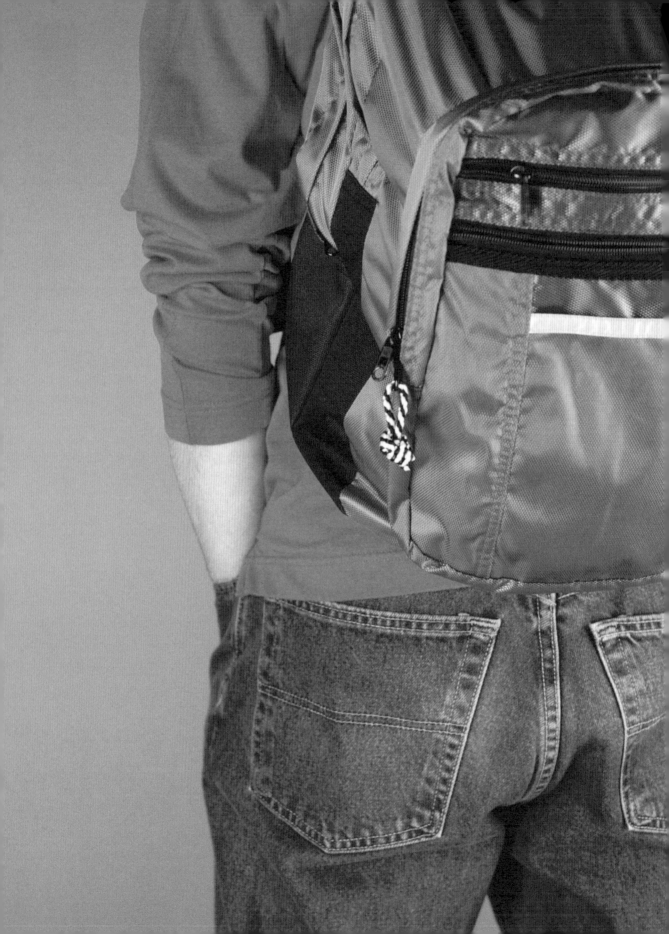

Starting university – leaving home

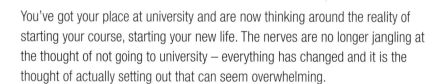

Student tip

'It will be weird leaving my family but I now see that moving out is just part of the uni experience and am excited to see what next year will bring. Change can be very scary but it is something we all need to get used to.'

You've got your place at university and are now thinking around the reality of starting your course, starting your new life. The nerves are no longer jangling at the thought of not going to university – everything has changed and it is the thought of actually setting out that can seem overwhelming.

The thing is to start planning as soon as you can, and to do things step by step.

www.ucas.com

UCAS would like to thank UNITE for their help and contribution to this chapter.

The heart of student living

UNITE is the UK's leading developer and manager of purpose-built student accommodation. UNITE has over 120 properties in towns and cities throughout England and Scotland in great locations, close to universities and city centres. They offer a wide choice of different room types for students in all years. Students can share with their friends or book a room individually, and all utility bills, internet access and contents insurance are included in the price.

Visit **www.unite-students.com** or call 0800 783 4213.

Accommodation

There are some key items you need to sort out if you are leaving home to go to university – and the first of those is accommodation. You may have already checked out the accommodation available at your firm and insurance choices, but now is the time to get serious. Contact your university to find out about the accommodation available. You can also search online to find out about other types of accommodation options available to you. Some providers offer virtual tours through their websites. Once your offer arrives, it is often a good idea to arrange a viewing at your choice of accommodation and to visit the local area before signing your tenancy agreement. If, however, you need to go through Clearing, then there's no need to worry. There will most likely be plenty of options still available to you as you complete the process. Check descriptions carefully so that you know what you're getting in terms of facilities, cleaning, sharing and so on.

As a student you will typically have three accommodation options open to you: uni accommodation, also known as halls of residence, managed by the uni; private houses or traditional student houses, managed by private landlords; and thirdly, purpose-built student accommodation provided by private companies such as

Student tip:

'If I'd checked beforehand I'd have known to bring lots of cleaning products and cooking utensils.'

UNITE, the UK's leading student accommodation provider. Your uni accommodation office will have further information on many of the different types of accommodation available to you, including contact details for private landlords if you're looking for a private house, as well as details on university halls of residence and purpose-built student accommodation. You can also search online to find out about the full range of accommodation available to you.

Price and quality for the different types of accommodation vary hugely, but there is something out there to suit everyone's taste and budget. Living in student accommodation while at uni is a great way to meet new people and make new friends easily. If, however, you have chosen not to live in student accommodation and are staying at home instead, you will still have plenty of opportunity to meet new people from your course and through uni clubs and activities.

The arrangement of the accommodation in university halls of residence and private companies tends to be a large building divided into a number of flats or individual private rooms rented exclusively to students. In university halls of residence you can typically expect individual rooms with some communal living space, such as a common room and study area. You can also often choose between catered or self-catered halls, dependent on the level of cooking you are prepared to do! In shared flats, you can typically expect your own private bedroom with a study area and a shared kitchen and lounge area.

The majority of purpose-built student accommodation offers a choice of living spaces from single rooms to double studios, and is also likely to come complete with en-suite shower rooms and will often include utility bills, contents insurance and broadband. Students will have their own study space, a common room for socialising and could have the chance to share with up to nine people. Premium accommodation, which can include larger beds and mod cons such as wall-mounted flat screen TVs, may also be an option.

Student tip:

'I wish I'd known that halls of residence would be so much fun!'

There is also the option of private housing through a landlord. This can be either a house or apartment in a student area of the city or near to your uni campus, and, like some halls of residence and purpose-built student accommodation, allows you to choose who you share with.

Whatever your choice, when you arrive you will probably have to show the letter or email confirming that you have been allocated a room, plus some photographic ID, before you can sign your contract and be given your key. There might be a compulsory health and safety talk by the hall and property managers.

Check whether there are rules concerning keeping items in your room such as candles, posters and electrical equipment such as kettles and sandwich toasters. Make sure you stick to these rules if you wish to get your deposit back, be covered by insurance, etc.

When choosing what accommodation to apply for, you might ask yourself questions such as these.

Self-catering or full board?

Catered sounds great, with meals provided and no washing up or cooking. But be aware that communal meals have to be provided at set times so you will have to take breakfast between say 8-9.30 am whether you are ready for it or not, and probably not in your dressing gown. Some mealtimes might clash with lectures around midday so you might end up doing some self-catering anyway. If you want to keep it to a minimum then full board (or weekday board) can be a good idea, and can help ensure you have a varied diet and can turn your mind to other things. Just remember it can be a bit regimented, and ask yourself whether that suits you or not. Self-catering can be better at matching special diets.

If you go for self-catering check where the nearest shops are and what equipment you're likely to need to supply yourself; and it might be a good idea to bring a few basic initial foodstuffs with you – some pasta, some cheese, some fruit, some teabags or coffee and a pint of long-life milk, and a supply of your favourite snack.

En-suite or not en-suite?

Completely personal choice, but do question before you sign on the dotted line:

- whether the extra cost or saving is worth it

- how many people might be sharing the facilities

- what the cleaning arrangements are.

Be aware that the hot water supply might struggle if many en-suites are operating at the same time, and that if you use shared shower facilities the flow of hot water might benefit from the demand being paced. Some non-en-suite rooms have a hand-basin which can be useful, though again you might like to consider the relative costs. Fixed plumbing can restrict the options for rearranging the layout of your room.

Location

The location of your accommodation is important. Consider the balance of location against price carefully, as you might feel you're getting a bargain by opting for a cheaper area, but think about the added cost of travelling to and from uni or the city centre. Depending on the location of the accommodation you choose, getting around can be expensive. Weekly or monthly travel cards can shave pounds off your travel expenses and don't forget to see if there are student discounts – a Student Rail Card will save a third on rail fares.

You should also consider the security of a property and whether you would feel safe living there. Some properties will come equipped with 24-hour security cover as well as security cameras but this is not to be expected in all properties. In some purpose-built student accommodation, properties benefit from additional security facilities such as secure door entry systems and CCTV.

In 2009 over 30% of applicants travelled less than 12 miles from home to their accepted university, compared with 27% in 2000. Of these many, though not all, will have lived at home, and the increase is suspected to be as much the result of increased numbers of mature applicants as the increased costs of living away at university.

Mixed or single sex?

Again, personal preference will tell you what's right for you. If you're an outgoing person you will meet other people anyway, and there is always a variety of clubs and societies for interest, relaxation and socialising. Your accommodation is where you are based, and for some people can be a bolt-hole while for others it is the central place for everything to happen. Your course will also bring you into contact with many people of like mind even if not of like tastes, and you'll encounter all sorts at the student union and library. So even if you are not in hall, you'll not be left out of the social scene. The first year seems just to fly by, so make sure you do give the right amount of time to your social life.

Deposit

If you opt for a private rented flat or shared house, you will be asked to pay a deposit, usually equivalent to one or three months' rent or a fixed sum around £250. This can also be demanded by the university for the accommodation they run too. It will be returned to you when you leave provided that the place is in the same condition as it was when you moved in. The costs of repairs and cleaning can be deducted from the deposit returned to you, so read your tenancy agreement carefully to see what you might be liable for, and make careful notes of the condition of the rooms and their fixtures and fittings.

Before moving into furnished rooms, you might like to take photos of all marks, scratches etc, copy them onto a CD and seal it and hand it to the landlord. That way you might be more likely to get your deposit back.

You should also agree an inventory, or list of items such as furniture, kitchen utensils etc, so that both you and the landlord know what should remain when you move out. Your students union or the Citizens Advice Bureau can give you advice and tips – see their websites.

You rental deposit should be protected under a Tenancy Deposit Protection Scheme designed to stop landlords wrongly withholding all or part of the deposit and to help resolve any disputes – check before you hand over your deposit and sign the agreement.

During the holidays

Most tenancy agreements are for a fixed number of weeks so, depending on the length of the tenancy, holiday periods may be included. Tenancy lengths and start dates can vary, so before signing a tenancy agreement you should get clarification from your accommodation provider when the tenancy starts and its length in weeks.

Many properties run by companies such as UNITE offer 43-week tenancies which take you up until after your exams. There is also the option of extending your stay over the summer at a reduced rate. This can be useful if you're looking to stay in your university city to work over the holidays.

Managing accommodation costs

Accommodation prices vary by city with prices in London often higher than other parts of the country. When working out how much you can afford to pay, don't forget to make allowances for bills, contents insurance and a TV licence, which in some cases are not included in the rent. However, some accommodation providers include the price of utility bills, in-room internet access and contents insurance within the room price to make it easier for students to manage their finances.

It's vital that you read through a tenancy agreement before signing anything, as it's a legally binding document. The payment terms and options for different types of accommodation will vary considerably depending on the type of accommodation you choose. In some cases you may be required to pay the full term's rent in one sum at the beginning of your tenancy, while in other properties you have the option to pay in smaller instalments. A tenancy agreement is also likely to vary in length depending on the accommodation you choose and this will have an impact on your overall accommodation budget for the year.

Accommodation for international students

Students coming from abroad have access to the same accommodation choices as UK students and are often advised by their individual universities on the best places to live. It's a good idea for students from overseas to look at various accommodation options online for the full choice available to them.

If you're an overseas student, living in halls of residence or other purpose-built student accommodation is a great way to meet new people and mix with others from different backgrounds and on different courses; or the accommodation officer might be able to help you find a place with other students from your part of the world, if that is what you would prefer.

Being aware of the different accommodation options and knowing how to make the right decisions in choosing student accommodation will help you get off to the best start in your life at uni. Enjoy the experience!

Looking forward

After you've completed your first year at uni, you will once again be faced with a choice of accommodation for your second and third years. If you have been living in halls of residence, you will most likely need to look for alternative accommodation as halls are usually exclusively for first year students. Also, by now, you will have an idea if there's anyone you want to share with so will probably be looking for somewhere together to accommodate you and your friends. Whether you are looking for an apartment for two or a large house for eight, both purpose-built student accommodation and private houses may be able to cater for your choice. The accommodation office will be able to point you in the right direction or you can search online for providers or landlords.

In some cities students start searching for second year accommodation before the end of the first term of their first year, so be prepared to start looking early for a place to live next year.

Two students discuss their accommodation choices:

Chris was a resident at a UNITE property

'I did a lot of research into living options for my second year and UNITE was the most cost-effective option compared with a private house share.

'Utility bills and contents insurance were also included in my room rent which made it so easy to budget. With a private landlord, bills would have been in addition to rent which can be difficult if you live with other students.

'I think the best thing about living at Phoenix Court was the social aspect. In a house share you are just with the same set of people throughout the entire year, whereas I met so many people from different courses and universities. There was a big common room in the basement so lots of people would get together to watch films or sports. The atmosphere was great and I've made lots of good friends.'

Janie lives in university accommodation

'The decision to live on campus took a lot of deliberation; as a (very) mature student used to having my own house, it was going to be a big transition. However the trade-off of being a couple of minutes away from lectures, versus a long and expensive daily commute, plus the chance to be involved in uni life seemed well worth it.

'All the uni rents were inclusive of bills which helped massively with budgeting. I requested a room in a six-bedroomed flat as my first choice, along with a preference to live with other mature students.

'The day I arrived on campus I was extremely nervous; not knowing my housemates and being somewhat older, it felt like day one in the Big Brother house and I wondered if I had made the right decision. Upon arriving at the flat however, all my fears were allayed and I could not have been happier. It was basic but spacious and clean and, most importantly, my flatmates were all absolutely lovely! I think it would be least likely to win party flat of the campus but it kinda helps not having that as a distraction.

'Campus living also enables me to study with my coursemates in the evenings and weekends which is usually followed by a well-earned drink at the SU bar; living here is a great experience all-round and gives university another dimension!'

If you have a disability…

Find out in advance, either by contacting the university or by visiting and seeing for yourself, whether buildings and facilities are accessible to you. Buildings you are likely to use include the students' union, bars, canteens, libraries, computer rooms, sports facilities, lecture theatres, teaching rooms and any departmental rooms. If you are deaf or hard of hearing, check if lecture theatres and teaching rooms have induction loops. You may also need to find out if there is parking for disabled people, good lighting and helpful signs around the university or college.

Often, disabled students are able to gain early access to their accommodation, to help them get settled in to their new life and surroundings, so check whether this is the case and whether someone from the disability office can be on hand when you arrive to make sure it all goes smoothly. The connections they can make for you can be of many kinds, for instance at Oxford the Disability Advisory Service will liaise with the University Centre for Sport on behalf of disabled students who play a paralympic sport.

Do not be discouraged if some things are not right. Talk to the disability coordinator about your needs and discuss what adaptations can be made before you start.

Student tip:

'It's really important to know that the Disabled Students' Allowance (DSA) is there for people with less visible disabilities than wheelchairs etc – that if you are dyslexic you are eligible. You need to apply early.'

Under the Equality Act (2010), all higher education institutions are obliged to make reasonable adjustments to the physical features of premises, where these are helpful to disabled students. If there is a physical barrier to access, universities must remove it, alter it or provide a reasonable means of avoiding the physical barrier to access. The Act also states that, most of the time, the costs of reasonable adjustments cannot be passed on to the disabled person.

It is nearly always a reasonable adjustment to provide information in an accessible or alternative format.

Freshers' week will normally include provision or special events for students with disabilities or support needs.

Examples of support

Support can be given to you to make your life easier and to remove barriers. The following is a list of examples of support (for a longer list and further ideas, see **www.skill.org.uk**). Whatever your needs, do discuss them with the disability support officer at the university or college.

- Access to occupational therapist
- Adapted accommodation
- Alternative methods of assessment
- Braille note-taker
- Careful timetabling, to minimise stress or maximise use of interpreter's availability
- Computer with specialist software or hardware
- Ergonomic chair
- Exercise facilities for guide dog
- Extensions in coursework deadlines
- Extra tutorials
- Flashing light doorbell
- Fridge for medication
- Materials in literal language
- Support worker, interpreter, medical assistant.

If things go wrong and you want to make a complaint

The student population of the UK is just under two million and for all but a handful their time at university or college goes pretty smoothly. However, from time to time, you or someone you know at university may become dissatisfied with one of the services provided by your institution. If you want advice on dealing with such a situation, you should remember that all universities and colleges have complaints procedures which are broadly similar, and contain the following stages.

- A requirement to try to resolve the matter informally with the person or service causing the problem.

- If a problem cannot be resolved informally, the formal procedure will usually start with filling in a complaints form. The students union will be able to help with this if you wish and you will find information on your university website. You can search for "Complaint" – the relevant section of the website will usually be under "About us", "Customer service" or "If we don't come up to scratch" or something similar.

- The person dealing with complaints is usually the dean of school or faculty or the academic registrar.

- If the complaint is not satisfactorily resolved, there's usually a review procedure that operates at vice-chancellor level.

- Only if you have exhausted the official internal complaints procedure of your university can you go beyond it to the Office of the Independent Adjudicator for Higher Education (OIAHE) at **www.oiahe.org.uk**. Anyone who is registered as a student at a participating higher education institution can make use of the OIAHE procedures. (Please note that the Browne Review of October 2010 recommended a change in the location of the independent complaints function to a new HE Council.)

It seems a bit negative to focus here on what might go wrong. For most people, the transition to higher education goes well, but if you are unfortunate enough to encounter problems, it is as well to have in advance a general idea of what might happen next. That will help you to keep things in proportion, share your experiences and seek help for yourself or give appropriate support to someone else in difficulties.

Money: making it go further

Student loans are paid in three HUGE instalments and so one of your top priorities has to be learning how to budget properly. For many of you this will be the first time you will have had charge of such a large sum of money. If you go out and spend it all at once, by week three of the term you will be living off supermarket own-brand beans and will be fairly miserable too, besides possibly getting into debt.

When you get your funding it can seem like a lot of money, but it has to last you a whole term. (The only exception to this rule is NHS bursaries which are paid monthly.) Everyone's priorities vary but it's essential that you have enough money to pay your rent, food and utility bills. So pay your rent and any other essentials immediately and see what you have left for the rest of the term. You can work out a budget quite easily just by dividing this by the number of weeks until the next loan/grant payment. Life is very exciting at the start of your course and it is easy to slip into bad habits.

Think carefully before you get any other loans or a credit card. Credit card debt is an easy trap to fall into but extremely hard to escape. Other forms of debt you

Student tip:

'I wish I had known not to waste my student loan.'

should try to avoid include store cards, no matter how tempting the offer, they are one of the most expensive ways of borrowing money.

- Fill in the budget sheet for each term to learn more about managing your own finances.

Student budget sheet

Income	£	Expenditure	£
Loan		Rent/hall fees	
Part-time wages		Food	
Grant		Household	
Other		Mobile telephone	
Bursary		Gas/electricity/water	
		TV licence	
		Books/stationery/photocopying	
		Socialising	
		Travel	
		Clothes	
		Other	
TOTAL		TOTAL	

Student tip:

'It can come as a surprise how much you have to spend on facilities like photocopying, books, etc.'

- If your expenditure is more than your income, see if there are ways to increase your income – for example, getting a job. Maybe also contact the university for a 'Wealth Check' to make sure you are getting your full grant or loan entitlement.

- Once you have figured out how much you have left after paying your bills, set yourself a weekly amount for other costs and try to stick to it.

- Open your post! You should get in the habit of checking your bank statements as this will make it easier to keep track of your spending.

- Use cash rather than cards.

- Go to the cash machine once or twice a week rather than every day. If you go and withdraw £10 every weekday in term time you will be withdrawing over £1500!

- Make eating out a treat – not a daily event. This includes your lunch. Take your lunch with you (even if it is for only a few days a week) and save hundreds of pounds per year.

- Don't do your shopping in the convenience store next to your halls of residence – these are often far more expensive than a luxury delicatessen, let alone a regular supermarket. Use more economical shops, which often have a wider choice too. Get everyone in the flat to join in and help with the shopping.

- Buy supermarket own-brand toiletries and food.

- A student travel pass can save you a fortune each term, but do your sums. If you are not travelling the same route every day it may not be worth your while buying one.

- Look out for student discounts at the cinema, shops and restaurants – show your student card everywhere you go. Don't be embarrassed! If you live in a student town or city the shops and restaurants will nearly all offer discounts (but may not advertise them). We don't recommend you eat out but you will occasionally.

The majority of universities run free money management sessions either on a one-to-one basis or in groups. These are intended to be fun and interactive (not a lecture) and you will learn more about how to manage your money and get your spending habits under control.

Many universities are taking part in a national project supported by the Consumer Financial Education Body (CFEB) to provide proactive support to students. The idea is to avoid financial problems and develop good money management skills. These may be labelled 'Money Doctor' sessions, but they sometimes go by different names at different universities. The sessions are intended to make your life easier

Student tip:

'I was so incredibly grateful that the university finance service was there when I had problems paying my fees.'

by developing your skills and increasing your knowledge. Check out the student money advice pages on your university website to see if they are part of the project and find out what help is on offer.

Working as a student

As a student in employment you will be liable for income tax and National Insurance just like anyone else. Students like any other employee can earn a certain amount (called the basic allowance) before they have to pay income tax. If your employer deducts tax from your wages you may be able to reclaim this from HM Revenue & Customs (HMRC) at the end of the year if your income is below this threshold.

At the time of writing HMRC are planning changes to students and income tax. The website **www.hmrc.gov.uk/students/** can give you more information about your tax liability.

Almost everyone has to pay National Insurance – students included. Make sure you give your employer your correct National Insurance number and check it on your payslips. Getting this wrong can have serious repercussions on your state pension later in life. Unlike income tax you cannot claim any overpayments back at the end of the year.

See Employment section on page 331 for further information about getting employment during your studies.

Council tax

Most full-time students do not have to pay council tax. When you enrol on your course you will be given an exemption certificate. It is your responsibility to give this to your landlord if you live in a privately rented house. It is a good idea to keep a copy of the certificate in case you receive a bill.

Students who live in purpose-built student accommodation (halls of residence) do not have to pay council tax.

Health care costs

You can have free health care costs until your 19th birthday and even after this many students can get help with prescriptions, glasses or other health care costs, not because you are a student but because you have a low income. However, not many students know about this or make a claim.

You need to complete a form to be assessed. These are available from any large pharmacy, your university or can be downloaded from **www.nhsbsa.nhs.uk/792.aspx**.

Bank accounts

High street banks compete with each other for student business (they know that you should be a good earner over your lifetime and are likely to be too lazy ever to change banks) but don't be blinded by the free gifts on offer. Instead, look carefully at the level of support each bank offers and how they will treat you in various financial circumstances.

As a university student, you will normally qualify for an interest-free overdraft. This means that as long as you stay within the limit of your overdraft, you will not be charged for using it.

Most banks will require you to have all statutory funding, such as your maintenance loan and maintenance grant, paid directly into your bank account. Banks can and will close your account and ask for any overdraft back, if you do not pay your student funding into the account.

Domestic life

When you are living independently, the following points will be worth considering.

Safety and security

- Your landlord has a legal duty to have gas appliances checked for safety by a Gas Safe registered engineer and you should be given a copy of the safety check record. Faulty gas appliances which leak carbon monoxide can cause severe illness or even death. Carbon monoxide is odourless, so you cannot rely on recognising a smell of gas to protect you.

- Fires can be caused by electrical or other faults. Make sure that smoke detectors are installed and are working. Check the labels of all furniture and furnishings to see that they are made from fire-resistant material – if they are not, ask your landlord to replace them. Be careful about electrical wiring; plugging many items into one socket can overload the system besides leading to a tangle of wires over the floor. Make a mental note of the best means of escape in case of a fire.

- The first few weeks of the first term are often plagued by thefts as there are so many new faces around and nobody knows who is meant to be there and who is not. Think hard about leaving windows open, especially on the ground floor, and be careful about giving out entry codes to all and sundry. The NUS says that one in five students will be a victim of crime while at university – visit their website page The Lock (**www.nus.org.uk/Campaigns/The-Lock/**) for information and tips to help you protect yourself.

Insurance

- You might be covered by your family's domestic contents policy which sometimes includes the possessions of students away from home, though watch out for any proviso which excludes instances of forced entry or items worth over a certain figure (say £1,000).

- Hall fees sometimes include insurance – check before buying separate cover.

- Don't leave anything valuable over the holidays.

- Old, well-used equipment (for instance, a laptop) is far less likely to attract attention than a brand new top-of-the-range one.

Health

- Check whether there are conditions concerning health attached to your course – for instance if you're applying for courses to do with medicine or health care the UK health authorities recommend you should be immunised against Hepatitis B before you start training, and universities are likely to ask you for certificates to show that you are free of infection before confirming your place.

- Check your immunisation records. If there's an outbreak of something nasty it will help you to know where you stand.

- Take a small first aid box, with a cold cure included for 'freshers' flu'. Unfamiliar kitchen knives can inflict a nasty gash, so include a few plasters and antiseptic cream. Check that you understand when you should call 999.

- Find out where the campus health service is situated before you need it, or register with a local surgery.

- Inform yourself about alcohol and drug abuse before you get tempted.

- Be aware that, as in boarding schools, concentrations of similar people in similar circumstances can lead to particular health issues. For instance there have been recent outbreaks of meningitis and mumps among students, the majority of whom today are among those who have not been vaccinated against these diseases. Don't be alarmist but just log somewhere in your mind that the risks are slightly greater than back at home.

- Either you or some of those around you might be finding adjusting to student life particularly stressful. Try and look out for others and try and remember to look after yourself. Be active in looking for opportunities to make friends and for time to attend to your studies so that you don't fall behind. Remember that a chat to the student welfare office or your pastoral tutor can give you the benefit of volumes of experience both in sorting out your own problems or how best to deal with having a neighbour in hall who is causing you concerns.

Laundry

- Dark clothes are easier to keep looking clean! As are dark bedding, towels and tea-towels.

- Washing tablets are easier than powder and don't spill into a wasteful mess, though they are more expensive.

- Take a big "laundry bag" with a starter supply of small change (not too small) for the laundrette. And don't forget coat-hangers so that creases have the chance to fall out!

Eating

- If you don't cook, now might be a good opportunity to learn. Get a student cookbook such as *Nosh 4 Students*, or *The Classic 1000 Student Recipes*, *Grub on a Grant* or *Vegetarian Cooking for Students*. Start small and then it is only you who have to eat the results of your early experiments.

- Sharing cooking and eating is sociable and by sharing you can improve your cooking until you become a popular host yourself.

- Grilling is far healthier than frying!

Student tip:

'One of the most useful things I learnt was how to cook pasta for six people for £2.50!'

- Find the whereabouts of a good cheap breakfast so that you can start the day on the right foot even when the cupboard is bare.

- Check out the catering in the students union.

- A list of basic equipment for self-catering might include: crockery for two, cutlery for two, a mug or two, two wooden spoons (to avoid your custard being tainted with the taste of onions), pair of saucepans, a frying pan and an oven tray, cheese grater, strainer, can opener, corkscrew, couple of tea-towels, wooden chopping board and sharp knife, measuring jug. But there is also a case to be made for taking less rather than more – you don't know what is supplied (but can always ask) and most university towns will have cheap outlets for basics, though this needs a budget. If you're getting into cooking a slow cooker can be great.

Accommodation miscellany

- Big cushions can be useful to use as either chairs or spare beds.

- Don't take too much unless you know the size of your room – some are very compact indeed and can just about accommodate you and one sock. On the other hand, the further away from home you are, the harder it is to pop home to stock up from the family store.

- If you bring a television or a computer capable of relaying or replaying television programmes you must make sure you are covered by a valid TV licence.

- If you are eligible for Disabled Students' Allowance you may be able to receive support in the form of extra equipment, see pages 311-312.

Practical matters

Important documents to bring with you

- Your AS12 Confirmation letter from UCAS confirming your place on your course

- Documents from Student Loans Company or equivalent, bursary administrator, etc

- Letter from accommodation office with details of your university accommodation

- National Insurance number and tax details

- Passport, birth certificate, marriage certificate, immigration papers, national identity document or card etc (check with your university exactly what you need to bring)

- Driving licence, insurance and MOT

- Any other insurance certificates, or copy of your home insurance if it covers you at university – see page 322

- Medical card, details of repeat prescriptions, your home doctor's and dentist's details

- Travel discount card and travel tickets

- Bank details and bank, credit and debit cards, including recent statement from a UK bank, or a recent statement from a non-UK bank showing you have the funds to pay your fees.

You should check carefully that you are able to bring with you everything you need to enrol – check your university's website for full details. If you do not have all the necessary documents, you will not be able to enrol. This can mean withdrawal of your student entitlements, and if you are unable to supply documentation by a given deadline, you may even be excluded from the course.

Emergency contact

You will need to give the name and details of an emergency contact, so make sure you have up-to-date phone details and the email address of whoever it is you would want to be called in to help you in a crisis.

Getting around

- You'll probably need an ID card or pass to enter certain buildings or areas so enquire how they are supplied. This may be included as part of your enrolment onto your course, and might involve production of your passport or driving licence or similar, or a photograph.

- Phoning up before a journey, even when travelling to the station, might get you a cheaper option than the ticket office.

- It is always worth checking the price of two singles as well as the price of a return on any public transport.

- Check parking availability before you go – how close is it to where you'll live, how secure, how expensive? Consider taking a bicycle instead of a car, especially if the university or college aspires to a green image. The only parking might be on side-streets which are potentially less safe and can antagonise the local population.

Induction and freshers' week

Induction days and freshers' weeks are designed to help you find your feet and settle in for the duration of your course. They are also very important for reminding you that extracurricular activities are an important part of the higher education experience. Details are often on university websites. You might have to book in advance for very popular options. Beware of signing up for very esoteric clubs which might be very grateful for your joining fee but then fail to hold many or any meetings. Don't forget that if there is no club catering for your pet interest you can always start one yourself!

- Plan your freshers' week carefully with a variety of events around your course, your leisure interests and your location. Be aware that freshers' week will involve a mixture of campus-wide events and events devised to be of special interest to those in your department or faculty.

- Sometimes there are events that welcome parents and other family members.

- Most universities will have an orientation week for international students before the UK students move in, and sometimes airport pick-ups can be arranged. This will give you extra time to settle in and will help you find your way around the town and the campus, with special emphasis on the international clubs and societies and introductions to the international officers and where possible native speakers of newcomers' languages. Check the UKCISA website for information of general interest too; for instance every international student can benefit from reading the UKCISA information sheet on culture shock available at **www.ukcisa.org.uk/student/info_sheets/culture_shock.php**.

- Induction will involve an outline of your course or at least its early stages, introductions to key staff, notes on assessment and course work expected, and other important matters such as tours of key or specialist facilities, introduction to library usage, and will also have a section or two on more general matters such as student welfare and the students' union. You will often find out about student ambassadors during induction, who are usually second year students who remember just what it is like to be in your position.

- Study timetables might not be available until very near the start of the study year – check with your tutor or students' union who should be able to tell you where to look on the university or college website. Timetables are often a bit provisional at first, so check for updates even after you have found it.

Things to avoid

Some people see groups of new students as ripe for exploitation – so protect yourself by applying your common sense.

- Don't sign up for things you don't want or haven't had time to think about – store cards, credit cards, indeterminate commitments.

- Try not to deal with too many novelties or difficulties at once. There are many sources of help – make use of them. It might all be very different from what you expected; if this is the case, have a word with your pastoral tutor or find someone to talk to about it at the students' union or the welfare office, or you may find your new friends are feeling the same but hadn't liked to admit it.

- Avoid being caught by scams – there are ever-increasing cases of email scams where a site looking just like a high street bank or the Student Loans Company, for instance, contacts you and asks you to confirm your personal details. No reputable institution would ever ask for such information to be verified in this way, so if you receive anything that arouses your suspicion, send it on to the real company. They will let you know if it is real and if so, how to deal with it. If it is a mistake or a scam they will be very grateful to you for helping them to stamp out such practices.

www.ucas.com

Employment

Nowadays two-thirds of students undertake paid work to help finance their studies. Roughly one in four work during term time, about half of whom are in paid employment for 14 or more hours a week. Keeping the financial wolf at bay all adds to the stress of trying to succeed in your studies and social life. How to keep a healthy balance between building up debt and dedicating time to earning funds is delicate and different for every student. Again, the university authorities will have seen many solutions to this conundrum and will have advice to offer. You can't begin to plan to work until your timetable and study commitments are clear.

Universities usually have recommended maximum employment hours for students, and there is a legal maximum of 20 hours for overseas students which makes a good rule of thumb. Talk to your tutor or welfare officer if you are tempted to work more than this to help cover your expenses. There might be employment possibilities within the university or the student union in the bars or shops for example, and these jobs might be easier to fit around your timetable as the employers will be sympathetic, and in any case try to get work nearby if you don't have transport otherwise the costs in time will be out of proportion to your earnings.

It might be worth while giving a little attention to writing a CV before you go to university so that you can jump in quickly with your application while other people are worrying about how to apply! If you get the outline done beforehand, with your school results, hobbies, interests and what you are studying, you can fill in any last minute details about availability once these become clear. Have a look at **www.e4s.co.uk**, **www.justjobs4students.co.uk** or **www.student-jobs.co.uk** to get a flavour of the kinds of jobs that may be available.

It is a bonus, but one well worth giving some thought to, if you can find employment that could help your future career development. It is well known that employers are more likely to take on someone who has already spent time in their line of business, and even work placements elsewhere count with four in ten employers as a mark in your favour. Progression within any sphere is worth mentioning on your CV: so make the most of any opportunity that comes your way. But try also to be aware that a highly competitive transient workforce is also ripe for exploitation, and check out anything that looks too attractive as the sting in the tail can be difficult to escape – remember to check whether you can work more flexibly when you are taking exams, for instance, and whether you are committed to working the same hours or shifts in holiday and term time, or if you are offered a premium for unsocial hours do check what these actually are and what the transport implications are. You need to stay safe, too, and walking home alone in an unfamiliar area in the small hours may not be the best way to do that.

Parents, grandparents, guardians, and other family members

Saying goodbye to you is probably something new for them as well as for you. They'll regard you as more adult when you come home for the Christmas holidays than they do now. For them it might seem like only last week that they brought you home from the maternity hospital (they're sometimes silly like that) and now you're suddenly very grown up and they're having to do a lot of adjusting in a very short time. If you're living at home while you study you'll have more chance to explain but they might be less aware of the changes going on around you than if you were physically far away. So the potential problems are different if you are living at home while studying: your family might not recognise how much things are changing for you and might not realise the new ways in which you need both freedom and support. You'll still be a part of the student community and fully involved in evening events and weekend outings, which will be different from your life before university. If you have children they might take time to adjust to the new you!

You'll be developing your initiative and confidence, and learning responsibility, how to apply for jobs, contribute to projects or presentations, and how to represent yourself independently, all on top of what you learn in your course. This could be a new element in your relationships – but is all part of growing up and in some ways how your family deals with such things will be known to you already. If you've moved out, your family will find it strange at home without you and might expect you to spend more time with them during the holidays than you really want. They will be worrying about money, about your marks and results, about your happiness and safety. You might be worrying about them. It is kind to stay in touch beyond those times when you need support, just to let them know you are safe and enjoying life. Some parents might try and contact their son or daughter's tutors direct – work out whether this is likely and what your reactions would be, so that you can try and keep in charge of the situation.

Strange things can happen. You might miss them more than you think, and they might miss you for unexpected reasons – are you the one who always removes spiders from the bathroom? Try to see the funny side if you can.

Did you know?

Unis have loads of societies you can join

Each uni has a long list of groups you can join, from political and religious societies to social societies – one uni has a cheese and chocolate club… Joining a society is a great way to meet people with the same interests. Check the unis' websites or speak to the students' union.

Myth buster

You're not on your own

Although you might be nervous about starting uni on your own, you're not alone. Everyone is going through the same experience, and if you have any concerns when you're at uni, there's always someone available to help. Most unis have their own welfare, advice or guidance centres.

Whatever your problem, big or small, they'll be able to advise you or point you in the right direction for help. To find out what your uni offers, go to their website and look up student support, or go into the students' union and ask staff there.

Chapter checklist

These are the things you should be doing and thinking about in Step 6 of your applicant journey:

- ☐ Check the correspondence you receive from your university or college and take the relevant action on:

  - accommodation options

  - reading lists

  - preparation advice for your course

  - assembling your important papers and documentation

  - liaising with the disability officer

  - booking your place on freshers' week events.

- ☐ Check out your accommodation options if you want to be independent of the uni.

- ☐ Finalise your finance arrangements.

- ☐ Meet people through yougo and other social networking sites.

- ☐ Pack bags and make travel arrangements, if moving away from home.

- ☐ Think about part-time work options.

www.ucas.com

Resources

This section of the book will help you understand some of the jargon you may hear when making your UCAS application, including information about the UCAS Tariff. We've also included links to other organisations you may find useful during your journey into higher education and a map of the UK to help you locate your institutions.

www.ucas.com

UCAS Tariff

What is the UCAS Tariff?

The UCAS Tariff is the system for allocating points to qualifications used for entry to higher education. It allows students to use a range of different qualifications to help secure a place on an undergraduate course.

How do universities use the UCAS Tariff?

Universities use the UCAS Tariff to make comparisons between applicants with different qualifications. Tariff points are often used in entry requirements, although other factors are often taken into account. Entry requirements and conditional offers that use Tariff points will often require a minimum level of achievement in a specified subject (for example '300 points to include grade A at A level Biology', or '260 points including SQA Higher grade B in Mathematics'). Entry Profiles on Course Search at **www.ucas.com** provide a fuller picture of what admissions tutors are looking for (see page 64 for more information about Entry Profiles).

How does the Tariff work?

- Students can collect Tariff points from a range of different qualifications, eg GCE A level with BTEC Nationals.

- There is no ceiling to the number of points that can be accumulated.

- There is no double counting. Certain qualifications within the Tariff build on qualifications in the same subject. In these cases only the qualification with the higher Tariff score will be counted. This principle applies to:

  - GCE Advanced Subsidiary level and GCE Advanced level

  - Scottish Highers and Advanced Highers

  - Key Skills at level 2, 3 and 4

  - Speech, drama and music awards at grades 6, 7 and 8.

- Tariff points for the Advanced Diploma come from the Progression Diploma score plus the relevant Additional and Specialist Learning (ASL) Tariff points. Please see the appropriate qualification in the Tariff tables to calculate the ASL score.

- The Extended Project Tariff points are included within the Tariff points for Progression and Advanced Diplomas. Extended Project points represented in the Tariff only count when the qualification is taken outside of these Diplomas.

- Where the Tariff tables refer to specific awarding organisations, only qualifications from these awarding organisations attract Tariff points. Qualifications with a similar title, but from a different qualification awarding organisation do not attract Tariff points.

Although Tariff points can be accumulated in a variety of ways, not all of these will necessarily be acceptable for entry to a particular course. The achievement of a points score therefore does not give an automatic entitlement to entry, and many other factors are taken into account in the admissions process.

Use Course Search at **www.ucas.com** to find out what qualifications are acceptable for entry to specific courses.

In July 2010, UCAS announced plans to review the Tariff. This review will take between 18 months and two years, and will therefore have no impact on applications to HE during 2011.

The following pages list which qualifications are included in the Tariff and provide tables showing the number of Tariff points allocated to a qualification. Further information about the Tariff, including the review plans, is available at www.ucas.com/students/ucas_tariff.

What qualifications are included in the Tariff?

The following qualifications are included in the UCAS Tariff. See the number on the qualification title to find the relevant section of the Tariff table.

1	AAT NVQ level 3 in Accounting
2	AAT level 3 Diploma in Accounting (QCF)
3	Advanced Diploma
4	Advanced Extension Awards
5	Advanced Placement Programme (US and Canada)
6	Arts Award (Gold)
7	ASDAN Community Volunteering qualification
8	Asset Languages Advanced Stage
9	British Horse Society (Stage 3 Horse Knowledge & Care, Stage 3 Riding and Preliminary Teacher's Certificate)
10	BTEC Awards (NQF)
11	BTEC Certificates and Extended Certificates (NQF)
12	BTEC Diplomas (NQF)
13	BTEC National in Early Years (NQF)
14	BTEC Nationals (NQF)
15	BTEC QCF Qualifications

Updates on the Tariff, including details on the incorporation of any new qualifications, are posted on **www.ucas.com**.

UCAS TARIFF TABLES

1

AAT NVQ LEVEL 3 IN ACCOUNTING	
GRADE	TARIFF POINTS
PASS	160

2

AAT LEVEL 3 DIPLOMA IN ACCOUNTING	
GRADE	TARIFF POINTS
PASS	160

3

ADVANCED DIPLOMA

Advanced Diploma = Progression Diploma plus Additional & Specialist Learning (ASL). Please see the appropriate qualification to calculate the ASL score. Please see the Progression Diploma (Table 44) for Tariff scores

4

ADVANCED EXTENSION AWARDS	
GRADE	TARIFF POINTS
DISTINCTION	40
MERIT	20

Points for Advanced Extension Awards are over and above those gained from the A level grade

5

ADVANCED PLACEMENT PROGRAMME (US & CANADA)	
GRADE	TARIFF POINTS
Group A	
5	120
4	90
3	60
Group B	
5	50
4	35
3	20

6

ARTS AWARD (GOLD)	
GRADE	TARIFF POINTS
PASS	35

7

ASDAN COMMUNITY VOLUNTEERING QUALIFICATION	
GRADE	TARIFF POINTS
CERTIFICATE	50
AWARD	30

8

ASSET LANGUAGES ADVANCED STAGE			
GRADE	TARIFF POINTS	GRADE	TARIFF POINTS
Speaking		Listening	
GRADE 12	28	GRADE 12	25
GRADE 11	20	GRADE 11	18
GRADE 10	12	GRADE 10	11
Reading		Writing	
GRADE 12	25	GRADE 12	25
GRADE 11	18	GRADE 11	18
GRADE 10	11	GRADE 10	11

9

BRITISH HORSE SOCIETY	
GRADE	TARIFF POINTS
Stage 3 Horse Knowledge & Care	
PASS	35
Stage 3 Riding	
PASS	35
Preliminary Teacher's Certificate	
PASS	35

Awarded by Equestrian Qualifications (GB) Ltd (EQL)

UCAS TARIFF TABLES

10

BTEC AWARDS (NQF) (EXCLUDING BTEC NATIONAL QUALIFICATIONS)			
GRADE	TARIFF POINTS		
	Group A	Group B	Group C
DISTINCTION	20	30	40
MERIT	13	20	26
PASS	7	10	13

11

BTEC CERTIFICATES AND EXTENDED CERTIFICATES (NQF) (EXCLUDING BTEC NATIONAL QUALIFICATIONS)					
GRADE	TARIFF POINTS				
	Group A	Group B	Group C	Group D	Extended Certificates
DISTINCTION	40	60	80	100	60
MERIT	26	40	52	65	40
PASS	13	20	26	35	20

12

BTEC DIPLOMAS (NQF) (EXCLUDING BTEC NATIONAL QUALIFICATIONS)			
GRADE	TARIFF POINTS		
	Group A	Group B	Group C
DISTINCTION	80	100	120
MERIT	52	65	80
PASS	26	35	40

13

BTEC NATIONAL IN EARLY YEARS (NQF)					
GRADE	TARIFF POINTS	GRADE	TARIFF POINTS	GRADE	TARIFF POINTS
Theory				Practical	
Diploma		Certificate		D	120
DDD	320	DD	200	M	80
DDM	280	DM	160	P	40
DMM	240	MM	120		
MMM	220	MP	80		
MMP	160	PP	40		
MPP	120				
PPP	80				

Points apply to the following qualifications only: BTEC National Diploma in Early Years (100/1279/5); BTEC National Certificate in Early Years (100/1280/1).

www.ucas.com

UCAS TARIFF TABLES

14

	BTEC NATIONALS (NQF)						
GRADE	TARIFF POINTS		GRADE	TARIFF POINTS		GRADE	TARIFF POINTS
Diploma			Certificate			Award	
DDD	360		DD	240		D	120
DDM	320		DM	200		M	80
DMM	280		MM	160		P	40
MMM	240		MP	120			
MMP	200		PP	80			
MPP	160						
PPP	120						

15

BTEC QUALIFICATIONS (QCF) (SUITE OF QUALIFICATIONS KNOWN AS NATIONALS)				
EXTENDED DIPLOMA	DIPLOMA	SUBSIDIARY DIPLOMA	CERTIFICATE	TARIFF POINTS
D*D*D*				420
D*D*D				400
D*DD				380
DDD				360
DDM				320
DMM	D*D*			280
	D*D			260
MMM	DD			240
MMP	DM			200
MPP	MM			160
		D*		140
PPP	MP	D		120
	PP	M		80
			D*	70
			D	60
		P	M	40
			P	20

16

CACHE LEVEL 3 AWARD, CERTIFICATE AND DIPLOMA IN CHILD CARE & EDUCATION					
AWARD		CERTIFICATE		DIPLOMA	
GRADE	TARIFF POINTS	GRADE	TARIFF POINTS	GRADE	TARIFF POINTS
A	30	A	110	A	360
B	25	B	90	B	300
C	20	C	70	C	240
D	15	D	55	D	180
E	10	E	35	E	120

17

CAMBRIDGE ESOL EXAMINATIONS	
GRADE	TARIFF POINTS
Certificate of Proficiency in English	
A	140
B	110
C	70
Certificate in Advanced English	
A	70

18

CAMBRIDGE PRE-U					
GRADE	TARIFF POINTS	GRADE	TARIFF POINTS	GRADE	TARIFF POINTS
Principal Subject		Global Perspectives and Research		Short Course	
D1	TBC	D1	TBC	D1	TBC
D2	145	D2	140	D2	TBC
D3	130	D3	126	D3	60
M1	115	M1	112	M1	53
M2	101	M2	98	M2	46
M3	87	M3	84	M3	39
P1	73	P1	70	P1	32
P2	59	P2	56	P2	26
P3	46	P3	42	P3	20

19

CISI INTRODUCTION TO SECURITIES AND INVESTMENT	
GRADE	TARIFF POINTS
PASS WITH DISTINCTION	60
PASS WITH MERIT	40
PASS	20

www.ucas.com

UCAS TARIFF TABLES

20

CERTIFICATE OF PERSONAL EFFECTIVENESS (COPE)	
GRADE	TARIFF POINTS
PASS	70

Points are awarded for the Certificate of Personal Effectiveness (CoPE) awarded by ASDAN and CCEA

21

DIPLOMA IN FASHION RETAIL	
GRADE	TARIFF POINTS
DISTINCTION	160
MERIT	120
PASS	80

Awarded by ABC Awards

22

DIPLOMA IN FOUNDATION STUDIES (ART & DESIGN AND ART, DESIGN & MEDIA)	
GRADE	TARIFF POINTS
DISTINCTION	285
MERIT	225
PASS	165

Awarded by ABC, Edexcel, UAL and WJEC

23

EDI LEVEL 3 CERTIFICATE IN ACCOUNTING, CERTIFICATE IN ACCOUNTING (IAS)	
GRADE	TARIFF POINTS
DISTINCTION	120
MERIT	90
PASS	70

24

ESSENTIAL SKILLS (NORTHERN IRELAND)	
GRADE	TARIFF POINTS
LEVEL 2	10

25

ESSENTIAL SKILLS WALES	
GRADE	TARIFF POINTS
LEVEL 3	20
LEVEL 2	10

26

EXTENDED PROJECT (STAND ALONE)	
GRADE	TARIFF POINTS
A*	70
A	60
B	50
C	40
D	30
E	20

Points for the Extended Project cannot be counted if taken as part of Progression/ Advanced Diploma

27

FREE-STANDING MATHEMATICS	
GRADE	TARIFF POINTS
A	20
B	17
C	13
D	10
E	7

Covers free-standing Mathematics - Additional Maths, Using and Applying Statistics, Working with Algebraic and Graphical Techniques, Modelling with Calculus

28

FUNCTIONAL SKILLS	
GRADE	TARIFF POINTS
LEVEL 2	10

UCAS TARIFF TABLES

29

GCE AND VCE									
GRADE	TARIFF POINTS	GRADE	TARIFF POINTS	GRADE	TARIFF POINTS	GRADE	TARIFF POINTS	GRADE	TARIFF POINTS
GCE & AVCE Double Award		GCE A level with additional AS (9 units)		GCE A level & AVCE		GCE AS Double Award		GCE AS & AS VCE	
A*A*	280	A*A	200	A*	140	AA	120	A	60
A*A	260	AA	180	A	120	AB	110	B	50
AA	240	AB	170	B	100	BB	100	C	40
AB	220	BB	150	C	80	BC	90	D	30
BB	200	BC	140	D	60	CC	80	E	20
BC	180	CC	120	E	40	CD	70		
CC	160	CD	110			DD	60		
CD	140	DD	90			DE	50		
DD	120	DE	80			EE	40		
DE	100	EE	60						
EE	80								

30

HONG KONG DIPLOMA OF SECONDARY EDUCATION					
GRADE	TARIFF POINTS	GRADE	TARIFF POINTS	GRADE	TARIFF POINTS
All subjects except mathematics		Mathematics compulsory component		Mathematics optional components	
5**	No value	5**	No value	5**	No value
5*	130	5*	60	5*	70
5	120	5	45	5	60
4	80	4	35	4	50
3	40	3	25	3	40

Points come into effect for entry to higher education from 2012 onwards.
No value for 5** pending receipt of candidate evidence (post-2012)

UCAS TARIFF TABLES

31

IFS SCHOOL OF FINANCE (NQF & QCF)			
GRADE	TARIFF POINTS	GRADE	TARIFF POINTS
Certificate in Financial Studies (CeFS)		Diploma in Financial Studies (DipFS)	
A	60	A	60
B	50	B	50
C	40	C	40
D	30	D	30
E	20	E	20

Completion of both qualifications will result in a maximum of 120 UCAS Tariff points

32

LEVEL 3 CERTIFICATE / DIPLOMA FOR iMEDIA USERS (iMEDIA)	
GRADE	TARIFF POINTS
DIPLOMA	66
CERTIFICATE	40

Awarded by OCR

33

INTERNATIONAL BACCALAUREATE (IB) DIPLOMA			
GRADE	TARIFF POINTS	GRADE	TARIFF POINTS
45	720	34	479
44	698	33	457
43	676	32	435
42	654	31	413
41	632	30	392
40	611	29	370
39	589	28	348
38	567	27	326
37	545	26	304
36	523	25	282
35	501	24	260

34

INTERNATIONAL BACCALAUREATE (IB) CERTIFICATE					
GRADE	TARIFF POINTS	GRADE	TARIFF POINTS	GRADE	TARIFF POINTS
Higher Level		Standard Level		Core	
7	130	7	70	3	120
6	110	6	59	2	80
5	80	5	43	1	40
4	50	4	27	0	10
3	20	3	11		

UCAS TARIFF TABLES

35

IRISH LEAVING CERTIFICATE			
GRADE	TARIFF POINTS	GRADE	TARIFF POINTS
Higher		Ordinary	
A1	90	A1	39
A2	77	A2	26
B1	71	B1	20
B2	64	B2	14
B3	58	B3	7
C1	52		
C2	45		
C3	39		
D1	33		
D2	26		
D3	20		

36

IT PROFESSIONALS (iPRO)	
GRADE	TARIFF POINTS
DIPLOMA	100
CERTIFICATE	80

Awarded by OCR

37

KEY SKILLS	
GRADE	TARIFF POINTS
LEVEL 4	30
LEVEL 3	20
LEVEL 2	10

38

MUSIC EXAMINATIONS					
GRADE	TARIFF POINTS	GRADE	TARIFF POINTS	GRADE	TARIFF POINTS
Practical					
Grade 8		Grade 7		Grade 6	
DISTINCTION	75	DISTINCTION	60	DISTINCTION	45
MERIT	70	MERIT	55	MERIT	40
PASS	55	PASS	40	PASS	25
Theory					
Grade 8		Grade 7		Grade 6	
DISTINCTION	30	DISTINCTION	20	DISTINCTION	15
MERIT	25	MERIT	15	MERIT	10
PASS	20	PASS	10	PASS	5

Points shown are for the ABRSM, Guildhall, LCMM, Rockschool and Trinity College London Advanced level music examinations

39

NPTC LEVEL 3 LAND BASED QUALIFICATIONS				
EXTENDED DIPLOMA	DIPLOMA	SUBSIDIARY DIPLOMA	CERTIFICATE	TARIFF POINTS
D				360
M	D			240
	M			160
P		D		120
	P	M		80
			D	60
		P	M	40

Points come into effect for entry to higher education from 2011 onwards.

40

OCR LEVEL 3 CERTIFICATE IN MATHEMATICS FOR ENGINEERING	
GRADE	TARIFF POINTS
A*	TBC
A	90
B	75
C	60
D	45
E	30

41

OCR LEVEL 3 CERTIFICATE FOR YOUNG ENTERPRISE	
GRADE	TARIFF POINTS
DISTINCTION	40
MERIT	30
PASS	20

UCAS TARIFF TABLES

42

OCR NATIONALS						
GRADE	TARIFF POINTS	GRADE	TARIFF POINTS	GRADE	TARIFF POINTS	
National Extended Diploma		National Diploma		National Certificate		
D1	360	D	240	D	120	
D2/M1	320	M1	200	M	80	
M2	280	M2/P1	160	P	40	
M3	240	P2	120			
P1	200	P3	80			
P2	160					
P3	120					

43

PRINCIPAL LEARNING WALES	
GRADE	TARIFF POINTS
A*	210
A	180
B	150
C	120
D	90
E	60

44

PROGRESSION DIPLOMA	
GRADE	TARIFF POINTS
A*	350
A	300
B	250
C	200
D	150
E	100

Advanced Diploma = Progression Diploma plus Additional & Specialist Learning (ASL). Please see the appropriate qualification to calculate the ASL score.

45

SCOTTISH QUALIFICATIONS							
GRADE	TARIFF POINTS	GRADE	TARIFF POINTS	GRADE	TARIFF POINTS	GROUP	TARIFF POINTS
Advanced Higher		Higher		Scottish Interdisciplinary Project		Scottish National Certificates	
A	130	A	80	A	65	C	125
B	110	B	65	B	55	B	100
C	90	C	50	C	45	A	75
D	72	D	36				
Ungraded Higher		NPA PC Passport					
PASS	45	PASS	45				
		Core Skills					
		HIGHER	20				

www.ucas.com

UCAS TARIFF TABLES

46

SPEECH AND DRAMA EXAMINATIONS							
GRADE	TARIFF POINTS	GRADE	TARIFF POINTS	GRADE	TARIFF POINTS	GRADE	TARIFF POINTS
PCertLAM		Grade 8		Grade 7		Grade 6	
DISTINCTION	90	DISTINCTION	65	DISTINCTION	55	DISTINCTION	40
MERIT	80	MERIT	60	MERIT	50	MERIT	35
PASS	60	PASS	45	PASS	35	PASS	20

Points shown are for ESB, LAMDA, LCMM and Trinity Guildhall Advanced level speech and drama examinations accredited in the National Qualifications Framework and LAMDA's Certificate in Communication and Certificate in Performance accredited on the Qualifications and Credit framework (QCF). Tariff points are available for both the NQF and QCF PCertLAM.

47

SPORTS LEADERS UK	
GRADE	TARIFF POINTS
PASS	30

These points are awarded to Higher Sports Leader Award and Level 3 Certificate in Higher Sports Leadership (QCF)

48

WELSH BACCALAUREATE ADVANCED DIPLOMA (CORE)	
GRADE	TARIFF POINTS
PASS	120

These points are awarded only when a candidate achieves the Welsh Baccalaureate Advanced Diploma

Jargon buster

When applying through UCAS, you may hear or read the commonly used words and phrases shown below. To help you, we've provided this list, with a summary of their meanings.

APEL: Accreditation of Prior Experiential Learning.

APL: Accreditation of Prior Learning.

Apply: the UCAS online application system for applying for higher education courses.

Adjustment: applicants who have met and exceeded the conditions of their firm choice are given an opportunity to look for an alternative place while holding their original confirmed place.

Clearing: a system used towards the end of the academic cycle. If you have not secured a place, it enables you to apply for course vacancies.

Conditional offer: an offer made by a university, whereby you must fulfil certain criteria before you can be accepted on the course.

Confirmation: when conditional offers that you have accepted become unconditional or are declined. Confirmation is usually dependent on your qualification or exam results.

Deferral: holding an offer of a place until the following year.

Entry Profiles: comprehensive information about individual courses and institutions, including statistics and entry requirements. Entry Profiles are found on Course Search at **www.ucas.com**.

Exam board: an organisation that sets exam questions and is responsible for marking them and distributing results. Also known as examination board, awarding organisation, or awarding body.

Extra: the opportunity to apply for another course if you have used all five choices and not secured a place. Extra runs from the end of February until the end of June.

FE: further education.

Firm offer: the offer that you have accepted as your first choice.

Fresher: a first year undergraduate student.

HE: higher education.

Institution: a university or college offering higher education courses.

Insurance offer: the offer that you have accepted as your second choice, in case you do not meet the requirements for your firm offer.

Invitation: an invitation from a university to attend for interview, audition, or provide a portfolio, essay or other piece of work.

NSS: National Student Survey.

Oxbridge: a term used for the Universities of Oxford and Cambridge.

Personal ID: a 10-digit individual number assigned to you when you register to use Apply. It is printed on every letter we send you and is displayed in the format 123-456-7890. You will be asked to provide this number if you contact our Customer Service Unit.

Point of entry: your year of entry to the course, for example, 2 refers to the second year of the course.

Scheme Code: used in conjunction with your Personal ID to uniquely identify your application.

Track: a system where you can track the progress of your application at **www.ucas.com**, reply to any offers received, and make certain amendments, for example, change of address or email.

UCAS Card: this scheme is the start of the UCAS journey. Registered students have access to a host of information about courses, life in higher education, the application process and a free discount card that can be used in the high street.

UCAStv: our video guides to help you apply to university and find out what other students think about higher education. You can learn how to use our systems and make the most of the resources available at **www.ucas.tv**.

Unconditional offer: an offer given to you by a university if you have satisfied the criteria and can attend the course.

Unistats: a website for students who want to research and compare subjects and universities before deciding where to apply. You can also look at student satisfaction ratings and explore the figures about getting a graduate job after completing a course. It includes the results of the latest National Student Survey. Visit the Unistats website at **www.direct.gov.uk/unistats**.

Unsuccessful: you have not been accepted by the university concerned.

Withdrawal: either you or a university cancels a choice before a decision has been made – a reason will be included if the withdrawal was issued by an institution.

yougo: yougo is the UCAS student network, where you can meet people doing your course or going to your university before you start. You can also access university profile pages and contact UCAS advisers online. Find out more about yougo at **www.yougofurther.co.uk**.

Useful contacts

In this section we've provided contact details for other sources of information and advice you may find helpful.

Higher education – general advice

Your school or college: if you are currently studying at a school or college, you can contact your tutor for help. You may also have a school careers adviser who can look at your skills and interests and help you identify suitable courses.

Careers centres: contact your local careers advisory service and careers library for more advice and guidance.

Connexions: provides advice on a range of topics for 13-19 year olds living in England and has a careers database – **www.connexions-direct.com**

www.yougofurther.co.uk: 'yougo', as it is more commonly known, is the UCAS student network. On yougo you can make friends with other applicants who are going to the same university or college and/or who are going to be on the same course.

Unistats: www.direct.gov.uk/unistats is the website to help you make an informed choice when deciding which UK university or college to apply to. It includes the results of the latest National Student Survey.

The Complete University Guide: includes university league and subject tables – **www.thecompleteuniversityguide.co.uk**

Department for Education: formed in May 2010, the Department for Education is responsible for education and children's services – **www.education.gov.uk**

Quality Assurance Agency for Higher Education (QAA): safeguards quality and standards in UK higher education, checking how well universities and colleges meet their responsibilities – **www.qaa.ac.uk**

National Union of Students (NUS): is the national voice of students, helping them to campaign, get cheap student discounts and provide advice on living student life to the full – **www.nus.org.uk**

Students with disabilities and special needs

Skill: National Bureau for Students with Disabilities

Skill is a UK independent charity that promotes equality in education, training and employment for disabled people: **www.skill.org.uk**

Royal National Institute of Blind People: **www.rnib.org.uk**

Royal National Institute for the Deaf: **www.rnid.org.uk**

British Dyslexia Association: **www.bdadyslexia.org.uk**

Disabled Students' Allowances (DSAs): more information can be found at **www.direct.gov.uk/dsa**

Student finance

Depending on where you live, contact the relevant organisation below for advice:

Student Finance England – **www.direct.gov.uk/studentfinance**

Student Finance Northern Ireland – **www.studentfinanceni.co.uk**

Student Awards Agency for Scotland – **www.saas.gov.uk**

Student Finance Wales – **www.studentfinancewales.co.uk**

EU students (living outside the UK) who want to study in England, Northern Ireland or Wales should visit **www.direct.gov.uk** for further information. EU students who want to study in Scotland should visit **www.saas.gov.uk**

At the time of writing, the Government has proposed student finance changes. If you're applying from 2012 onwards, you'll be affected – see **www.bis.gov.uk/studentfinance** to find out more.

Lifestyle and accommodation

UNITE was established over 15 years ago and is the largest provider of student accommodation in the UK – **www.unite-students.com**

Studentpad.co.uk was set up in December 1999 as an independent adviser and provider of a database of private and university accommodation.

Push.co.uk is the 'ruthlessly independent guide' to UK universities, student life, gap years, open days and student finance.

Cheap and healthy recipe ideas for students and anyone else on a budget can be found at **www.beyondbakedbeans.com**

Getting support when you're at university or college

Students' unions: your students' union will probably be the hub of your university or college. The union is responsible for social events, sports events, discounts, music and, most importantly, for representing students. Details of students' unions within UK universities and colleges are available on the UCAS website at **www.ucas.com/students/startinguni/studentsunions**. (Also see NUS details above.)

Nightline: Nightline is a confidential and anonymous listening, support and information service, run by students for students. Nightline operates in many universities and usually offers a phone service through the night. Email services and drop-in centres are also available in many universities – **www.nightline.ac.uk**

Lifetracks: Lifetracks offers help and advice for students at university or college. It contains useful articles, videos, features and a free question and answer service, all aimed at helping you while you're studying, and when making choices about your future – **www.lifetracks.com**

International students

Passport and visa requirements

For the latest information visit the visa services guidance page for students on the UK Border Agency website at **www.ukvisas.gov.uk/en/aboutus/features/studyingintheuk**

Guidance on documents you will need to study in the UK is available from UKCISA (UK Council for International Student Affairs): **www.ukcisa.org.uk**

You can make further enquiries as to whether you will be able to come to the UK as a student by contacting the Visa Application Centre (VAC), or where there is no VAC, the British Embassy or High Commission, in the country where you live. Find your nearest visa application centre and access their local visa service information at **www.ukvisas.gov.uk/en/howtoapply/wheretoapply**

All visa applicants are required to submit their biometric details. For more information visit **www.ukvisas.gov.uk/en/howtoapply/biometricvisa**

English language courses

Most universities and colleges provide English language courses and other forms of support to help you with your studies. The British Council also provides information about English language support at **www.britishcouncil.org/new**

You may want to take English classes when you arrive in the UK. English UK is the world's leading language teaching association with more than 400 members – all accredited by the British Council – including private language schools, educational trusts and charities and language centres in further education colleges and universities. More information can be found at **www.englishuk.com**

If you are also interested in improving your academic listening skills, ease (essential academic skills in English) may be able to help:
www2.warwick.ac.uk/fac/soc/al/leap/listeningandspeaking/

Other links you may find useful:
Prepare for success: an interactive web learning tool for international students who are getting ready to come to the UK for study in further or higher education – **www.prepareforsuccess.org.uk**

Education UK: a website brought to you by the British Council to inspire and guide you throughout your study abroad journey in the UK – **www.educationuk.org**

UK NARIC: the national agency responsible for providing information, advice and expert opinion on vocational, academic and professional skills and qualifications from over 180 countries worldwide – **www.naric.org.uk**

Mature students

Access to HE courses
Access to HE courses are specially designed for entry into higher education and provide the underpinning knowledge and skills needed to progress to a degree or diploma course at a university or college. More information and a course search for QAA-recognised Access courses in England, Wales and Northern Ireland can be found at **www.accesstohe.ac.uk**

Information about Access courses in Scotland is available on the Scottish Wider Access Programme (SWAP) website at **www.scottishwideraccess.org**

Advice from further and adult education
If you are currently studying in further or adult education, it is worth asking your tutor for help, as well as your careers advisory service and careers library.

Advice from higher education
School and college liaison units within universities and colleges will also help mature applicants. Some institutions have city centre advice shops.

Association of British Colleges (ABCC)
The only trade association in the UK dedicated to distance learning providers: **www.homestudy.org.uk**

Careers companies
Some local careers companies offer an all-age information and advisory service. This is sometimes free, but a modest charge may be made. Look in your local telephone directory under Careers Service.

C2 – The Graduate Careers Shop
Operated by the University of London Careers Service, but open to any graduates at any point in their careers, C2 offers impartial, independent advice on any matter related to jobs and careers. Several services are available, on a sliding scale of charges: **www.c2careers.co.uk**

Directgov
Directgov is the website of the UK Government providing information and online services. Information about options for older people looking to get into higher education, and ways to combine study with work and family life can be found at **www.direct.gov.uk/maturestudents**

Educational Grants Advisory Service (EGAS)
Provides advice on funding available for post-16 education and training within the UK. Primarily concerned with helping disadvantaged students: **www.family-action.org.uk**

Information, advice and guidance (IAG)
Local IAG services for adults are delivered by a variety of organisations, including Careers Scotland, educational institutions, and voluntary and community bodies. They offer free information and advice to individuals. You can find contact details for your nearest IAG service at your local library.

Learndirect

Guidance about training and employment opportunities. Working to rigorous standards monitored by the Department for Education: **www.learndirect.co.uk**

Lifelong Learning Networks

Lifelong Learning Networks (LLNs) focus on progression into and through vocational education. They aim to create new learning opportunities; forge agreement across institutions on how qualifications are valued; and produce publicity to help people understand how they can progress through the system **www.lifelonglearningnetworks.org.uk**

National Extension College

With over 150 home-study courses, the NEC offers a range of nationally recognised qualifications in a wide variety of subjects: **www.nec.ac.uk**

Next Step

Next Step is a publicly funded service, helping adults get the advice they need for future skills, careers, work and life choices: **https://nextstep.direct.gov.uk**

Open College Networks (OCNs)

The National Open College Network (NOCN) is the leading credit-based awarding organisation in the UK, offering high quality, flexible, credit-based qualifications: **www.nocn.org.uk**

The Open College of the Arts (OCA)

The OCA is an educational charity established in 1987 to widen participation in arts education. Students can study courses to develop their skills or to gain credits towards a degree: **www.oca-uk.com**

The Open University (OU)

The OU is the UK's only university dedicated to distance learning: **www.open.ac.uk**

Workers' Educational Association (WEA)

The UK's largest voluntary provider of adult learning: **www.wea.org.uk**

Gap years

Year Out Group: to help you find a suitable and worthwhile project. Year Out Group provides references and resources to help you make the most of a year out – **www.yearoutgroup.org**

Foreign & Commonwealth Office travel & living abroad: provides travel advice by country, guidance to travellers before embarking on their trip, tips on staying safe and healthy and travel news – **www.fco.gov.uk/en/travel-and-living-abroad**

vinspired: connects 16-25 year olds with volunteering opportunities in England – **http://vinspired.com**

Gapwork is an independent information and educational provider for anyone planning a gap year: **www.gapwork.com**

CSV is a volunteering and training charity, founded in 1962: **www.csv.org.uk**

Publications

Our online bookstore – **www.ucasbooks.com** – contains details of all our UCAS guides as well as books carefully selected from other publishers. It includes, for example, *Open Days, How to Complete Your UCAS Application, Personal Statements, Student Finance* and *The Times Good University Guide*.

The publications listed will help you prepare for all aspects of higher education and can be ordered online.

UK map of major cities and airports

Acknowledgements

UCAS is tremendously grateful to the many individuals and organisations for their invaluable contributions to our new guide. Without their help we would not have been able to make the book come alive with their experiences and knowledge.

Individuals: Dr Nina Reeve, GP; Caroline Queen, veterinary surgeon; Liz Reece from St. Clare's, Oxford.

Case studies: Olamide Agboola, Mike Williams at Bournside School in Cheltenham, Alice Hancock, Shona Heath, Jordan Hodge, Kevin Minors, Hameed Nazham Ahmed, Daniella Nzekwe, Caryn Wright.

Universities and colleges: Andy Howman at University of Bath, Dr Helen Johnson at University of Birmingham, Claire Powell and Frances Shea at University of Bristol, Tayma Cannon and Sarah Hannaford at University of Cambridge, Jamie Bradford at De Montfort University, Helen Charlesworth and Julia Paolitto at University of Oxford, Sue Davey at Peninsula College of Medicine & Dentistry, Margaret Kilyon at The Royal Veterinary College, Marjorie Coulter, Tom O'Neill and Alan Scott at University of Ulster and Lynsey Hopkins at University of Warwick.

Organisations: Bernard Kingston for The Complete University Guide, Alex Sharratt for the Gap-Year Guide at John Catt Publishing, Mark Jones at Higher Education Statistics Agency (HESA), Jo Gibson at National Association of Student Money Advisers (NASMA), Anne Brook at Skill: National Bureau for Students with Disabilities, Lauren Amos and Elisabet Sanchez at UNITE.

Special thanks to all the students who gave us their UCAS experiences on the yougo forums.

Finally, thanks must also go to our UCAS colleagues, not only for their contributions, but also their enthusiasm and encouragement toward the production of the guide.